IDEAS FOR
Families

Phyllis Pellman Good
and
Merle Good

Good Books
Intercourse, PA 17534

Cover artwork by Cheryl Benner

Design by Dawn J. Ranck

IDEAS FOR FAMILIES
Copyright © 1992 by Good Books, Intercourse, PA 17534
International Standard Book Number: 1-56148-076-2
Library of Congress Card Catalog Number: 92-41577

Library of Congress Cataloging-in-Publication Data

Good, Phyllis Pellman, 1948—
    Ideas for families / Phyllis Pellman Good and Merle Good.
        p. cm.
    ISBN 1-56148-076-2 (pbk.) : $9.95
    1. Family--United States--Miscellanea. 2. Family recreation--United
States--Miscellanea. I. Good, Merle. II. Title.
HQ536.G658   1992
306.85--dc20   92-41577
                                                              CIP

Table of Contents

Introduction

Establishing, and then maintaining, strong family life is a matter of interest and concern for many of us.

We lead lives full of demands from our jobs and careers. Sometimes we seem to have too many commitments, and we find ourselves shortchanging those we care most about. Many of us do not live close to our extended families. We feel alone in our efforts to hold things together.

This book is a collection of modest practices, natural ideas, suggestions that adapt easily—all of which can enhance the quality of a family's life together.

We gathered these ideas from many people and places. Most are simple to put into practice; few require the purchase of particular supplies or the presence of special skills.

What all 1,000-plus ideas have in common is a deliberateness, a conscious effort to value and cultivate family relationships.

This is a collection of actual things to do. It is not a book of theory. Implicit in this compendium, however, is a respect for children, parents and grandparents, and regard for connections to friends as well as family. Here, too, is an acknowledgement of the relentless passing of time, and the realization that family and friendship configurations change.

Most of the persons whose ideas are a part of this book are members of the Mennonite community of faith. A people with a history and tradition of strong families, Mennonites know as well the stresses that the current world brings to families. Many of the stories in this book reflect both the way things used to be, and the way practices have changed, now that both parents work away from home in many families, that one's social life is no longer centered around church, and that outside interests compete daily for everyone's time and energy.

These gathered ideas are likely to trigger your memories of life in your childhood home. If that happens, you may want to find a way to bring back those practices, or adapt them, along with any new ideas which you find here.

We hope this host of tried and weathered activities inspires all who browse and read it to revive family relationships. There is material here for singles and grandparents, for life with infants and junior-highers, for ordinary moments and special seasons.

We sincerely thank the hundreds who contributed ideas to this book. It is a gift to all of us. We deeply appreciate your sharing the occasions and gestures of meaning from your own experiences in families.

1.

Ordinary Fun Times

▼ When I'm working around the house, the children like to play "Sneak." They love to try to sneak from room to room without me seeing them. I usually sing a song about where I'll go next so they are forewarned. This works well when I'm putting wash away or tidying up. The children love to "fool" me and I always pretend that I'm worried that they're gone.

▼ When I need a break, I fill the tub with warm water and bubbles and let the children play in the tub, while I sit in the bathroom and read or write letters. This is great when they're feeling tired and so am I.
—*Anita and Randy Landis-Eigsti, Lakewood, CO*

▼ During the summer months we hang our hammock under the shade of our beautiful oak tree. The girls and I get cozy and sing songs, tell stories or look for acorns up in the tree. Sometimes we are silent. Just being together is fun!
—*Jenny and Dave Moser, Bluffton, OH*

▼ Singing makes a lot of things go better. I sometimes make up songs to suit the occasion: "It's a hot, hot day/and Rachel's riding in the car/and she's very hot and sweaty/so what should we do when we get home?/Maybe we'll have a cold, cold drink/maybe we'll have a nice cold drink/because it's a hot,hot day." Sometimes I use songs like Raffi's songs about brushing teeth, taking a bath, etc. The children especially like the ones in which I include their names.
—*Rod and Martha (Yoder) Maust, Indianapolis, IN*

▼ Being a parochial school teacher, I have always had a modest salary which restricted how much we could spend, so we found other ways to have fun. Ordinary fun has been taking walks in the woods behind our house, visiting relatives and cousins, and taking occasional day-trips—to Cleveland Indians ball games and to historical sites (with stops at McDonald's). We have played lots of card games on wintry evenings with the fire blazing in the fireplace and watched videos or TV as a family.
—*Jim and Dee Nussbaum, Kidron, OH*

▼ We like "campfires" where we can toast marshmallows, as part of camping in the backyard or sleeping out on the porch.

▼ Breakfast is special cooked outside.

▼ Our garden usually has kid paths and special "road" signs—"Bunny Path," "Turtle Highway," and "Bug Street," for example.

▼ We build marble rolls in the sandbox, making sand towers with marble runways and tunnels.
   —*Ann James Van Hooser, Princeton, KY*

▼ We received as a family Christmas gift an elaborate bird feeder with a one-way mirror in the center. We can watch the birds close up and they can't see us. This has developed into a very interesting family pastime. All of us have become avid birders.
   —*Glennis and Mark Yantzi, Kitchener, ON*

▼ After having four sons, we decided to move onto a farm. This meant we would not be able to have many going-away vacations because of the dairy herd we had. One of the fun things we learned to do was to have foreign meals and eat them in a special way. We ate our African meal of *ugali* on the lawn, all seated around the food and eating with our fingers, in the customary African style. Our Javanese meal was prepared by a missionary friend, who also showed us her slides of Java. Then there was the Chinese meal where we learned to eat with chopsticks. The children would read in the encyclopedia about the country we were featuring.
   We laughed hardest on the occasion we created when we decided we needed more American manners at our mealtimes. We arranged to have a formal American meal. We dressed up for each other; Dad seated Mother and everyone put on their best manners. Soup was the first course, with other courses following. Our four-year-old placed his elbows on the table, then suddenly drew them off again, producing laughter. The children had read about manners prior to the meal in a small booklet we had bought from the bookstore!
   —*Stephen and Sadie Yoder, Quarryville, PA*

▼ Through the years we had many visitors from around the world in our home, especially because we lived in Luxembourg. It was important to us that the children always ate at the table with the adults and mingled with the guests. They listened to the conversations, asked questions and learned a great deal about the larger world and about the larger church from these guests. I recall especially visitors from Tanzania, Somalia, the Middle East and Indonesia, as well as North

Americans, who sat at our table and in our living room and responded engagingly to the many questions our children put to them. The children loved having guests. They felt connected to a larger world community as it passed through our home.
—*Wilma Beachy Gingerich, Harrisonburg, VA*

▼ Our family has become international in food tastes. While in India we fell in love with rice and curry—the hot and spicy variety. Our daughter married an M.D. from Ethiopia and together they have become superb cooks of Chinese food. Our son married a woman of Russian Mennonite background so she has added that style to our meals. For a family who thought meat and potatoes were just fine, we have become a family who loves to try the exotic!
—*Harvey and Erma Sider, Fort Erie, ON*

▼ Since returning to the U.S., we often ask international students over for meals and invite them to tell us about their countries. We like to cook international foods for guests, inviting these friends and family to chop vegetables with us for Chinese egg rolls or to help us make tortillas and chapatis.
—*Richard and Jewel Showalter, Chad, Rhoda Jane, and Matthew, Irwin, OH*

▼ We like baking bread together.
—*Ron and Betti Risser, Lancaster, PA*

▼ Weird-Night-Dinners means creating uncommon combinations or colors—purple milk, blue eggs, pink ice cream with carrot sticks. The children may choose anything in the cupboards or something that I can reasonably make. *I pick the night!*
—*Christine Certain, Fresno, CA*

▼ Our house had a fireplace in the basement family room, so sometimes in the winter (on Saturday or Sunday evenings) we spread a plastic tablecloth on the rug and had an indoor picnic, roasting hot dogs and, later, marshmallows in the fireplace. Then we'd play table games until it was bedtime. When I worked outside our home, we'd go out to eat on Friday night to an inexpensive place to celebrate the end of the week.
—*Joyce Rutt Eby, Goshen, IN*

▼ A family I know has "winter picnics" with their young children. When the family room is very warm from a roaring fire in the woodstove, they dress in summer clothes, spread out a blanket and

have a picnic which might include roasting wieners over the fire and eating ice cream cones.
—Arlene Kehl, Kitchener, ON

▼ Sometimes on weekends, or whenever one of us was in the mood for some casual celebrating, we would have a picnic-on-the-rug. We have an old yellow-checked vinyl tablecloth we'd spread out on the family room floor, and then we'd gather around for a finger-food meal, usually pizza.
—Phyllis and Merle Good, Kate and Rebecca,
Lancaster, PA

▼ *Friday* nights are *family nights.* We usually have pizza (in or out) and choose an activity like roller-skating, biking, board games, and, occasionally, a video or movie.
—Elizabeth Loux and Don Kraybill, Matthew,
Micah, and Ashley, Harleysville, PA

▼ Friday evening is family night. No family member schedules an out-of-family activity without checking with the rest of us. As a four-member family, we each take our turn on one Friday night of the month to plan or be in charge of the evening's activities. In the months that have five Friday evenings, all four of us plan the evening together. The activities range from games, shopping, concerts, fairs and anything else of interest—that is cheap!
—Millard and Pris Garrett, Kimmi and Krissie, Lancaster, PA

▼ We try to do a lot of walking together. We walk to church, to parks, or just around town. We walk to visit elderly friends from church. We hike in the mountains, identifying flowers, trees, or birds.

▼ Don remembers that sometimes his mom would make a picnic lunch for just him and his friends to go off by themselves to eat.
—Joan Schrock Woodward and Don Woodward,
Elizabethton, TN

▼ We are fortunate to have a long lane at the edge of our property. It has been important in our children's lives and, almost more so, in our grandchildren's. We have taken many hikes, observing bugs, butterflies, and birds. We find interesting rocks and often pick wildflowers for bouquets.

At the mention of the lane, Lisa, now 7, grabs the toy picnic basket and packs anything available. It might be cookies and lemonade or water and graham crackers. Way back by a wooded area a neighbor has some farm tools parked. There we tell stories, read a few books, do imaginary farming and get into some good discussions. When Mark was old enough to drive the riding mower, we often loaded the trailer with teddy bears for a teddy bears' picnic.

We stop by the iron gate to talk to the neighbor's heifers; they are all named. Our family pet, Teddy, a Pomeranian, often accompanies us on these trips.

This has been such a popular activity that quite often we spend time back there during the day and again in the evening. We have made a scrapbook with lots of pictures to help us preserve these memories.
—*Mattie Miller, Sugarcreek, OH*

▼ We walk around the farm or lawn, listen to the many sounds, and try to identify them. Or we look for insects, fish, and frogs around the pond. We also watch for different birds and other wildlife—ducks, ducklings, geese, foxes, groundhogs, and rabbits. We've watched a bird's nest being built, then the eggs laid and hatched, and finally the little birds learning to fly. We draw parallels to our own experience—a child growing older, then finally leaving mother and father and becoming independent, with God helping them in making many decisions in their lives.
—*Erma Kauffman, Cochranville, PA*

▼ When the children were preschool and school age we would find caterpillars on milkweed. We placed them, along with a part of the plant, into a large jar and put cheesecloth secured with elastic over the opening. To watch a caterpillar spin a chrysalis and later emerge as a butterfly was a thrilling experience to share.
—*Arlene Kehl, Kitchener, ON*

▼ Every morning Alice and I get the day off to a fast start. We take a 20-minute hike to the mountain creek and back. Whether it's zero degrees or 70 degrees we do our daily ritual. It gives us a chance to talk if we feel like it—that usually happens on the way to the creek. On the return we might sing, pray out loud, share a scripture by memory or just meditate. You are right, we're in our early 60s and our four children are married and on their own.

Benefits? Better health, better communication, better schedule and better togetherness! When Alice suggested this idea over four years ago after reading of another couple who did a daily walk, I wasn't all that excited. But we've found it to be a wholesome practice—physically, emotionally, and spiritually.
—*Eugene and Alice Souder, Grottoes, VA*

▼ We took early morning bird hikes along the woods and the river, then followed that with an outdoor breakfast over an open campfire.

▼ We enjoyed spring walks in the woods noticing birds, flowers, and mushrooms. Sometimes we did this on Sunday morning as our family worship.
> —*L. Glen and Allie Guengerich, Kalona, IA*

▼ We joined the church youth in a 20-mile bike excursion along a mountain riverside, making the weekly 20-mile drive to church meaningful to our family
> —*Orpah and Elam S. Kurtz, Jefferson, NC*

▼ We have invested in a fleet of mountain bikes. Living in a rural area we enjoy all the back roads and trails, either all of us together or in two's and three's.

We each have a pair of cross-country skis, and we all like to have a winter picnic, including roasting hot dogs in the snow, when we're out skiing.
> —*Tom and Lois Marshall, Naomi, Christine and Jonathan, Spruce, MI*

▼ In spite of concern about conserving gasoline, one of our favorite events as a family when the girls were young was taking a drive in the countryside, especially in the early evening. We'd stop to watch the cows, collect leaves, skip stones in a brook, or visit a little store or country hideaway.
> —*Phyllis and Merle Good, Kate and Rebecca, Lancaster, PA*

▼ In the fall we rake the leaves into a huge pile, then make a nest and have a lunch in our nest.

▼ During winter snows we made trails through the snow and played Follow the Leader.
> —*John and Marilyn Burkhart, Mount Joy, PA*

▼ On lovely spring and fall days (when I don't work away from home) we take a tray outside for Teatime. We make it complete with china tea cups, silver teaspoons, cloth napkins and small crackers or cookies. This is very appropriate for boys. Our son loves it!
> —*Kelli Burkholder King and John King, Jacob Hans and Suzanne Marissa, Goshen, IN*

▼ I like just *being* with our grandchildren and pretending their stories.
—*Shirley Kirkwood, Mt. Solon, VA*

▼ One summer the girls and their friends spent a lot of time writing a play, making the costumes, practicing together, and finally producing it for family and friends.

▼ Making a tree house together was a fun project for the children and their dad.

▼ Taking care of a pony that the children wanted was a cooperative venture for all of us.
—*Ben and Lorraine Myers, Dillsburg, PA*

▼ When the children were younger, we had family secret pals which included some of the pets. We pulled names and throughout the year spontaneously and secretly surprised our pal. The big revelation was at Christmastime—if the "secret" part of the pal lasted that long!
—*Ernest and Lois Hess, Lancaster, PA*

▼ Our daily life is not very ritualistic. It revolves around church, school, and lessons. Our daughter Kate loves when we do something spontaneously. Once (I can't remember when) I decided to break one of my own rules at her request (I bought a luxury item in the grocery store—without a coupon!). I just popped it into the cart and said "Oh, why not!" Her eyes popped out with delight. It was the spontaneity, not the product, which delighted her most. Of course, if we wouldn't have such frugal rules in the first place, it wouldn't be so much fun to break them!
—*Shirley H. and Stuart W. Showalter,*
Goshen, IN

▼ My mother and father had the uncanny ability to take the routine and make it into something special.

My father was a minister and during my childhood conducted numerous meetings in various churches throughout our local Conference. It was not uncommon for our entire family (however many there were at the time) to accompany him nearly every night to these two-week events.

If the drive home from church was in the vicinity of the Lancaster Airport, Dad would have us search the skies for an approaching airplane. And if we spotted one, we would drive into the airport and watch the passengers embark and board. We watched for as long as we could, and as we made our way back to the car, Dad would inevitably comment, "You don't see how that thing gets off the ground."

Or we would stop at the Lancaster train station, walk up to the fence and watch in amazement as the conductor paced back and forth, looking at the big pocket watch attached to his belt-keeper by a long silver chain. We strained to see inside the dining cars, trying to imagine what it must be like to ride, eat, and sleep in a moving train. Then, as the destinations were announced over the loudspeaker, the large engine moved the cars down the tracks. Again, we watched as long as we could, and as we made our way back to the car, Dad would say, "Just think, tomorrow that train will be in Chicago."
　　　—Melvin Thomas, Lancaster, PA

▼ All of us enjoyed doing things spontaneously sometimes—playing games indoors and outdoors, taking short trips to visit relatives and friends, making jaunts to the zoo, Franklin Institute (in Philadelphia), the shore, mountains, museums, art galleries, etc.
　　　—Richard and Betty Pellman, Millersville, PA

▼ When we first moved to New York City the Metropolitan Museum of Art was a frequent afternoon stop. Our children were 4½ and 2½. Often we would only "stop to visit" three or four works featuring children with which our children were familiar. They included the Roman sculpture, "A Boy With a Thorn in His Foot," Goya's "Don Manuel," and Van Gogh's "First Steps."
　　　—Joan and Larry Litman, Hoboken, NJ

▼ We played carrom, Authors (which helped to acquaint us with authors and their works), Parcheesi and Dominoes.

Our daughter often said, "Tell me a story about when you were a little boy."
　　　—Laurence and Marian Horst, Goshen, IN

▼ Our family has always enjoyed playing a variety of games together. Our favorites now include Upword, Scrabble, Boggle, Spill and Spell, Ipswich, and Crossword Dominoes. Even though our visits are infrequent, we continue to enjoy this type of fun time together.
　　　—Lois G. Dagen, Lancaster, PA

▼ Our family has always enjoyed playing games—from Uncle Wiggly to Sorry, to Clue, to Yahtzee, to Racko, to Monopoly, to Rook. As the children were growing up, and now that they are adults and married, we still enjoy playing games when we get together.

Shanghai, Scum, and Up and Down the River (or 7 Up and 7 Down) are favorites now, because any number can play. These games are played using regular playing cards, and extra sets of cards can be added as needed to accommodate the number playing.
—*Ken and June Marie Weaver,*
Harrisonburg, VA

▼ Spending time at the basketball hoop—gender- and age-inclusive in various combinations—occupied much of our time. So did listening to and critiquing new music;sharing articles and cartoons at meals; limited TV-/movie-viewing together.
—*Jim and Janalee Croegaert and family, Evanston, IL*

▼ Both of us parents enjoy singing together at the piano. Sometimes the girls join our duets with variations of their own.
—*Phyllis and Merle Good, Kate and Rebecca,*
Lancaster, PA

▼ When our oldest child was less than a year old, we began singing hymns to her at bedtime (and fussy times). We'd get the hymnal and start at the beginning and sing until she quieted. We've continued singing hymns with her through the years, and now, at age five, she knows many hymns and perks up during church when the congregation sings one of "her" songs.
—*Tom and Sue Ruth, Lancaster, PA*

▼ When the children were small (pre-eight), I rewarded them for getting up early by reading stories/books. That solved the problem of sleepyheads, since they valued that time together.
—*Ervin and Bonita Stutzman, Mount Joy, PA*

▼ Library books are an important staple of our family life. I often read to the older ones while nursing the baby.
—*Rod and Martha (Yoder) Maust,Indianapolis, IN*

▼ My mother loved to read and often read stories to us—especially when we had to wait for my father at mealtime. That taught me to be patient. She also read entire books to us in the evenings—in serial style.
—*Elma Esau, North Newton, KS*

▼ Over the years we've usually read a chapter from a book after dinner. And we always read a book while traveling.
—*Marlene and Stanley Kropf, Elkhart, IN*

▼ We enjoy reading to each other when we drive (especially James Thurber short stories).
—L. Lamar Nisly, Newark, DE

▼ Because Mommy (Phyllis) loves to read more than eat (and she relishes food!), we've tried as often as possible to give her "Reading Mornings." This was especially true on Saturday mornings when the girls were younger. It was worth the effort, because Mommy was renewed after three or four hours by herself, and we all enjoyed each other more.
—Phyllis and Merle Good, Kate and Rebecca, Lancaster, PA

▼ With the birth of our first child I started a "Family Memories" book—a simple blank, hardcover book I purchased at a stationery store. Through the years, I've jotted down special family memories, details about vacations we took, the children's accomplishments and lots of funny things they've said or done along the way. Our children absolutely love to get our book out and read aloud the funny stories from when they were younger.
—Miles and Dawnell Yoder, Lancaster, PA

▼ A fun thing for me was to tell the children stories about the pieces of furniture in our house that I grew up with. So much of our furniture, our pictures, and our art have stories behind them. Now I am beginning to tell the grandchildren those stories.
  We own quite a few postcards of famous artists' works, starting that collection in Fine Arts class in college. These cards were always stored on a table or in a cupboard within easy view and reach of our children, beginning when our eldest was quite small. They became a favorite quiet-time play, and are still available to our grandchildren.
—Charlotte H. Croyle, Archbold, OH

▼ As a grandmother I want to write down all my favorite Bible verses and give them to my grandchildren. I will challenge them to learn them word-perfect and offer them 25 cents for each one they recite back to me.
—Lorna Sirtoli, Cortland, NY

▼ We become babysitters to four of our grandchildren on special religious holidays like Ascension Day and Old Christmas. Our daughter, who is a speech pathologist in a local school system, must work on those days, although her Amish helper observes those holidays and cannot care for the children then. We always play lots of games.

We also make a special effort to attend the graduations of our older grandchildren.
—*Milton and Ella Rohrer, Orrville, OH*

▼ When the children return home during college breaks or from a vacation, we light a candle in their respective bedroom windows to signal an eager welcome.
—*Ernest and Lois Hess, Lancaster, PA*

▼ Our daughters don't like to be surprised by our absence. If one of us needs to travel out of town, for instance, they adjust better if we don't spring it on them at the last minute. They like to know a day or so ahead of time—but not too far ahead of time, either.

▼ When one of us parents is on a trip, we buy three post cards and send them home, one to the other parent and one to each girl—but with a twist. We lay all three cards beside each other and write our message across all three, so that those at home have to put all three cards together after they receive them in the mail. Otherwise, none of the cards makes sense.
—*Phyllis and Merle Good, Kate and Rebecca,*
Lancaster, PA

▼ After preschool or when I return from work, we have a "Special chat" over a healthy snack. It might be only five to ten minutes, but it helps us reconnect.
—*Kelli Burkholder King and John King, Jacob*
Hans and Suzanne Marissa, Goshen, IN

▼ I like to tuck little notes in our son's school lunchbox or put a surprise sticker on his napkin.
—*Allen and Roseanne Shenk family, Strasburg, PA*

▼ I keep a collection of cartoons which I find particularly amusing. When the boys were in high school, I occasionally added a cartoon to their lunches, or an encouraging note on exam day, or a valentine on Valentine's Day.
—*Arlene Kehl, Kitchener, ON*

▼ We all like to go to garage and yard sales or attend flea markets. Everyone looks for their own treasure.
—*Clive and Margaret LeMasurier, Plainville, CT*

▼ At our house we have an Odd and Silly Box. Family members finding an odd or silly object (not intentionally made by persons) contributes to this box. Our box contains a stone shaped like a kidney bean, a malformed nut, and misshapen pretzels, to name a few. Garden vegetables such as carrots can be quite freakish, though it's impractical to add them, so they are saved as long as possible and always remembered when we check our box once each year.

—*Lois and Randy Zook, Lancaster, PA*

▼ Routines give us an opportunity to measure time in ways that children can understand better than the days of the week. They also allow us to look forward to little fun times together. We all anticipate Thursday evenings when we curl up on the floor, often with a bowl of fruit, in front of the TV. The content of the programs is not so important (often the children do not understand all of it), as the fact that we are all there, not doing anything but being together.

—*Daryl and Marlisa Yoder-Bontrager, Lancaster, PA*

▼ Rituals seem to be important in our family. I find the more we do something regularly, the more we enjoy ourselves and the activity. Taking walks with our children has given me much joy. There is little energy required to initiate the activity and no money has to be invested.

▼ After a year of pushing our two boys to help with meal preparation and cleanup they are finally beginning to feel a sense of accomplishment and competency. When I keep their participation a priority, I have the energy to encourage them to help. When I focus on meals as just a task to be gotten out of the way, rather than as an opportunity to enjoy the task and my children, I lose my energy.

—*Donna M. Froese and Don E. Schrag, Samuel and Joseph, Wichita, KS*

▼ I often found that the young children enjoyed as much being involved in everyday chores, as having us play children's games with them.

—*Arlene Kehl, Kitchener, ON*

2.

Specific Practices for Routine Times

Mealtimes _____

▼ Supper together is close to sacrosanct. Cynthia and I usually refuse to participate in any adult activities that require us to miss supper with our family.
—David and Cynthia Shank, Joshua, Benjamin, Nathaniel, and Caleb, Mt. Crawford, VA

▼ I deliberately don't schedule many breakfast meetings. We eat practically all suppers together as a family.
—Ervin and Bonita Stutzman, Mount Joy, PA

▼ If the phone rings during mealtime, the caller is told that we are eating, and that the call will be returned after the meal. In this way we tell each other that this time together is very important.
—Jane-Ellen and Gerry Grunau, Winnipeg, MB

▼ It is a priority for our family to eat together, which may mean that the time of our meal in the evening is adjusted—from early (4:30) to late (7:30-8:00), so that all can be there.
—Jim and Nancy Roynon, Brad, Taryn, Drew and Colin, Archbold, OH

▼ With three teenagers (two drive), and one 11-year-old, our biggest challenge is having a meal together. Even though I (Rachel) work, I plan complete fast meals and we sit and visit if possible. We rarely use mealtime to discuss grades or discipline issues. TV and radio and phone conversations during meals are off-limits.
—Marvin and Rachel Miller, Indianapolis, IN

▼ We try to keep mealtimes as a time of family togetherness. A family rule is "No Reading at the Table" (unless it is shared with everyone)!
—Roy and Hope Brubaker, Mifflintown, PA

▼ During the meal we recounted school events, as well as anything else of interest that had occurred that day. This was a tradition I (Leroy) brought from my family. My dad was a great storyteller and it was only natural to follow the pattern for our family. Suppertime has been storytime for us and our children.
—*Leroy and Sarah Miller, Chesapeake, VA*

▼ While in a service program in Nigeria we read a continued story at mealtime when the kids were with us on holidays. (They always begged to read "just a little more.")
—*Jim and Dee Nussbaum, Kidron, OH*

▼ On Saturdays and at mealtime we often played "Come-je-come." One person began by saying "Come-je-come." The others would answer, "What do you come by?" The one that was "It" replied, "I come by the letter ____." The beginning letter of an object was used, and the rest of us were to guess that object. For instance, "It" said "C" and thought of "chair." Whoever guessed "chair" became "It."
—*Herbert A. and Jessie T. Penner, Bakersfield, CA*

▼ At suppertime we often take turns saying one good thing that happened to us that day and one bad thing that happened. This is a good way to get conversation going.
—*Roger and Pamela Rutt, Lancaster, PA*

▼ At dinner in the evening everyone answers the question, "What's the best thing that happened to you today?" Occasionally the question gets reversed: "What's the worst thing...?" It's been a good way to keep us up-to-date about what's important to each of us.
—*Marlene and Stanley Kropf, Elkhart, IN*

▼ We spent a lot of time around the kitchen table with three teens, discussing summer plans, career possibilities, church or spiritual issues, music ideas, school teachers and reminiscing about childhood happenings. It was open season for serious or good humored conversation, or hilarious brain pickins'. I hardly remember what definite decisions were made or specific problems solved, but the memory of goodwill and animated conversation will remain with me forever.
—*Mrs. Robert Sauder, York, PA*

▼ Although my parents raised a large family on a limited budget, my mother found creative ways to make ordinary meals fun. One of my favorite memories involves three different types of mystery meals. In the first, everyone except my mother was banished from the kitchen, during which time all items on the menu were individually wrapped and creatively disguised with the help of aluminum foil. All wrapped food items were placed on a pile in the center of the table. We were then instructed about the number of packages we could choose for our meal. What we took became our meal. No finger poking and no trading of packages were allowed!

The second type of mystery meal involved a trip to the local grocery store. Each child (there were six) was given a set sum of money with which to buy any food item he/she wished. Then, one at a time, we would go into the store and make our selection. We could hardly contain our secret until one-by-one we would unveil our selection around the kitchen table. These meals usually consisted of all junk food (a rare treat)—from corn curls to marshmallow cookies—except for the one healthful food contributed by my mother.

The last kind of mystery meal is the one most commonly known. It involved a menu of creative names for common foods. For example, "dirty mattress" was really an ice cream sandwich and "naughty hen mixture" was a deviled egg. Each person received a menu and then ordered their food items in four courses. The order in which one chose one's food was the order in which those items were served. Flatware and drinks also needed to be ordered.
    —*Cheryl and Jerry Wyble, Salunga, PA*

▼ When the children were young, sometimes as often as once a month, we'd have a company meal, just for us. The meal was simple, but always it was elegant with a pretty tablecloth, perhaps candles, and always some of the serving dishes were family antiques. I felt that our children would care about our family things only if we used them and talked about them regularly.
    —*Charlotte H. Croyle, Archbold, OH*

▼ Children like to make name cards for guests and family on special occasions. We use small pictures that fit a theme, such as light, hearts, singing, etc., and each person is given a verse to read that is related to our theme. Themes can be chosen to coincide with the season, holidays, or special events.
    —*Mattie Miller, Sugarcreek, OH*

▼ We've extended suppertime to include Teatime. For Teatime, the adults have tea and the little one (18 months) has "tea" in a special

cup: a cup of milk, with a few dribbles of tea. It's often messy, but he feels very grown up.
—*Ann and Byron Weber Becker, Kitchener, ON*

▼ When the refrigerator is full of leftovers, we list the leftovers on a piece of paper (menu). Diners order from the menu. Leftovers are much more exciting this way.
—*Suzann Shafer Bauman, Lima, OH*

▼ My father used to prepare and serve breakfast to us high-schoolers before the rest of the family so we could catch our early bus. It was a special point of contact with him.
—*David and Louisa Mow, Farmington, PA*

▼ When our children complained at mealtime about the food, we established a "Grumble box." A complainer paid a five-cent fine out of his/her allowance. It worked! On one occasion, a child was complaining about a certain dish of food. Suddenly the child remembered what he was doing and quickly exclaimed, "But that's the way I like it."
—*Omar A. and Delphia Kurtz, Morgantown, PA*

▼ We had a custom that helped decrease mealtime disappointments when something spilled or broke: whoever made the mess cleaned it up (with parents' help, if needed), without being reprimanded. It was an accident, and nothing was more important than the person.
—*Enos and Erma Shirk, Thornton, PA*

▼ Monday through Friday we all (except our four-year-old) get up early enough to have 10-15 minutes for devotions and prayer together before the boys leave for school at 7:30 a.m. We usually pray specifically with our sons about their protection and their school day.
—*David and Cynthia Shank, Joshua, Benjamin, Nathaniel and Caleb, Mt. Crawford, VA*

▼ One simple dilemma—whose turn it is to pray at our evening meal—was solved by our son praying on even dates and our daughter on odd dates. (Adam's birthday is on an even date and Amanda's is on an odd date.)
—*Gretchen Hostetter Maust and Robert Maust, Adam and Amanda, Keezletown, VA*

▼ When our daughters, who are now 21, 19, and 13, were younger, we tried to provide fun ways for them to participate in mealtime prayers other than just reciting memorized prayers. We would pray through the alphabet. Each evening at dinner we would take a different letter of the alphabet, starting with "A." We would go around the circle and each person would thank God for something that began with that letter of the alphabet. (This was especially fun when the girls were learning to read.) The letter would be posted so they could think throughout the day of something that began with that letter.

As autumn approached we made the outline of a large tree with bare branches on a poster board. Out of fall-colored construction paper we would cut a variety of leaves. Each evening at mealtime we placed leaves on two or three persons' plates. Those persons would pray for someone or something and write that on their individual leaves, then tape those leaves to the tree. After several weeks, when the tree was full of colorful leaves and the trees outside had started to lose their leaves, we started removing the leaves from the tree, two or three each evening, praying again for the person or thing on the leaf and thanking God for answers to prayers prayed weeks previously.
—Herb and Sarah Myers and daughters, Mount Joy, PA

▼ Our family uses Martin Luther's table grace, which our son learned at age two: "Come, Lord Jesus, be our guest, Let these gifts to us be blest. In the name of the Father, Son and Holy Spirit. Amen."
—Beth A. Schlegel and David Stoverschlegel,
North Wales, PA

▼ We take turns saying grace before meals. Sometimes we sing the "Doxology" as our grace, or a prayer song or chorus. Sundays we usually pray the Lord's Prayer together, unless we have guests and one of them prays.
—Anne Long, Mt. Joy, PA

▼ We hold hands during prayer or songtime before the meal—when the children were very young, they clapped at the end.
—Lorna Chr. Stoltzfus, New Holland, PA

▼ At suppertime we hold hands for prayer, read a short Bible story, and tell each other one new thing we learned that day.
—Shirley H. and Stuart W. Showalter, Goshen, IN

▼ We acquired some worn hymnals that we sing from before meals. The children love learning the new words and tunes and are delighted if the song is sung at church the next Sunday. We also take them when we travel in the car to pass the time. With the more familiar songs the children like to take turns singing solos on the verses.
—*Sue Aeschliman Groff, Kinzer, PA*

▼ We use the *Rejoice!* devotional magazine at breakfast and a different devotional book at bedtime. We often sing before meals, especially when married children or guests join us, and in the evening.
—*LaVerna and Lawrence Klippenstein, Winnipeg, MB*

Work

▼ We don't have children of our own, but we had a great method for making work a pleasure in the family in which I grew up. I am the oldest of seven children. We loved to read! When it was time for dishes, snipping beans for canning, or any other tedious task, out came one of the *Little House* books or one of the *Anne of Green Gables* books (or whatever was currently being enjoyed). One person read and the rest (Mom and the sisters) worked. Time flew!
—*Don and Ruth Hartman, Brutus, MI*

▼ All our children (three years old, 16 months and 16 months) are regular visitors at both of our work places. This works very well, even though we both teach in post-secondary settings.
—*Richard Harris and Caprice Becker, Manhattan, KS*

▼ When I (Ruth) returned to teaching, we had a family conference about how each of us could contribute to our family living. Kevin, Duane, and Bruce each became responsible for one supper a week. The person who prepared the meal is excused from doing dishes.

We try to follow garden and lawn work with swimming at our neighbor's pool.
—*Clayton and Ruth Steiner, Dalton, OH*

▼ We work together! We live on a 15-acre farm and grow strawberries and other produce. Our children aren't always happy about working, but there is something good about watching things grow and then harvesting the fruit of your labors together.
—*Roy and Hope Brubaker, Mifflintown, PA*

▼ We work alot together in the garden. Our four-year-old son has a pair of work gloves, a shovel and wheelbarrow. It all keeps him busy for hours and helps him understand the wonderful world of nature and where food comes from.
—*Jim, Carol and Jonathan Spicher, Mountville, PA*

▼ Each spring we have accumulated a pile of sticks, seed pods and fruit tree prunings on an edge of our garden. This pile becomes the fuel for the first hot dog roast of the season in late April. For young children, the love of roasting hot dogs and marshmallows is good incentive for spring clean-up work.
—*Stan and Susan Godshall, Mt. Joy, PA*

▼ Our youngest, now 23, looked forward to his dad helping him wash and wax his "new" truck, recently, when we visited him in another state where he now lives. They had a good time talking about sports (local and national) and work, among other things.
—*Jim and Dee Nussbaum, Kidron, OH*

Evenings

▼ We sing together after supper with instruments (fiddle and guitar); we sing lullabies at bedtime.
—*Joan Schrock Woodward and Don Woodward, Elizabethton, TN*

▼ After dinner, since the piano is beside the table, I usually play and we all sing.
—*Valerie A. Metzler and William D. Minter, Chicago, IL*

▼ On sunny summer evenings, we enjoy taking a drive in our convertible and finding different spots in the county to go for ice cream.
—*Mike and Kim Pellman, Matt and Brooke, Bird-in-Hand, PA*

▼ On summer evenings we frequently ate freezers of ice cream with neighbors.
—*Martin and Sadie Hartzler, Mill Creek, PA*

▼ A walk/ride around the block in the little red wagon was almost a daily event when Dad came home from work in the evening.
—*Robert and Miriam Martin, East Earl, PA*

▼ At dusk we play hide-and-seek, now with our children *and* grandchildren.
> —*David M. and Rhonda L. King, Cochranville, PA*

▼ We have two children, Jesse, five, almost six, and Jacob, two, almost three. After supper we have an "activity." Some evenings we choose something the four of us can do together; other nights each child chooses to do something alone with Mom or Dad.

A favorite activity for the four of us is listening to children's tapes and dancing or running or acting out the songs. Other times we play rhythm instruments to accompany the tapes.
> —*Anita and Randy Landis-Eigsti, Lakewood, CO*

▼ We set aside one night as "Family Night" when we choose an activity for the evening for all of us to do together. The children submitted ideas that we keep on a page to choose from.
> —*Galen and Marie Burkholder, Jed, Kara, and Gina, Landisville, PA*

▼ For a number of years, my father and I played a game of ping-pong virtually every night before we went to bed.
> —*L. Lamar Nisly, Newark, DE*

▼ We have always read books as a family in the evenings. Because of the wide range in our children's ages, now 18, 16, 11, and nine, we have not always expected all the kids to sit and listen. In the last several years, as we have read primarily to the younger two, we have quietly observed the two older ones lingering in the living room to listen, particularly to books they enjoy remembering.
> —*Lois and Jim Kaufmann, New Paris, IN*

▼ We often do crossword puzzles together, passing them to each other when we're stymied. The one in the daily paper has become a nightly ritual and keeps three of us huddled over it, sometimes until near midnight.
> —*LaVerna and Lawrence Klippenstein, Winnipeg, MB*

▼ We have tea at 10:00 p.m. daily. All other activity ceases, and we (family of four) sit around the kitchen table. While our children attended high school, they would frequently bring their friends home for tea and goodies—always at 10:00.
> —*Irvin and Leona Peters, Winkler, MB*

Bedtime _____

▼ Our daughters remember joining me on warm, moonlit summer nights, lying under the stars on a specific old orange blanket in our backyard. We'd count falling stars, name constellations, tell stories, giggle, then snuggle together when it grew chilly or the mosquitoes got too thick—and put off bedtime forever.
>—*Charlotte H. Croyle, Archbold, OH*

▼ Our one daughter dislikes the end of an activity. So rather than abruptly stopping, we've learned to say, "We need to go to bed soon—shall this be the last game?" She agrees, and the transition seems much easier for her.
>—*Phyllis and Merle Good, Kate and Rebecca,*
>*Lancaster, PA*

▼ There was no better way to end the day then snuggled up to my mother, drifting to sleep with the adventures of Christopher Robin or Laura Ingalls in my head.

Later we read together such classics as *Treasure Island* and *Little Women*. I am certain that my love of literature as an adult comes from memories of those wonderful, warm childhood evenings.
>—*Kristine Platt Griswold, Falls Church, VA*

▼ Ernie read through the *Narnia* series several times with the children at bedtime.
>—*Ernest and Lois Hess, Lancaster, PA*

▼ Bedtime usually includes a half hour of reading aloud after the children are ready for bed. After that they talk quietly with each other or read until they wind down and go to sleep.
>—*Louise S. Longenecker, Oxford, PA*

▼ When the children are ready for bed, we read a Bible story. We have used various Bible storybooks; my favorite is Cornelia Lehn's *God Keeps His Promise*. We then tuck the kids in and sing to them. Either parent does this routine; occasionally we do it together.
>—*Rod and Martha (Yoder) Maust, Indianapolis, IN*

▼ At bedtime we had two stories—one of the children's choice and one from *The Children's Story Bible*.
>—*Ellen S. Peachey, Harpers Ferry, WV*

▼ At bedtime we have used a series of child-oriented Bible stories when the children were between two and six years of age. After that they graduated to morning devotions. We make a special effort to tell the boys of our love as they go to bed. When our sons were six months to four years old, I repeated a ritual at bedtime, "Special boy, precious son, one of a kind, I'm glad you belong to me."

> —*David and Cynthia Shank, Joshua, Benjamin,*
> *Nathaniel, and Caleb, Mt. Crawford, VA*

▼ At bedtime we have our devotions, do the "Trivia" questions in our daily newspaper and read 15-20 minutes from a book. We read nonfiction, true adventure, books by Mennonite writers, humor, and historical fiction.

> —*Mr. and Mrs. Nelson Schwartzentruber, Lowville, NY*

▼ I sat on the stairway to read to the children when they were all in their teens and were sleeping in two rooms, three boys in one and two girls in the other. We never had a bedtime problem that I can remember. Now I read to the grands when they are here.

> —*Allen and Doris Schrock, Goshen, IN*

▼ From birth, up to and sometimes during, their early high school years, our children's bedtime routine included a story or chapters from a children's book—something just hot off the press (Helen worked as a children's book buyer)—a song and, always, falling asleep listening to classical music.

> —*Ken and Helen Nafziger, Jeremy, Kirsten, and Zachary,*
> *Harrisonburg, VA*

▼ I am a music teacher and have our own children in class, so our daughter and son request "private songs." These bedtime songs are ones which were never sung at school!

> —*Joan and Larry Litman, Hoboken, NJ*

▼ At bedtime we spend 30 minutes or more singing with guitars and harmonicas.

> —*Mary Hochstedler and Ruth Andrews, Kokomo, IN*

▼ At bedtime, after baths, the children and one of us parents would sit snuggled together on the sofa and read stories aloud. Then it was into the bedroom for a prayer, followed by a backrub. After the backrub I played piano and sang softly for a time. All four children

still remember the words and tunes to many of the songs in Lois
Lenski's book of peace songs, entitled *We Are Thy Children.*
—*Charlotte H. Croyle, Archbold, OH*

▼ Instead of a bedtime story, my son's family sometimes plays
charades. It's great fun for all ages.
—*Helen G. Kennell, Eureka, IL*

▼ Daddy's bedtime stories made that time of the day one to be
anticipated. Daddy usually did not read stories; instead he made
up stories. Sometimes they were stories based on an event in his
childhood, sometimes they were about the girls' dolls or stuffed
animals, sometimes they were disguised stories about one child, but
most often they were animal stories with a moral or lesson to be
learned. The story just grew as he told it.
—*Herb and Sarah Myers and daughters, Mt. Joy, PA*

▼ Like many of today's families, we live far from other relatives and the
people we grew up with. As our daughter grew older, we realized
that she would not gain a sense of family history unless we provided
it for her. As a result, we started telling "when I was little" stories as
part of her bedtime ritual. She loved to hear about our early lives,
and we soon discovered that the stories she liked best related
directly to her world as well. (After a trip to the doctor's office, she
would say "Mommy, tell me when you were little and got sick."
When she got a new trike, her daddy had to tell about when he had
a bike.)
　　Second, the stories didn't need to have a clear beginning, middle
and end, or a clear moral. The most popular stories were short and
described the day-to-day realities of our childhood worlds and the
ways we related to parents, siblings, and friends ("Mommy, tell me
about when you got a new baby" was a very frequent request for the
first six months after her baby brother was born.).
　　Third, details about how we felt or what something looked like or
what we said always improved the story. But woe to the storyteller
who told the story again and left out a detail or two!
　　Finally, my husband and I found that our own relationship was
enriched. By "eavesdropping" on each other's stories we learned
new things about one another.
—*Susan and Scott Sernau, Sierra and Luke, South Bend, IN*

▼ Howard began telling stories about "Monkus," a monkey and his adventures in the forest, when our children were young. Now when he puts the grandchildren to bed, they ask for stories about "Monkus."
—*H. Howard and Miriam Witmer, Manheim, PA*

▼ At bedtime I develop another episode of Chip and Gale, with the enthusiastic participation of the younger children. Chip and Gale are two friendly chipmunks who live in a hollow tree located next to a river in a forest. They are able to communicate with other animals and birds, and they become involved in rescues, daring adventures, Good Samaritan acts, solving mysteries and dealing with almost-human problems. After I set the stage, the children may guess what happens next and give ideas, enabling the story to go on indefinitely.
—*Cornelia and Arlie J. Regier,*
Overland Park, KS

▼ Our little ones respond to a ride to bed "by camel" (on my shoulders) or "by elephant" (on my back) or for special, a "cloud ride," carried aloft on a pillow. Saturday nights we play family games, and on Sunday nights I read to them or we sing.
—*David and Louisa Mow, Farmington, PA*

▼ Our younger son, Steve, loved stuffed animals and had a bed full of them. At bedtime when he employed delaying tactics to keep from going to his room, my husband or I simply said, "Steve, your animals are crying. They're saying, 'Where's our little boy? We can't sleep until our little boy comes.'" Steve would listen and then run to his waiting animals and bed. Dick and I always looked at each other and laughed. We expected Steve to see through our ploy, but it worked for years.
—*Dick and Nancy Witmer, Richard and Steve,*
Manheim, PA

▼ To get youngsters upstairs at bedtime Mom cut large shoes from the *Sears* catalog (it takes alot!), making a trail around chairs, under tables—wherever—then up the stairs.
—*John and Marilyn Burkhart, Mount Joy, PA*

▼ At bedtime, as a way of discovering feelings or even information about the day, we sometimes ask these questions: What in your day made you happy? What made you sad? What would you do differently? What were you glad you did?
—*Galen and Marie Burkholder, Jed, Kara, and Gina,*
Landisville, PA

▼ For a period of time (several months), Ernie was "Answer Man," traipsing to each child's room after they were settled in for the night to answer their question of the day.
> —*Ernest and Lois Hess, Lancaster, PA*

▼ Our daughters, at different ages, have asked for something to think about when they're trying to go to sleep. A few ideas: 1) 10 favorite memories with your cousins; 2) 25 words which rhyme with "pray;" 3) name 20 streets in our city and put them in alphabetical order; 4) hum quietly a part of 12 pieces of music you enjoy (including hymns or school songs); 5) see how many persons you can name from our church who are 10 years old or younger. There are literally hundreds of fun, warm lists one can suggest.
> —*Phyllis and Merle Good, Kate and Rebecca,*
> *Lancaster, PA*

▼ Dave and I each put a child to bed, and we alternate from one night to another. My own mom gave me a back rub at the end of each day and we always talked together.
> —*Jenny and Dave Moser, Bluffton, OH*

▼ At bedtime at least one parent always talked and prayed with each child individually. During high school those sharing times often extended past midnight.
> —*Mary and Nelson Steffy, East Petersburg, PA*

▼ Bedtime always includes this rhyme—"Good night, sleep tight, wake up bright, in the morning light, to do the right, with all your might!"
> —*Ilse and Larry R. Yoder, Goshen, IN*

▼ Most nights we have bedtime prayers together as a family. Occasionally, to liven things a little, we choose a favorite hymn as our prayer, and then sing it through as fast as we can, each of us racing to be the first one finished.
> —*Phyllis and Merle Good, Kate and Rebecca,*
> *Lancaster, PA*

Saturdays

▼ Friday evening Roger stops at a bakery on the way home from work to pick up a special sweet treat for breakfast Saturday morning. He often doesn't let anyone peek inside and makes us guess what it is when he brings the box out Saturday morning. We all look forward to both old favorites and new treats.

—Roger and Pamela Rutt, Lancaster, PA

▼ A routine we have is pancakes for breakfast on Saturday mornings. In fact, as the children were learning the days of the week, Saturday was called Pancake Day more often than Saturday.

—Daryl and Marlisa Yoder-Bontrager, Lancaster, PA

▼ Saturday morning we like to eat a bigger than usual breakfast together, often having waffles or pancakes made in the shape of specific animals with raisins for their eyes and mouths.

—Wayne and Mary Nitzsche, Wooster, OH

▼ Saturday mornings the children could stay in their pajamas until noon, and Mom would make whatever they wanted for breakfast— usually either French toast or pancakes and sometimes both.

—Mary and Nelson Steffy, East Petersburg, PA

▼ On Saturday mornings, usually throughout the school year, the kids go out with their dad to breakfast and then get the mail and "visit" work. It gives Mom a chance to catch up after the hectic school week.

—Mike and Kim Pellman, Matt and Brooke, Bird-in-Hand, PA

▼ Weekday mornings we have cereal or something simple for breakfast. Saturday morning is different. We all make breakfast together. Rebekah (five) and Laura (three) help Daddy scramble eggs. We mix up orange juice and make toast. While the eggs are cooking, we set a pretty table together and enjoy a nice big leisurely breakfast.

After eating we gather in the living room and listen to Saturday morning children's radio programs—Bible stories and songs. This has been a wonderful substitute for Saturday morning TV and begins a Family Day. Everyone loves Saturdays because Daddy stays home and we do fun stuff around the house together.

—Keith and Brenda Blank, Rebekah, Laura, and Matthew, Philadelphia, PA

▼ We like big pancake and waffle breakfasts Saturday mornings before each getting a list of jobs for the day.

—Richard and Jewel Showalter, Chad, Rhoda Jane, and Matthew, Irwin, OH

▼ Saturday is work day at our house—usually lawn work. When the children were young, we worked at projects together—weeding, mulching, mowing, etc. The younger children helped by serving iced tea or water or emptying weed baskets, etc. When everyone worked, we frequently bought hoagies for lunch.

Our current routine is to go out for Saturday breakfast before the work begins. If the children are coming home for the weekend, they check on the time we'll be going for breakfast so they can go along, with their friends or whoever is here. We have several hours together in a little "greasy spoon" place just to talk.

—*R. Wayne and Donella Clemens, Souderton, PA*

▼ Mom and Dad eat Saturday morning breakfast out each week, leaving the teenagers on their own. Parents share that as "special time."

—*Keith Schrag, Ames, IA*

▼ My wife and I have started a Saturday morning custom of having brunch; that is the meal in the week that I always prepare.

—*L. Lamar Nisly, Newark, DE*

▼ We prefer to make Saturdays a "together" time, maybe a work day, but not doing routine work like laundry or housecleaning. We usually work outside, tackling a special project of some sort. We try to finish up kind of early even if we're planning to be home in the evening so that we can be rested for Sunday church. Sometimes we spend some time watching several public television programs.

—*Allen and Roseanne Shenk family, Strasburg, PA*

▼ When our children were young, we declared one Saturday a "Backwards" day. Everything that could be done backwards was done so. We had dinner in the morning and breakfast in the evening. We all wore our clothes backwards, brushed our teeth before eating, ate dessert before the main part of the meal and the children played awhile before doing their homework! Not only was the day a real hit with the children, it made them think about the order in which they do things.

—*Don and Faye Nyce, Grantham, PA*

▼ Saturday evenings we have pizza for supper (usually the frozen ones we pop into the oven) and a lettuce salad and Pepsi. We set up TV trays in the living room and eat in there while we watch some taped Christian kid's programming from Saturday morning.

—*Judy Stoltzfus, Colorado Springs, CO*

▼ Friends make Saturday night Sloppy Joe and Potato Chip Night.
—*Harvey and Erma Sider, Fort Erie, ON*

▼ For many years as our family was growing, we went to my parents for Saturday night supper. We inevitably talked about some particular subject that would send my dad to check the encyclopedia, and we would have what we fondly called "Grandpa's lesson." While my parents are older now and we don't see each other every Saturday night, we still get together and often have our "lesson."
—*Clive and Margaret LeMasurier, Plainville, CT*

Sundays

▼ To let us know it was time to get up on Sunday mornings, my mother usually played a hymn or two on the piano.
—*Louise S. Longenecker, Oxford, PA*

▼ Sunday morning wake-up for the children was the sound of sacred music from the stereo.
—*Richard and Betty Pellman, Millersville, PA*

▼ Sunday mornings Mom always sang her made-up song while rubbing each youngster's back. "Today we go to Sunday School" (repeat 3 times) to learn more about Jesus." Then each child ran down the hallway and jumped into bed with Daddy. A grand bunch—six children! And a full bed!
—*John and Marilyn Burkhart, Mount Joy, PA*

▼ On Sunday morning we held hands before church, sang a hymn, such as "I Owe the Lord a Morning Song," and together prayed for the service.
—*J.C. and Ruth D. Wenger, Goshen, IN*

▼ Sunday mornings my husband makes omelettes for breakfast while "we girls" get ready for church. This started when our daughters were small and I needed to work with sashes, bows, etc.! Dad's omelettes are a much looked-forward-to family favorite.
—*Janet E. Dixon, Berne, IN*

▼ Sundays, after church, several families with small children go out for a fast-food lunch. The toddlers get to sit at their own table and feel very grown up.
—*Richard Harris and Caprice Becker, Manhattan, KS*

▼ Sundays we either have guests or we are guests in others' homes. When we host, the menu is chili, salad, and dessert.
—*Mary Hochstedler and Ruth Andrews, Kokomo, IN*

▼ Since I (Rachel) work, we treasure Sunday dinner at home as a family, but we use Sunday evening for entertaining—casual, usually with popcorn, pizza, and salad.
—*Marvin and Rachel Miller, Indianapolis, IN*

▼ Some things are so ordinary that no one quite remembers when they became special. This happened to us when our older daughter came home with her husband, Tony. We had attended church and then came home for dinner at our house. Tony went up and changed into everyday clothes. When he came down to eat, we were all surprised since it's our custom to come home for Sunday dinner and eat with our good clothes on. We had not thought to tell him because it was just natural to us!
—*Sam and Joyce Hofer, Morton, IL*

▼ We never work on Sundays, not even bed-making, and I try to have the main meal prepared ahead of time. Sunday is a complete day of rest. The children decide what we do—picnic, go to museums, sightsee, stay home and play board games, or play soccer baseball or kickball in the yard. This means, however, that we all work hard during the week and on Saturdays to get the duties done.
—*Miki and Tim Hill, Woodstock, MD*

▼ Sunday is the day for visiting my mother, the children's grandmother. Although we live 45 minutes away, very rarely do we not visit her on Sunday. Usually my mother makes a big Italian dinner, which lasts all afternoon, during which time we recap the week's events. Sometimes I make dinner at my home and just heat it up at her house.

This weekly visit has given my children and me a sense of tradition, belonging, and long-lasting memories. It gives my mother a sense of being important in our lives and keeps her connected in a way similar to her childhood in Italy, where grandparents were always respected and loved.
—*Marie Palasciano, Hazlet, NJ*

▼ We like to have company for Sunday dinner—visitors or other families and friends from church. We may each invite friends, especially if our guests don't include children our age.
> —*Richard and Jewel Showalter, Chad, Rhoda Jane, and Matthew, Irwin, OH*

▼ At Sunday dinner we ask, "What is one thing you heard or experienced in worship this morning?" We started this custom years ago when our children were small, as a way to help them learn to pay attention in church. They used to joke about listening just long enough to be able to answer the Sunday dinner question.
> —*Marlene and Stanley Kropf, Elkhart, IN*

▼ Sunday after church we have a light lunch (like sandwiches) and then go for a drive or to Granny and Grandpop's, usually stopping for ice cream to finish off the afternoon.
> —*Elizabeth Loux and Don Kraybill, Matthew, Micah, and Ashley, Harleysville, PA*

▼ During the summer when our children were younger we had to check on cattle 20-30 miles away in the Flint Hills area. So on Sunday afternoons we all piled in the car, and after we counted the cattle we looked for wildflowers on rocks or in crevices. In the winter we went ice skating.
> —*Wilma Schmidt, Walton, KS*

▼ When our children were in elementary school, we often rode bike on Sunday afternoons to one of the city or county parks. Sometimes we rode bike to church on Sunday in the summer.
> —*Joyce Rutt Eby, Goshen, IN*

▼ After church on Sundays we like to visit museums, zoos, and parks or just drive, although we're stopping aimless driving because of the damage it does to the environment.
> —*Valerie A. Metzler and William D. Minter, Chicago, IL*

▼ Often on Sunday afternoons during World War II our family visited the neighbors. We hitched up one of the work horses to the buggy and visited relatives and friends within a mile and a half. We weren't Amish, and there weren't any in our area or even close to us, so we were quite a spectacle. But we saved gas, for it was rationed during the War, and it was a lot of fun.
> —*Dorothea M. Eigsti, Morton, IL*

▼ We like to spend Sunday afternoons fishing at a nearby farm pond.
   —*Heidi and Shirley Hochstetler, Kidron, OH*

▼ On Sunday afternoons we take a walk down our long lane, around the barnyard, around the garden and, as Bess says, we "collect nature."
   —*Jenny and Dave Moser, Bluffton, OH*

▼ Sunday *faspa* (afternoon snacks and socializing) included "junk food" for our family and any friends they might bring home. Since our children could eat as much of this one meal per week as they wanted, they never spent their allowance on junk food. In the long run this saved them and us a lot of money.
   —*Irvin and Leona Peters, Winkler, MB*

▼ At our house we plan nutritious meals for every day of the week, and each person is expected to eat at least a small serving of every item. For the children that sometimes seems a monumental task. However, to offer some relief from that, Sunday evening supper is designated the "Get whatever you want" meal. It has become a fun time to search the cupboards and the refrigerator and enjoy the "no vegetables or fruits required" policy.
   —*Martha and Rich Sider, Lancaster, PA*

▼ Sunday breakfast was a light meal so I always planned a hearty dinner. Sunday supper was sort of a "fix your own," with sandwiches and often a baked rice pudding for dessert (still a favorite when the family come visiting).
   —*Iona S. Weaver, Lansdale, PA*

▼ Sunday night suppers at our house are what our sons have named "snacky suppers." The meal consists of crackers, cheese, apple wedges, carrots, cookies, and other easy things. The meal is eaten somewhere other than the kitchen—sometimes with folding trays on the sofa, sometimes on a sheet spread on the living room floor. We tell stories, play games, or just visit. It's become the favorite meal of the week.
   —*Kenny and Rachel Pellman, Nathaniel and Jesse, Lancaster, PA*

▼ Our children make the Sunday evening meal, even when visitors come. The meal is grilled cheese-sweet bologna open-faced sandwiches and sugar-cinnamon butter toast, both done on cookie sheets in the broiler.
—*Lorna Chr. Stoltzfus, New Holland, PA*

▼ Every Sunday night we have grilled cheese sandwiches, fruit salad, and popcorn for supper. If company comes, we just add or subtract some ingredients but maintain the same basic menu. I love having one day when I don't have to think about what to serve for a meal.
—*Nancy and Clair Sauder, Tim and Michael, Lancaster, PA*

▼ On the Sunday evenings when we do not have church we've made a tradition of renting a good family film (often nature oriented). For our supper we have cheese, carrot sticks, apple slices, and a huge bowl of popcorn, and we all sit on a blanket, picnic-style in the family room, and view the film together.
—*Miles and Dawnell Yoder, Lancaster, PA*

▼ If we don't have company for Sunday supper, our family really likes to make a meal, I'm almost embarrassed to admit, of popcorn and muffins, or sometimes even banana splits, and then watch Walt Disney together. It's been a lot of fun, doing two things which we usually discourage—not eating a balanced, healthy meal, *and* watching TV!
—*Jane-Ellen and Gerry Grunau, Winnipeg, MB*

▼ Sunday evening is "ice cream, popcorn, and game night" at our house.
—*Herb and Sarah Myers and daughters, Mount Joy, PA*

▼ Sunday evenings during the winter include supper by the living room fireplace, candlelight, classical music, and conversation.
—*Louise S. Longenecker, Oxford, PA*

3.

Celebrating Birthdays

▼ We wake up our birthday child with a song and lighted candles.
— *David and Louisa Mow, Farmington, PA*

▼ We always review the events of the day on which the birthday person was born: when Mother went into labor, how long the labor was, when they went to the hospital, and other tidbits that come to mind.
— *Marian J. Bauman, Harrisonburg, VA*

▼ I told our children the story of their births each year on their birthdays. The surprise of two baby girls when we were only prepared for one was an exciting story in itself, and our son was a very welcomed change four years later. I hope they caught the excitement and importance of their comings into our life, and I believe they did with this yearly ritual.
— *Ken and Eloise Plank, Hagerstown, MD*

▼ We kept the complete newspaper from the day each of our daughters was born. We also keep the complete newpaper from each of their birthdays through the years. When they become adults, this will be a gift to remember what was happening each year of their childhood and youth.
— *Phyllis and Merle Good, Kate and Rebecca, Lancaster, PA*

▼ The honored guest wore a homemade crown and was considered "King/Queen for a Day." The "Master of Ceremonies" gave program assignments to each member of the family. This included singing, piano lesson renditions, poems, jokes, riddles, original essays or recollections of birthdays of long ago by us as parents. We all gathered in the living room seated on chairs in rows facing the "MC" to give the atmosphere of a real production at a theater. The applause helped encourage creative expression.
— *L. Glen and Allie Guengerich, Kalona, IA*

▼ In my husband's family, the one celebrating a birthday was made king or queen for the day. The special person was permitted to stay home from school, choose the dinner menu, and select a family activity—anything from a board game at home to a trip to the zoo or a

ball game. Rules were not entirely suspended but were certainly relaxed! We've found this way of celebrating so enjoyable that we have adopted the practice for our own family.
—*Kristine Platt Griswold, Falls Church, VA*

▼ We tried to make birthdays occasions when the birth person's uniqueness was recognized, rather than focusing on gifts and parties. The choice of meals was theirs, they were not required to help in the preparation, the prayer before the meal included thanksgiving for the life of the birthday person and her/his contribution to our family and our world. We finished the meal with a homemade decorated cake with a personalized theme. If guests showed up on these days, as was the case on several occasions, they were welcomed and included in the ritual. The sixth, sixteenth and twenty-first birthdays were larger affairs, with some special guests invited and fun games planned.
—*Norman and Ruth Smith, Ailsa Craig, ON*

▼ For birthdays we always set the table with candles, a tablecloth and the red "you're special" plate.
—*Marvin and Rachel Miller, Indianapolis, IN*

▼ On birthdays each person around the table shares a special memory of the birthday person from the past year as we enjoy his/her favorite menu, cake, and ice cream. We also read from Lois' journal of events from the birthday person's younger years, which always inspires shared laughter over wonderful memories.
—*Ernest and Lois Hess, Lancaster, PA*

▼ Something that has been fun for birthdays has been to think back over the past year and to gather together items that represent that individual's year. We try to use small objects because I arrange them as a centerpiece on the table, a sort of montage of the birthday person's stage of life.
—*Allen and Roseanne Shenk family, Strasburg, PA,*

▼ We follow a custom brought from Russia by our parents. When a child has a birthday, he/she sits on a chair, and is lifted—chair and all—into the air, once for each year.
—*Marie K. Wiens, Hillsboro, KS*

▼ Birthday celebrations revolve around a theme. We have had a Decorate-Your-Bike and Clown Make-Up Party that resulted in a

parade. Another party included Olympics with the high jump and running races with staggered starts for various age groups. We created our own version of the Double Dare Game with an obstacle course exercise.
—*Suzann Shafer Bauman, Lima, OH*

▼ We usually celebrate birthdays by picking some theme and carrying it through the celebration. When Daryl's birthday present was an umbrella, his birthday cake was shaped like an umbrella. When we were in Florida over Yovana's birthday, one of her presents was a dress with a pink flamingo on it. Her cake was shaped like a flamingo.
—*Daryl and Marlisa Yoder-Bontrager, Lancaster, PA*

▼ Our older son's birthday is December 6, so we always buy a Christmas tree on his birthday and decorate it that evening. The house is dressed in Christmas festivity for his birthday. Our younger son's birthday is September 21, so on his day we go to a local farm market and buy pumpkins and Indian corn to celebrate fall.
—*Kenny and Rachel Pellman, Nathaniel and Jesse, Lancaster, PA*

▼ On our family birthdays we give the kids a chance to choose between going away for a weekend or having a birthday party and inviting grandparents, aunts, uncles, and cousins.
—*Mike and Kim Pellman, Matt and Brooke, Bird-in-Hand, PA*

▼ One of our favorite birthday adventures was a trip to the Philadelphia Zoo after a heavy snow. It was early February and Kate had just turned two. Walking on paths through the deep snow between the buildings and watching the animals cavort in the white stuff was great fun. And there were no lines!
—*Phyllis and Merle Good, Kate and Rebecca, Lancaster, PA*

▼ The birthday child could invite a guest for each year that he/she was old. The birthday person helped make decorations, choose games, and decide on refreshments. Not only that, but we had a birthday dinner with the grandparents as well. We also gave a special gift to the child *not* celebrating a birthday, which the children remember *more* than the presents they got when it was their own birthday!
—*Sam and Joyce Hofer, Morton, IL*

▼ Birthdays have been primarily family experiences. Parties with friends invited were limited to the children's sixth, twelfth and sixteenth birthdays. Grandparents often joined us for the birthday meal which was planned by the birthday child.
—*Lois and Jim Kaufmann, New Paris, IN*

▼ We have always invited both sets of grandparents to our daughters' birthday suppers. As the girls have gotten older, we've asked the grandparents to tell stories about when they were the age of the birthday person. This last year, when our older daughter turned 15, I (Phyllis) decided to be a little more deliberate about the storytelling, in an effort to bridge the generations. I wrote to each grandparent before the event and asked them to come prepared to answer three questions: What was their favorite thing to do when they were 15? What was their favorite food? What was their favorite music?
Each came with stories and, as the evening progressed, they inspired each other with more memories. Not only did we learn new things about people we thought we knew well, the evening opened new avenues of conversation for granddaughters and grandparents.
—*Merle and Phyllis Good, Lancaster, PA*

▼ On the years our children didn't have a birthday party, we invited a friend and that person's family for a birthday supper.
—*Norman and Dorothy Kreider, Harrisonburg, VA*

▼ The birthday person is always given breakfast in bed by the rest of the family on the Sunday closest to his/her birthday.

▼ Our gifts are generally not bought, but made, or are gifts of time or actions. For example, "I will help you pick out some good books at the library." "I will make lasagna for supper one day". . . , etc.

▼ Birthdays are a good excuse to have a family celebration. For the children we generally have three parties per birthday: one for just our own family, one with the child's friends, and one with the extended family. Our extended family is not the usual. We do not have family within the city, so as our children have grown, we have nurtured a "chosen" extended family. This has included a few families our own age with children the same age as ours, as well as families where the adults are the ages of our parents, or somewhere in between. This extended family has become very special to us.
—*Jane-Ellen and Gerry Grunau, Winnipeg, MB*

▼ Our family gets together once a month to celebrate that month's birthdays. No birthdays that month? We get together anyway for a light evening meal.
 —John and Marilyn Burkhart, Mount Joy, PA

▼ We wrap birthday gifts in odd shapes with newsprint or used gift wrap to save the earth. We always sing "Happy Birthday" often throughout the day, but at least once *loud* and *off key* to raise the roof.
 —David and Martha Clymer, Shirleysburg, PA

▼ In our daughters' teen years, Dad always remembers their birthdays with flowers.
 —Clive and Margaret LeMasurier, Plainville, CT

▼ Instead of giving gifts to my nieces, we celebrate their birthdays by taking them to an ethnic restaurant, to a play, or by visiting a special place. Memories of these events outlast any gift we could give.
 —Suzann Shafer Bauman, Lima, OH

▼ Birthdays are times for cards, calls, or special cakes. We sisters search all year to find the perfect hilarious birthday card for each other...the kind you can only send to folks who *know* you love them!
 —Shirley Kirkwood, Mt. Solon, VA

▼ Children as young as two or three years old can help choose birthday cards and cake decorations for parents' or siblings' birthdays.
 —Richard Harris and Caprice Becker, Manhattan, KS

▼ We planted a tree at my parents' farm when our son was born. We try to take a photo of him beside the tree on his birthday each year.
 —Jim and Carol Spicher and Jonathan,
 Mountville, PA

▼ As each baby was born, we bought a rocking chair in which that baby would be rocked. The chair is destined to be *that child's* chair and will accompany him/her to college, apartments, and houses, and perhaps someday will rock his/her babies.
 —Ken and Helen Nafziger, Jeremy, Kirsten, and Zachary,
 Harrisonburg, VA

▼ Birthday celebrations are special if they include a special prayer (written by one family member or with everyone contributing), thanking God for the birthday person.
—*Nancy Nussbaum, Elkhart, IN*

Practices for Particular Years

▼ Soon after your child turns four years old, take her to a garage sale, auction, or dime store. Invite the child to pick out a special plate that will be hers and hers alone! Purchase the plate and take it home. Whenever your child has something special to talk about or show at dinner, or whenever something special has happened, she may request her special plate. This will signal to everyone in the family that there is something to listen to that night! Use the special plate on birthdays and "gottcha" days (for adoptive children) as well.

All family members should have their own plates for such occasions. You will be amazed at the significance these plates take on. And when your children get married, buy another special plate, wrap both up and give them to the bride and groom as wedding gifts. And the circle continues!
—*Nancy Nussbaum, Elkhart, IN*

▼ At 10 or 11 years of age, each child spends a special weekend with the same sex parent to "prepare for adolescence." Making this a fun and exciting time provides a foundation for ongoing openness about relationships, sex, finances, education, and decision-making in general.
—*Chuck and Robyn Nordell, Fullerton, CA*

▼ On birthdays we show a slide history of the birthday kid. Dad takes the 10-year-old on a two-day camping trip as a rite of passage.
—*Keith Schrag, Ames, IA*

▼ On our children's tenth birthdays they were honored by a party with school classmates of their same sex.
—*Clayton and Ruth Steiner, Dalton, OH*

▼ One grandmother I know has a special gift for each grandchild on his/her eleventh birthday. She takes the child on a "heritage tour" which includes a visit to her childhood home and school 25 miles from her present home. They visit a cemetery where her parents are

buried, her church, and other places and people of special
significance in her life. The event includes restaurant meals, an
overnight, games, and individual attention.
—*Arlene Kehl, Kitchener, ON*

▼ We make a special presentation of a Bible when our children turn 12.
—*Virginia Buckwalter, Scarborough, ON*

▼ When each child turned 12, Ernie wrote a letter to the birthday
person that had been years in the making.
—*Ernest and Lois Hess, Lancaster, PA*

▼ Our church has a mentor program. At age 12 each child chooses an
adult mentor and that event is celebrated with a special ceremony in
church.
—*Shirley H. and Stuart W. Showalter,*
Goshen, IN

▼ When a child turns 13, we have a BIG sleepover with a movie and
permission to stay up all night.
—*Marvin and Rachel Miller, Indianapolis, IN*

▼ Our small group has developed an important ritual when our
children turn 13. We give the birthday child an oak box designed by
a friend and crafted by a local Amish woodworker. The box has a
secret drawer. In the box is a special letter from the whole group to
the new "man" or "woman." Each member of the group gives a
small symbolic gift to fit in the box. For the presentation ceremony,
the 13-year-old chooses the menu; the parents share slides,
pictures, and stories; the group gives the box.
—*Shirley H. and Stuart W. Showalter, Goshen, IN*

▼ When the children turn 13 and 16, we invite their friends to special
parties.
—*Dick and Cathy Boshart, Carolyn and Jeff, Lebanon, PA*

▼ When a child turns 16, we celebrate with a family dinner at a fancy
restaurant of the birthday person's choice. We also plan a party if
the child wants one.
—*Marvin and Rachel Miller, Indianapolis, IN*

▼ On a child's sixteenth birthday we parents take that person on an overnight trip, just the three of us, giving special attention to the child and what she or he wants to do.
    —*Marian J. Bauman, Harrisonburg, VA*

▼ Turning 16 always meant a little more special birthday gift—in the case of our daughters, a piece of sterling silver jewelry which, hopefully, they will have for years to remember.
    —*Clive and Margaret LeMasurier, Plainville, CT*

▼ To recognize the new privilege/responsibility of age 16, when the children are eligible for a driver's license, we have given them a sturdy key chain with a house key and keys for both cars. Presenting them with their own keys symbolizes the expectations and trust we have as they become more independent.
    —*Stan and Susan Godshall, Mt. Joy, PA*
    —*Ben and Lorraine Myers, Dillsburg, PA*

▼ We gave a birthday letter to each of our children when they reached age 16, telling them of our appreciation for them, highlighting their strong characteristics, and giving them the family blessing for the future.
    —*H. Howard and Miriam Witmer, Manheim, PA*

▼ When a niece or a nephew turns 16, we take him/her out for a meal and a movie. It's become a way to establish a more adult relationship with each one.
    —*Merle and Phyllis Good, Lancaster, PA*

▼ When the children became 21 years of age, we planted a young tree in our yard in their honor. I (Mother) wrote a poem for each child at 21 to recap important events of their lives and presented them with their baby books and records of their growth and accomplishments.
    —*Dick and Cathy Boshart, Carolyn and Jeff, Lebanon, PA*

▼ Each child received a special letter written by Clayton on his/her 21st birthday. In it he summarized the values we've tried to pass on.
    —*Clayton and Ruth Steiner, Dalton, OH*

Birthday Food_____

▼ The birthday child gets to pick a sweet cereal for her/his birthday.
   —*Christine Certain, Fresno, CA*

▼ On a child's birthday, the birthday child could select the menu for the evening meal and decide how the cake should be decorated. Later, Scott decided he'd rather have homemade pizza or a cherry pie for his special dessert.
   —*Joyce Rutt Eby, Goshen, IN*

▼ My mother, Bette Weaver Metzler, started the tradition of making the menu of our birthday meals be the food that the *rest* of the family ate just *before* we were born (i.e. on our birth day).
   We continue the tradition. My husband, my mother (who was visiting to help with our son Ezra's birth), and I ate ham, green beans, and potatoes for supper before we all went to the hospital for Ezra's birth. Now we eat ham, green beans, and potatoes on Ezra's birthday!
   —*Valerie A. Metzler, Chicago, IL*

▼ One year, for each child's birthday, the birthday person, in addition to selecting the menu, helped Mom serve the meal in mystery supper-style.
   —*Don and Faye Nyce, Grantham, PA*

▼ For birthdays and Mother's and Father's Days, we give "gift certificates" for breakfast. Most often they are from child to parent (but have been parent to child and even, occasionally, sibling to sibling!) and are "redeemed" at a local restaurant in the weeks or months following the birthday. Sometimes the "coupon" is part of a homemade birthday card; sometimes it is a separate "fashioned-by-the-giver" certificate or coupon.
   Jim and I have really treasured these outings as extra opportunity for individual times with our kids.
   A few times when our children were younger, these events were backpack-bicycle-trip-breakfasts to a nearby park.
   —*Jim and Janalee Croegaert and family, Evanston, IL*

▼ Since our children were in junior high, we have always gone to a special Chinese restaurant for birthdays.
   —*Linda and Ron Gunden, Lisa and Angela,*
   Elkhart, IN

▼ After our children went to college, we modified an earlier tradition of taking them out to eat alone on their birthdays. We sent them money with instructions to "take yourself out to eat."
—*Charlotte H. Croyle, Archbold, OH*

▼ Ned's family often has a "cup of blessing" for each person's birthday. The birthday person is "toasted," with each person at the meal having a cup of grape juice, wine, or cranberry juice and saying why the birthday person is special to her or him.
—*Marie and Ned Geiser Harnish, Hannah and Nathan, Indianapolis, IN*

▼ Beginning at age four, each daughter went out with Daddy to breakfast at the place of her choice. At 13 he took them out for dinner in honor of their becoming a teenager and presented them with a special gift like a gold necklace with their initial on it. At 18 both parents took the birthday girl out for dinner.
—*Herb and Sarah Myers and daughters, Mount Joy, PA*

▼ Since our children no longer live with us, we miss the occasional contact with their friends, so for their birthday meals at our house, we often invite several of their friends, of their choice, to dine with us. Our family is small, so we enjoy additional persons.
—*Edwin and Rosanna Ranck, Christiana, PA*

▼ If birthdays fall on a school day, one parent takes time off work to go to school and eat in the cafeteria with our celebrant. This is a big deal in elementary school, but may not be "cool" later on.
—*Gretchen Hostetter Maust and Robert Maust, Adam and Amanda, Keezletown, VA*

▼ We're not into decorating cakes—but have special desserts like blueberry cheese cake, rhubarb custard, or pumpkin torte at birthday times.

▼ We also ask if the child wants friends or extended family guests at the special birthday time. When the children were in grades one through eight, they often chose a Mystery Supper party over things like T-bone steak, etc. They wanted to be surprised and eat the meal in the jumbled three-course style of a mystery supper.

Here are two suggested menus for mystery suppers. The guests, of course, see only the left-hand column:

Spring Theme

Spring Thaw	— chocolate cake with ice cream
Puddles	— glass of water
Robin's Delight	— spaghetti and meat balls
Grass	— green beans
Daffodils	— roll with pats of butter
Trowel	— fork
Flower Bed	— colorful jello salad
Twigs	— celery and carrot sticks
Little Dipper	— spoon
Mower	— knife
Bugs and Slugs	— pickles and olives
Bird's Nest	— napkin and toothpick

Valentine/Lovers Theme

Lovers' Mess	— tacos
Sweet and Sassy	— spiced cider
Ribbons and Lace	— napkin
Betwixt Two	— fork
Love Sick	— spoon
Wedding Ring	— pineapple upside-down cake
Peacemaker	— knife
Cupid's Dart	— toothpick
Flaming Passion	— salsa
Fragile	— corn chips
Complements	— refried beans and rice
Unquenchable	— glass of water

—*Richard and Jewel Showalter, Chad, Rhoda Jane, and Matthew, Irwin, OH*

Birthday Cakes

▼ Being a farm family, we usually all had breakfast together. The birthday cake (baked the previous day) and the gift were brought to the breakfast table immediately following devotions. We didn't eat the cake until after school or in the evening, but I always felt that the *entire* day was special because of the early start.
—*Elma Esau, North Newton, KS*

▼ For birthdays Papa makes shaped birthday cakes (butterfly, goose, rabbit, elephant, etc.).
—Rod and Martha (Yoder) Maust, Indianapolis, IN

▼ For their birthdays, Jesse and Jacob choose the kind of cake they want and then help make and decorate it. So far we've had a lamb, spider, giraffe, giant cookie face, and a tractor cake. The children are already planning their next cakes. Jesse wants a beautiful cake with pink flowers. Jacob wants a "dragon dinosaur with fire in its mouth."
—Anita and Randy Landis-Eigsti, Lakewood, CO

▼ I always made special birthday cakes and decorated them, such as a train with an engine and several cars, with one car having licorice sticks for logs and one a coal car with chocolates. I also made airplanes, boats, and dolls. Last year our grandson asked for a train cake, "like you used to make," he said.
—Bob and Doris Ebersole, Archbold, OH

▼ Angel food cake has always meant that it's birthday time at our house. Before our grandchildren were old enough to bake cakes for their mother (as I always did for her before she was married), I continued the tradition of baking a cake for her special day. But I let the decorating for the grandchildren to do after they arrived at our house for dinner on her special day. Peanut M&Ms and birthday candles were planted in the frosting by willing hands and hearts of love. It was a way I could still celebrate my daughter's birthday, yet let the children contribute, too, to the fun of celebration. (We've tried more delicate decorative candies too, but M&Ms are a favorite in spite of the fact that they make the cake look gaudy!)
—Ruth Naylor, Bluffton, OH

▼ Our two youngest boys have the same birthday so we always have two cakes at their birthday meal. Last year, 10-year-old Drew had a 10-layer birthday cake!
—Jim and Nancy Roynon, Brad, Taryn, Drew, and Colin, Archbold, OH

▼ One year we had each guest place a candle on the birthday cake and say something they appreciate about the birthday person.
—Ken and June Marie Weaver, Harrisonburg, VA

Birthday Parties

▼ When the children were young, they usually had three birthday parties: one with their friends, a second one with the maternal family and a third one with the paternal family. We have a small house and it was one way to include everyone in the celebration.
—*The Sfrisi family, Lodi, NJ*

▼ Our sons always have birthday parties. They make out the invitation list and often ask one or two special friends to sleep over. We ask our boys to write thank you notes for all the gifts they receive. We see that as a teaching opportunity.
—*David and Cynthia Shank, Joshua, Benjamin, Nathaniel, and Caleb, Mt. Crawford, VA*

▼ For David's third birthday, we went with his two best "older" child friends to a museum where we have a membership and guest privileges. The next day I invited his best "little" friend and a few adult friends of ours, along with immediate family, to our house to celebrate. David was not overwhelmed trying to divide his time among lots of kids, and the adults could have relaxed conversation, too. I did not have planned activities, but simply allowed David to play with his friend and enjoy the attention and affection of all present as he felt able. It worked very well!
—*Beth A. Schlegel and David Stoverschlegel, North Wales, PA*

▼ One of the most favorite games we played with our children's birthday party guests was *Topfschlagen*, literally translated "beating the pot." Whoever would be "It" was blindfolded, given a cooking spoon, and cheered on to find the cookpot on the grass or living room floor (depending on the season), crawling on all fours, groping with the spoon. When the spoon hit the pot, the finder's

blindfold would be removed and he/she was entitled to the small gift hidden under the pot.
—*Reinhild K. Janzen, Newton, KS*

▼ I probably allowed more "messes" in the house than most parents would be willing to stand. For a birthday party one year I set up the tent (freestanding kind) in the dining room (a very large room) for a slumber party. Because the birthday was in January, the weather wasn't conducive to a camp-out. It was a spectacularly successful

party. I let homemade tents or "camps" stand in the house for days until their usefulness in play diminished.
—*Ann James Van Hooser, Princeton, KY*

Birthday Gifts

▼ Even if the children have a birthday party with friends, we always celebrate the birthday as a family also. First we sit in a circle with the birthday person in the center. Each person says one thing they appreciate about that person or mention a way he or she has changed and matured over the past year. Then, one person says a prayer for the birthday person.

Beforehand each person wraps a gift—some gifts are small—and hides it. During this circle time, we take turns giving clues about where the gifts are hidden—usually on another floor in the house. The birthday person searches for the gifts. The birthday person's pleasure in figuring out the clues and running up and down the stairs adds to the celebrative mood. This method also makes gift opening last longer, and makes it more of an adventure and more exciting for the observing siblings.
—*Sue Aeschliman Groff, Kinzer, PA*

▼ Because both Stan and I enjoy good books, we decided to give each of the children a very special book for every birthday and Christmas. Now when they look at the row of birthday and Christmas books on their shelves, they also see a record of their changing interests over the years. We also give them a Christmas tree ornament each year so they will have their own collection when they leave home.
—*Marlene and Stanley Kropf, Elkhart, IN*

▼ Grandma gives the boys money for their birthdays, then takes them shopping so they can buy presents. She even cooperates with their "comparative shopping" wishes, and has been known to cover the entire mall and nearby stores and then retrace steps to where they found the best buy.
—*Nancy and Clair Sauder, Tim and Michael, Lancaster, PA*

▼ Our two oldest children have birthdays one day apart between Thanksgiving and Christmas. Rather than a party and presents, we have often given them the option of a day and night in the city (Philadelphia). Each may choose a museum or special activity. It is

always a special way to celebrate, with other gatherings and gifts coming so close. (Many hotels run special family rates.)
—*Elizabeth Loux and Don Kraybill, Matthew,*
Micah, and Ashley, Harleysville, PA

▼ Birthdays are a time for giving "blessings." We make placemats for the special birthday person with affirmations and recognition for what she or he accomplished during the year. This includes words and pictures and a special wish for the coming year for growth. These are laminated and placed in a scrapbook.
—*Mark and Leone Wagner, Lititz, PA*

Adoption Celebrations

▼ We go out to eat at a restaurant of our child's choice on her "special day." "Special day" is the anniversary of the day we brought each of our adopted daughters home.
—*Paul and Elaine Jantzen, Hillsboro, KS*

▼ We adopted twin girls into our family. They were 11 months old when they came to live with us on a cold January day. Their birthday is in February, and the adoption became final in September, 18 months later. We celebrate all three events, with the birthday being the biggest event for them, and "Homecoming," or the day they came to live with us, being the most memorable for the rest of the family. Adoption day is important but is usually low-key because it was anticlimactic for us as a family, and sometimes we almost forget it.

For us parents, the Homecoming was the girls' "birthday," and it was a celebration to bring them home. Had they been newborns, the Homecoming probably wouldn't have been so important. But they were 11 months old and their infant days were nearly over. We have no pictures or memories of that time; therefore, their birthday has little meaning for us, other than the fact that they are a year older. Since they are twins, it feels especially right to celebrate all three events.

We usually have cakes and some kind of gift. Homecoming Day is a private event with just family. We tell about our going to get them and bringing them home, complete with pictures of the event which replace infant pictures for us. Most often the birthday is shared with friends as well as family, sometimes with a party, or an event such as ice or roller skating, or a sleepover with a few friends.
—*Karen Martin, Evanston, IL*

4.

Advent and Christmas

Advent _____

▼ Many years ago, we decided to develop a variety of traditions around Christmas so that receiving presents would not be the focal point. We always bake peppernuts. Even toddlers can help cut the rolls of dough into little pieces. For a few years we put handmade symbols on a Jesse tree, beginning on December 1.

▼ Another fun tradition is to put on Christmas records or tapes when the first snows fall. Sometimes that happens in November, but that's okay. Living in northern Indiana, we associate Christmas with snow! After that first snowfall, the records are put away until closer to Christmastime.
                    —*Lois and Jim Kaufmann, New Paris, IN*

▼ On the eve of Advent the young people in our church go around and sing Christmas songs to families after they are in bed. We gather the next morning for a community breakfast to start the Christmas season.
                    —*David and Louisa Mow, Farmington, PA*

▼ The Advent season begins the Saturday before the first Advent Sunday, when we cut fresh branches from evergreens in the yard, mostly from cedars, to make a wreath into which we place four red Advent candles. We also fill a vase or two with evergreens, so that the whole house is filled with the wonderfully strong resin aroma.
     The first batch of peppernuts or some German Christmas *stollen* is baked on this day as well, adding to the special scents that announce the season. This is also the day when we place the Christmas music on the piano, some in German, still from my childhood.

▼ Each Advent Sunday morning we light a new candle while we sing an Advent song around the breakfast table.

▼ When the children were in school, the first of Advent was also the day when they could place a Christmas wish list on Mom's desk, to be passed on to Santa Claus. Of course the understanding was that Santa Claus would be most impressed by beautiful writing and illustrations. The understanding was also that "Santa Claus" was a

metaphor for clothing the material side of Christmas gifts in a shroud of magic.
—*Reinhild K. Janzen, Newton, KS*

▼ Our Advent candle is a 12-inch homemade one with the numbers one to 25 painted in spiral fashion from top to bottom. Holly leaves or other season designs go in between. Each day the candle is burned through the correct date. We give many away to others—church families, work colleagues with small children, etc. Now that our children are grown and have homes of their own, they anticipate the arrival of the candle package before December 1.
—*Bill and Phyllis Miller, White Pigeon, MI*

▼ About 30 days before Christmas, we hang a red, white, and green paper chain with 30 links. The children take turns removing a link each day.
—*Mr. and Mrs. Nelson Schwartzentruber,*
Lowville, NY

▼ One year we made an Advent log with 25 candles. We accompanied the daily lighting of them with a devotional reading and song. Just before Christmas we made clay ornaments of symbols which were part of the devotional readings: star of David, lamb, scepter, etc. We painted them, adorned them with glitter, and hung them on the Christmas tree. We gave them to guests in our home as ornaments for their trees.
—*Robert and Miriam Martin, East Earl, PA*

▼ For Advent we have a large cloth calendar with a pocket for each day in December. (There is also a little cloth mouse marker on a craft stick which is moved forward each morning.) I write a Bible reference pertaining to Advent on a card for each pocket and put it and a piece of candy in each pocket. After dinner each evening, one child (we alternate) pulls the card from the pocket, looks up the Bible verses, and reads them while we are all still at the table. When the card is returned to the pocket, the reader gets the candy. We usually try to discuss the meaning of the Bible verse. It's been interesting to see the children's comprehension of Old Testament prophecy develop over the years.
—*Gretchen Hostetter Maust and Robert Maust, Adam and*
Amanda, Keezletown, VA

▼ Starting on the first day of December, our family counts the days until Christmas by using an Advent calendar. The calendar consists of a large piece of felt material with 25 numbered pockets on it. Each pocket contains a Bible verse and a felt object to stick onto the calendar. Every night at suppertime, we take turns reading the verse and putting the object up. On Christmas morning, we put up Baby Jesus, and our manger scene on the calendar is complete. This is a fun, educational way to learn what the Christmas season is really about.
—*Heidi and Shirley Hochstetler, Kidron, OH*

▼ Each year during Advent we've tried to learn a new Christmas or Advent hymn by singing it every night at suppertime. We light the Advent candles and oil lamps and eat supper by candlelight. Sometimes we'll sit by the Christmas tree for our Bible story at bedtime, and I'll tell parts of the Advent and Christmas story rather than using a book. I also choose Christmas songs for bedtime songs.
—*Rod and Martha (Yoder) Maust, Indianapolis, IN*

▼ One custom we keep is reading each day's assortment of Christmas cards and letters at the dinner table in the evening.
—*Marlene and Stanley Kropf, Elkhart, IN*

▼ We purchased special twisted candles that were purposely constructed to drip. Several weeks before Christmas, we began to burn a candle at each evening meal. We used various colors, creating our own special piece of art over the years. After Christmas we put it away and added to it the following year.
—*John and Trula Zimmerly, Jackson, OH*

▼ During Advent the children move Joseph and Mary on the donkey (from the nativity set, carved by Dad from styrofoam and dressed by Mom and the children), a little closer each day from the farthest corner of the house to the stable under the Christmas tree. On Christmas Eve shepherds and angels are added while Dad reads the account from Luke 2.
—*Dietrich and Mary Rempel, Hesston, KS*

▼ When our children were young, we set up the stable under the tree. Everything was there but Mary, Joseph, and Jesus. They traveled from room to room (or wherever the boys would move them) until Christmas morning when they arrived at the stable.
—*Hazel Miller, Hudson, IL*

▼ Between Thanksgiving and Christmas we take an evening to have a meal at our favorite Chinese restaurant in Philadelphia's Chinatown and then visit the Christmas displays in department store windows along Market Street and in the toylands inside. This annual event we often shared with cousins visiting from Lancaster and/or Maryland.
—Luke and Miriam Stoltzfus, Philadelphia, PA

▼ We burn a new candle on our Advent wreath each Sunday during Advent, and on Christmas day itself we light a special fifth candle. A scripture reading and meditation goes with each lighting. The children also each had their own Advent calendars. Each day they put an ornament on the special felt tree on their calendars.
—Dick and Cathy Boshart, Carolyn and Jeff, Lebanon, PA

▼ We have had an Advent calendar and "wreath" (really just four candles with a small wood carving of Mary and Jesus as a child placed in the center), partly to give the children a bit more understanding and an opportunity to ask questions about what we've done at church during the Advent candle-lighting. Church practices can be special in a certain way, but can sometimes lose something due to the lack of a two-way conversation.
—Allen and Roseanne Shenk family, Strasburg, PA

▼ We have also had an Advent candle in December. Some years on Sunday evenings we sat on the living room floor with candles, and I read stories.
—Lois and Jim Kaufmann, New Paris, IN

▼ A story in *Good Housekeeping* magazine inspired a tradition in our family which lasted quite a few years. We exchanged names each Sunday of Advent. Throughout the next week, the person whose name we drew became the recipient of as many small favors as we could think of and secretly accomplish. Each time we did a favor, we added a piece of straw to a small cradle that had been given to Grandma when she was a little girl. The aim was to have a soft bed for Jesus on Christmas Eve. And the pile of straw grew as Christmas drew near. We read the story the first Sunday of Advent, and then did additional readings and singing as we drew new names each week.
—Norman and Ruth Smith, Ailsa Craig, ON

▼ During Advent we invite a different family each year to come share a shepherd's supper with us. We instruct the guests to come dressed as shepherds and shepherdesses. We light our home with candle or lantern light. We eat what the shepherds may have eaten—black bread, cheese, figs, dates, venison stew, and fruit. If the guests have free imaginations, we sometimes each assume the role of a character from the Christmas story and talk together in that way over the meal. Some families have their imaginations stretched simply by coming as shepherds. We accept that and remember we are sharing joy and the story which we read together at the close of the meal.
    —*David and Martha Clymer, Shirleysburg, PA*

▼ At Christmas time I always plan family activities for the four Advent Sundays. On Sunday afternoon or evening we gather together for 45 minutes to an hour to focus on Jesus' birth. We usually read a story relating to Christmas, sing some carols, each say a prayer, and do a craft together. We often turn the lights off and have our together-time with just the Advent candles burning or the Christmas tree lights on. It's a great reminder to us and to our three children about what Christmas really means.
    —*Miles and Dawnell Yoder, Lancaster, PA*

▼ When our three children were young, we celebrated Advent by inviting folks over after evening church. We always included a family with young children, and a "Grandparent" couple since our children's grandparents lived a distance away. Sharing food and a devotional around the big kitchen table was a wonderful time.
    —*H. Kenneth and Audrey J. Brubaker, York, PA*

Christmas Eve

▼ Christmas Eve day is our "cookie baking day." We take cookies that the children make to friends. It is one time that I know the kids enjoy giving as much as receiving.
    —*Wendy Patterson, Shelby, NC*

▼ As a couple, we have established a Christmas Eve tradition that has become meaningful to us. In the late afternoon on Christmas Eve, we begin a pre-set round of holiday visits to elderly relatives who are either childless or single. We take along a simple gift, such as a red rose for each person or a fruit tray. Our visit at each home is short,

lasting only 45 minutes to one hour before we move on to the next home. Our elderly relatives have come to expect us. This tradition has filled what would otherwise be a quiet and lonely evening for all of us with much love and laughter.
—*Cheryl and Jerry Wyble, Salunga, PA*

▼ At sundown on Christmas Eve, we go as a family to give a small gift to each of our surrounding neighbors. It has become so traditional that we sit and talk, spending much of the evening catching up with how life is going for each of those families. At 11:00 p.m. on Christmas Eve we attend a Christmas Eve service, always choosing a different place each year!
—*Millard and Pris Garrett, Kimmi and Krissie, Lancaster, PA*

▼ For Christmas Eve our family gets together (usually at the family farm) for ham and bean soup. It began by my making bean soup in an iron pot over the fire in the fireplace. One year I forgot to put the ham into the soup, but it was such a good broth we didn't think about it until later! (I always put the cooked ham pieces in last.)
—*Arlene S. Longenecker, Oxford, PA*

▼ We ate a Shepherds' supper of soup, breads, cheese, and fruit on Christmas Eve by the family room fireplace. Then we slept on the "hillside" (family room floor) on Christmas Eve with one person "keeping watch" (keeping the fire going) throughout the night.
—*Ernest and Lois Hess, Lancaster, PA*

▼ We usually celebrate Christmas Eve with a fondue.
—*Marie and Ned Geiser Harnish, Hannah and Nathan, Indianapolis, IN*

▼ We always have an oyster stew supper on Christmas Eve.
—*Iona S. Weaver, Lansdale, PA*

▼ We read the Christmas story from all the gospels on Christmas Eve, following our oyster stew supper which we share with relatives or friends.
—*Ilse H. and Larry R. Yoder, Goshen, IN*

▼ The favorite (almost sacred!) Christmas tradition is our own family's Christmas Eve celebration. The evening begins with a dress-up, candlelight, fondue meal (cheese fondue with veggies and bread chunks, and chocolate fondue with fruit). Then we move to the living room lit only with the tree lights and zillions of candles. There we read the Christmas story from Luke 2, with each person reading a verse. We follow that with singing Christmas carols; each person leads a carol, starting with the youngest. (This tradition began in my husband's family. As one of the older children in a family of 12 kids and with friends and in-laws always included in this event, he had to have a good memory and repertoire!) Then we blow out the candles, turn on the lights, and open presents, one at a time and slowly, so the gifts are thoroughly relished.

This family night always includes a single aunt from Ohio who buys books as gifts. She is a vital part of our Christmas Eve tradition, always bringing trail bologna and baby Swiss cheese from Holmes County. The few times she has not been with us, the kids say it doesn't quite feel like Christmas.

▼ Christmas also means times with extended family and gift exchanges for the kids with a $10.00 limit on gifts, so that it is fun, but not a burden for the families.
—*Lois and Jim Kaufmann, New Paris, IN*

▼ When our boys were little, we often walked through our neighborhood on Christmas Eve to work off some energy and to admire the decorations. When we got back home, we would have a special dessert, often ice cream in holiday shapes.
—*Nancy and Clair Sauder, Tim and Michael, Lancaster, PA*

▼ We never opened our gifts on Christmas Eve until we had read the Luke Christmas story. So many other beautiful stories are written about Christmastime that we added one each year. They were usually so good we didn't mind waiting for the unwrapping of the gifts.
—*Herbert A. and Jessie T. Penner, Bakersfield, CA*

▼ We celebrate Christmas Eve with our extended family, which often involves singing carols or playing instruments and later opening gifts.
—*Merv and June Landis, Talmage, PA*

▼ We always have a time of prayer together on Christmas Eve.
—*Verna Clemmer, Leola, PA*

▼ Each Christmas Eve our children bring their sleeping bags and snacks, spend the night (it's quite a "spread" on our basement floor!), and stay for Christmas brunch together. Most everyone has another family get-together to go to after that.
—*John and Marilyn Burkhart, Mount Joy, PA*

Christmas

▼ As the Christmas holidays approached, we told our children that Christmas is celebrated in two ways. The most important is the birth of Christ. The other is a folk festival—trees, gifts, cookies.

We began in Advent with a wreath and calendars. On Christmas Eve (there was no service at church) we had a "family program" at which each one performed whatever they chose—music, poetry, stories. The youngest set up the creche and a parent read from the Bible. Then we watched "Amahl and the Night Visitors" and, finally, each child opened one gift.

Christmas morning the folk festival came to the fore with tree and gifts.
    —*Ellen S. Peachey, Harpers Ferry, WV*

▼ On the eve of St. Nicholas Day, December 5, our children, as well as their father, placed their best pairs of shoes in the hall near the front door, hoping that St. Nicholas would fill them with surprises during the night. Children who thought that the bigger their shoes, the more goodies there would be, were taught that St. Nicholas would not reward a greedy expectation. Instead, he appreciated clean shoes most and an attitude of modesty, as illustrated in Grandfather Kauenhoven's story: when once upon a time his youngest brother put out a washbasket for St. Nicholas to fill, all he found the next morning were broken cookies. That story made a big impression on our children!
    —*Reinhild K. Janzen, Newton, KS*

▼ We celebrate St. Nicholas Day on December 6 and focus the Santa story there. The gifts we exchange on December 24 and 25 are gifts to remember the Christ child who comes into our world. We have a birthday party for Jesus, with cake and candles on December 25.
    —*Beth A. Schlegel and David Stoverschlegel,*
    North Wales, PA

▼ Some years we made our own Christmas cards as a family project. The boys made Spirograph designs one year.
    —*J. Herbert and Cleo Friesen, Mt. Lake, MN*

▼ Make a Christmas wreath. Decorate it with little ornaments your children make which are symbols of Christmas (star, camels, dried figs, manger herbs). Place it on your front door. When guests come during the holiday season, give them one item per household from

the wreath as a reminder of what Christmas really means. This will initiate wonderful discussion of the true meaning of Christmas in your household and will help your children articulate their beliefs to others.
—*Nancy Nussbaum, Elkhart, IN*

▼ Every year on December 23, we have a birthday party for Jesus that includes cake and ice cream. We begin weeks in advance to prepare for the party, praying about what Jesus wants for His birthday this year. As a family, we choose what to do. One year we gave money to help reunite a refugee family. One year we sent needed items to an orphanage; one year we helped a family with medical bills they couldn't pay. The kids are very much a part of the gift, giving from their own giving money.
—*Melody Hall, Goessel, KS*

▼ The children are grown and gone from home, but we have preserved a tradition we began when they were growing up. At our family gathering, we recite in unison and, as much as possible by memory, the Christmas story as found in Luke 2. To ensure their rehearsing this before our gathering we send out typed copies of Luke 2 to each household and encourage them to memorize it.
—*Marie K. Wiens, Hillsboro, KS*

▼ More than gifts at Christmas we remember many plays our church staged. Practices were as much fun as watching the final production. The rewards were the many compliments from our audiences.
—*Herbert A. and Jessie T. Penner, Bakersfield, CA*

▼ We usually participated in singing a Christmas cantata at church. I realized the importance of that this year when my daughter "pieced together" portions of cantatas we had sung to teach her two-year-old the Christmas story from Scripture. Our two-year-old granddaughter could both say it and sing it.
—*Norman and Dorothy Kreider, Harrisonburg, VA*

▼ We take the children to the Hans Herr House at Christmas for their candlelight tour and hymn sing. (The Herr House was the home of an early Mennonite leader in Lancaster County, Pennsylvania, and was built in 1719.)
—*Lorna Chr. Stoltzfus, New Holland, PA*

▼ We didn't go visiting elsewhere on Christmas Day so the children could enjoy being home. Grandparents were welcomed, however!
—*Grace H. Kaiser, Phoenix, AZ*

▼ As our family was growing up, we invited international students from nearby colleges and universities to spend the holidays with us. We are still in contact with some of those former students. All of our children have since spent time living in other cultures. I trust that those early exposures helped to make their experiences profitable and enjoyable. At Christmastime we always visit someone who *never* gets caroled and the youngest member of our group presents that person with a small surprise of homemade goodies.
—*Helen G. Kennell, Eureka, IL*

▼ My grandparents entertained foreign students and foreign army officers in their home for years. Christmas was always an international affair for my family. Occasionally a foreign student would cook an international dish for us. None of us had ever traveled overseas, yet we knew people from many different countries around the world.
—*Dawn J. Ranck, Strasburg, PA*

▼ We have kept a tradition of having an extended (and sometimes extensive) program (sharing, singing, drama, etc.) before we open our Christmas gifts. Some years we've enjoyed the fellowship so much that the gifts are almost an afterthought. Even our small grandchildren prepare for the program weeks before Christmas. We sometimes record these events and play snatches from 20 or more years ago.
—*LaVerna and Lawrence Klippenstein, Winnipeg, MB*

▼ On Christmas Eve, we celebrated the "religious" aspect of Christmas by lighting candles and oil lamps and turning off the lights; then we would sing carols and read the Christmas story. On Christmas morning, we exchanged gifts, each person waiting on the others so we could all enjoy each other's gifts. After Christmas dinner, we played Monopoly all afternoon. At night, we viewed our family's collection of slides.

▼ My wife and I alternate our visits to our parents, visiting one family at Thanksgiving and the other at Christmas, and then reversing the order the next year. We have our own celebration on Christmas Eve, attending a service at a liturgical church and then exchanging gifts.
—*L. Lamar Nisly, Newark, DE*

▼ Now that our children are married, they come to our home with their spouses and children for a Christmas Eve supper. They all spend the night and we have Christmas Day together, sharing in providing meals. Every other year they spend Christmas Day with their spouses' families, so on those years we choose another date for our overnight and next-day gathering to celebrate Christmas.
—*Richard and Betty Pellman, Millersville, PA*

▼ Keith's family is scattered around the U.S. But at Christmastime we all gather for at least a week at Grandma and Grandpa's house. We all have our own rooms for our families to sleep in. The grandchildren love it. The meals are shared, each family taking turns in the kitchen. Each day we prepare a brunch and then an early supper with snacks available anytime.

The biggest priority of the week is "share time." One evening after all the children are sleeping or on an afternoon during naptimes for the little ones, the adults gather in a circle. Each couple or single adult shares what is new for them, or a specific prayer concern. We try to limit ourselves to 15 minutes each. After everyone shares we spend time in prayer for each other.
—*Keith and Brenda Blank, Rebekah, Laura, and Matthew, Philadelphia, PA*

▼ Each family member picks out a song that for them is particularly special (not necessarily a Christmas song). The song is played (tape or album or CD) and the whole family does a Christmas dance.
—*Janice Miller and David Polley, Ann Arbor, MI*

▼ Part of our Christmas evening celebration as an extended family is to form a caravan of cars and drive through the town to see Christmas lights. When we return home, we make hot chocolate for everyone and the holiday is complete.
—*Marie Palasciano, Hazlet, NJ*

▼ We celebrate the Twelve Days of Christmas. The day after Christmas the Wise Men from the nativity set are hidden. The children hunt for the Magi and for the paper with a clue placed under them. The clue leads them to small gifts—pencils, paper, candy bar, etc.
—*Suzann Shafer Bauman, Lima, OH*

▼ Each year at Christmas we bring out our special book in which we have recorded events of prior years. We review them just for fun.

Then we recall highlights and memories of the present year and record them in the book.

▼ We usually have a jigsaw puzzle going over the holidays. Many talks occur over it.
—*Janice Miller and David Polley, Ann Arbor, MI*

Christmas Tree_____

▼ Each Christmas Ken chooses an ornament for each child as their stocking stuffers. Hopefully, when they leave home they will have memorable ornaments for their own Christmas tree. We go as a family to a tree farm to cut our tree.
—*Ken and Helen Nafziger, Jeremy, Kirsten, and Zachary, Harrisonburg, VA*

▼ Trimming the tree is a family event. Part of that ceremony is giving each family member a new Christmas tree ornament. I choose a Scripture that somehow pertains to each ornament, which is read aloud before the ornament is unwrapped. From that the recipient, and then the others, guess what the ornament might be. Our children will take these ornaments with them when they establish their own homes.
—*Jim and Janalee Croegaert and family, Evanston, IL*

▼ In November we select a date when the whole family can go look for a tree. We also choose a date when the tree will be decorated (generally the first or second Sunday in December). Everyone participates in these days. They take precedence over all other schedule requests which come up.

▼ Every year on our summer vacation I find some special memento to make into a Christmas decoration for each member of our family. These become part of each child's Christmas decoration collection which they will have for the rest of their lives. Included in it are things they have made, extra special decorations which I have found/made, and decorations which their grandparents have sent them. There are many memories in those boxes, and there is great excitement when the boxes are taken out in December. (We have kept a careful record of where each ornament has come from.)
—*Jane-Ellen and Gerry Grunau, Winnipeg, MB*

▼ We keep the Christmas tree until Epiphany, lighting its candles on dark evenings.
                         —Reinhild K. Janzen, Newton, KS

Christmas Cookies _____

▼ Christmastime is cookie-baking time for our family. When our two children were younger, we would play our first Christmas record and bake our first batch of cookies on Thanksgiving Day. Whenever we baked cookies after that until Christmas, we always listened to Christmas records. Our daughter is now married, and she does her first batch of Christmas cookies on Thanksgiving. I still do that, and my co-workers all receive a bag of cookies at Christmas!
                  —Jim and Shirley Hershey, Bloomingdale, NJ

▼ We started several family traditions while we were on an overseas assignment that have carried through to the present. We make Christmas cookies together, especially gingerbread boys. I used the Molasses Crinkles recipe from the *Mennonite Community Cookbook*, and the children used the dough-like playdough to make whatever designs they wanted. We made the gingerbread boys not with cookie cutters, but by forming each body part, joining them together and flattening them to $3/8$- to $5/8$-inch thickness. We used raisins, cherries, and candied fruit peel for buttons and eyes. After they were baked, we also iced them.
                   —Roy and Hope Brubaker, Mifflintown, PA

▼ Dad and Daughter usually mix up the Christmas cookie dough, roll it out, and cut the cookies. Then the whole family gathers around the kitchen table (guests have been included) to enjoy a time of decorating the cookies.
                      —Mim and Roger Eberly, Milford, IN

▼ We always find one evening for all five of us to join in baking Christmas cookies.
                   —Stan and Susan Godshall, Mt. Joy, PA

▼ At Christmas we make cookies and deliver them to the local fire and police departments. We thank them for their service to us and tell them that we pray for them regularly.
                   —Chuck and Robyn Nordell, Fullerton, CA

▼ Baking Christmas cookies and "painting" them with colored egg yolk has become a favorite family affair.

▼ The month of January is our favorite time to make our gingerbread house. It offers something to look forward to after the Christmas rush.
>—*Lois and Randy Zook, Lancaster, PA*

Christmas Food _____

▼ At Christmas we bake a Jesus Birthday Cake—a version of a yule log.
>—*Ann James Van Hooser, Princeton, KY*

▼ For Christmas morning I made a tea ring and put a candle in the center for Jesus' birthday cake. We had that part of the celebration after opening our gifts. Our daughter is continuing this tradition with her family.
>—*Bob and Doris Ebersole, Archbold, OH*

▼ We schedule special dinners with aunts, uncles, and cousins during the Christmas season in an effort to keep in touch with the larger family.
>—*Richard and Betty Pellman, Millersville, PA*

▼ Our family enjoys hot oyster stew on Christmas morning!
>—*Phyllis and Merle Good, Kate and Rebecca,*
>*Lancaster, PA*

Christmas Games _____

▼ When the grandchildren were little, we adults often played games which excluded the children. So one Christmas I got a Bingo game we could all play. Now on Christmas afternoon they look forward to Bingo, even the married grandchildren. Prizes are given to the winner, who may trade the prize for one she or he would rather have from someone who had won it before. When the prize basket gets empty, those who have the prizes get to keep them.
>—*Grace Brenneman, Elida, OH*

▼ For years we got a new jigsaw puzzle and a game for Christmas. Both of these were "do together" things which we looked forward to. (Instead of filling the closets with used puzzles, they can always be given to rummage sales or a reuzit shop.) Now we seldom buy either for ourselves as the children keep us supplied with a new puzzle and game each Christmas.
—*Lois G. Dagen, Lancaster, PA*

▼ A tradition we began, upon receiving a jigsaw puzzle for Christmas one year, is to complete a puzzle the week between Christmas and New Year. It becomes the beginning of our puzzle craze during the winter months that follow! Younger children can help sort borders and colored pieces. When the puzzle comes to the difficult parts and the children no longer feel included, we work on the puzzle after the children are tucked into bed!
—*Lois and Randy Zook, Lancaster, PA*

▼ We often start a jigsaw puzzle during Christmas vacation.
—*Nancy and Clair Sauder, Tim and Michael, Lancaster, PA*

Christmas Gifts _____

▼ Since most of our children and their families live out-of-state, we always get together at some central location for Thanksgiving and Christmas. We celebrate both holidays at the same time. We all draw names to exchange gifts. But we also have a special missionary project. One of the families is designated each year to be in charge of the project; they distribute information during the year about the mission family they have chosen. This informs us all about what is going on in that particular mission field.

At the Christmas dinner they may give us a quiz or puzzle to see who can answer the most questions about the project. This has proven to be fun and also educational. The money we bring is then sent to the couple or mission of that year's choice. We hope this effort will promote interest in mission as well as create unselfishness in giving and receiving gifts.
—*Stephen and Sadie Yoder, Quarryville, PA*

▼ On Christmas morning *before* opening gifts, we light the five Advent candles and read the Christmas story. Then we each give a gift to

Jesus, bringing a gift of money and deciding together where to send it as a love offering. Of course, we have usually had to encourage the children to plan ahead to have some coins left after all the Christmas buying!
—*Mark and Pauline Lehman, St. Anne, IL*

▼ A cherished tradition at Christmastime was begun by John's parents when our children were very young. We continue it today with our grandchildren and refer to it as "the 5-Day Gifts." Since we always lived at a distance from his folks, and the same is true for our grandchildren today, the regular Christmas gifts are given when we get together for Christmas, but ahead of time we send five gifts for each child, numbered for Day 1 through 5 of the days before Christmas, December 20-24. These are small, inexpensive, and useful gifts like writing pads, Scotch tape, socks, or Christmas tree ornaments.

So far our task is easy; we have only two grandchildren with a third due to join us by next Christmas, but John's mother, now 90, has created a big job for herself each Christmas by now. She is still giving a set of five gifts (similar for all males or females for each day) to each of her two children, their spouses, and her seven grandchildren and their 5 spouses. We're easing into the tradition by taking over for the fourth generation, our grandsons.

Opening the gifts each of those five days prior to Christmas draws each family together around the tree five times, rather than only on Christmas Day, and of course it builds anticipation for the big day. It is usually a time to share a Bible verse or to sing a Christmas carol as well.
—*John and Alice Suderman, Kalona, IA*

▼ Before our children could read, we had a treasure hunt for their Christmas presents. I drew pictures on cards as the clues, and when they would come and wake us up early I would hand them the first card. At each place there was another card until the last one led them to their presents.
—*Harvey and Lavonne Dyck, Christina and*
Colleen, Viborg, SD

▼ At Christmastime, we open gifts over several days, beginning on Christmas Eve. They can "savor" gifts that way.
—*Ervin and Bonita Stutzman, Mount Joy, PA*

▼ During Christmas Eve night, we lay an unwrapped gift on the foot of each child's bed—something to keep them occupied in the early hours before they may waken us!
> —*Phil and Sandy Chabot, Becky and PV,*
> *Cromwell, CT*

▼ On Christmas morning our children could get up as early as they wanted and open everything in their stockings as quietly as possible. At 8 a.m. they could come into our room to waken us.
> —*Mary and Nelson Steffy, East Petersburg, PA*

▼ We begin opening presents about 9:00 a.m. and usually finish around 4-5:00 p.m. When a gift is opened, it is examined fully. If it is a game, we play it. In essence, each gift is thoroughly explored before the next person is given a gift to open. In this way each gift can be more fully appreciated by the recipient. We have found that Christmas Day is not a flurry of tearing paper off presents (or taking them out of special cloth Christmas bags which is now generally the case), but a wonderful family day in which we can participate together in gift-giving and gift-receiving.
> —*Jane-Ellen and Gerry Grunau, Winnipeg, MB*

▼ At Christmastime the children got a lot of pleasure from choosing or making a gift for each other. They loved watching the others open their gifts one at a time on Christmas morning. The emphasis was more on giving than getting.
> —*Ben and Lorraine Myers, Dillsburg, PA*

▼ As our children have reached the preteen and teenage years and have earning potential (babysitting jobs, etc.), our Christmas morning gift-giving has taken on a new flavor of mutuality and simplicity. We each hang a large stocking on the mantel on Christmas Eve. Then we take turns going into the room to stuff the stockings.

On Christmas morning one person at a time removes an item from her/his stocking and we try to guess who gave the item. We joke a lot and tease each other as gift items often reveal or highlight our personality quirks. This whole process of sharing is unhurried (can take as much as one-and-a-half hours) and we have a lot of fun with it.
> —*Martha and Rich Sider, Lancaster, PA*

▼ When we left the farm and moved to a smaller house, our daughters suggested that I share my excess needlework. (My mother had done much quilting and crocheting in her later years.) Now I see these old-fashioned doilies and decorative pieces in our children's homes.

Several times at Christmas when the family was together I set up a "grab table" with items of some value. Each individual was given a number; then they went, one by one, into a separate room and selected their choice from the table. It was a special time.

The past few years at Christmastime we have played the "Now you have it, now you don't" game of fun and gag gifts, with some specialties mixed in. It's been hilarious!
   —*Edna Mast, Cochranville, PA*

▼ Jake's family decided one Christmas to draw names and give only homemade gifts—sewn, composed literature, taped sermons, food, etc. It was a very creative Christmas experience.
   —*Jake and Dorothy Pauls, Winnipeg, MB*

▼ A friend of mine always saves one Christmas gift for each family member to open on Epiphany. It helps with the post-Christmas letdown.
   —*Elizabeth Weaver, Thorndale, ON*

5.

Seasons and Milestones

▼ Fondue has become our meal of special celebrations. I'm certain it is because of the relaxed atmosphere, the long time it takes to eat—you can't hurry fondue—and the pleasure of our all being together.
> —*Ken and Helen Nafziger, Jeremy, Kirsten, and Zachary, Harrisonburg, VA*

▼ I (Betty) like to send cards for special occasions and decorate the envelopes to either fit the occasion or the child's interest. I also like to wrap our family gifts in brown bags and then decorate them with drawings. It adds a special touch for the giver and the receiver.
> —*Richard and Betty Pellman, Millersville, PA*

▼ We usually answer Christmas cards in the spring, near February 14 or Easter, or we send letters of appreciation at Thanksgiving *instead* of sending Christmas cards in our culture's commercial way.
> —*Ilse H. and Larry R. Yoder, Goshen, IN*

▼ Read a special story at each holiday. Reread the same story year after year. Be sure to include multicultural stories.

Learn about Jewish celebrations as a family and practice them through the year.
> —*Nancy Nussbaum, Elkhart, IN*

▼ We consciously worked to not create traditions that one does "on cue" or that are expected, so that spontaneous gifts when one *felt* like it became our tradition. We gather at Thanksgiving and Christmas but not necessarily on the day or in a traditional way, in order to allow flexibility for young families needing their own time and space.
> —*Shirley Kirkwood, Mt. Solon, VA*

New Year's Day

▼ On New Year's Day we walk to a restaurant together to eat out, usually for mid-morning brunch.
> —*Ann James Van Hooser, Princeton, KY*

Lent

▼ Advent and Lent are special penitential times in our family life. The Christmas season and Easter season are big celebrations. Friends come over, we prepare special foods and do favorite activities. During Lent we do extra spiritual reading, we give up certain pleasures, we fast, we have no parties, we practice "early to bed and early to rise."
> —*Miki and Tim Hill, Woodstock, MD*

▼ When our children were young, we always observed Lent. One year we learned a new Lenten hymn each week. Another time we memorized the Apostles' Creed. One year we read related Scriptures and used litanies from a Lutheran booklet. One year we skipped desserts at supper and made a special donation to a cause.
> —*LaVerna and Lawrence Klippenstein,*
> *Winnipeg, MB*

▼ During Lent we usually cut out desserts, putting the money we saved in a bowl, and then giving it to a program for international relief.
> —*Tom and Lois Marshall, Naomi, Christine, and*
> *Jonathan, Spruce, MI*

Easter

▼ We use a Paschal candle (new every Easter) for Sunday supper. We use Scripture and ancient prayers of the church to keep the resurrection central to our Sunday celebration.
> —*Joan and Larry Litman, Hoboken, NJ*

▼ At Eastertime I use Easter songs and stories at our children's bedtime.
> —*Rod and Martha (Yoder) Maust,*
> *Indianapolis, IN*

▼ A couple of weeks before Easter, I plant grass seed in Andrew's Easter basket so that by Easter there's "real grass" in his basket. He enjoys watching the grass grow and anticipates the arrival of Easter.
> —*Ron and Betti Risser, Lancaster, PA*

▼ We share Maundy Thursday or Good Friday with another family from our church. Children and adults eat a meal together and then read the Passion story from the Bible. Each person holds a candle and lighting is done symbolically as we read the story. This small celebration together makes our Easter service at church on Sunday morning a special time.
> —*Kenny and Rachel Pellman, Nathaniel and Jesse,*
> *Lancaster, PA*

▼ For many years anyone in the family who wanted could go for a walk on Easter morning at sunrise with Dad. Often one or more of the kids went, while the rest stayed to help with dinner preparations.
> —*Jim and Dee Nussbaum, Kidron, OH*

▼ We have a community breakfast on Easter morning, after getting up early to see the sunrise. We have an egg hunt several days later so as not to distract from the real Easter experience.
> —*David and Louisa Mow, Farmington, PA*

▼ On Easter we go to a sunrise service and then have breakfast at church before the main Easter service. Our Easter baskets have Christian books or tapes and little candy.
> —*Phil and Sandy Chabot, Becky and PV, Cromwell, CT*

▼ We like attending Easter sunrise services together and then coming home to Easter breakfast of hot cross buns (made the day before) and other breakfast treats.
> —*Roy and Carol Sprunger, Monroe, IN*

▼ When our children were small, we woke them early on Easter morning to go with us to sunrise services. Following this, we drove to a park for our picnic breakfast and recreation. We enjoyed some beautiful sunny mornings, but occasionally had to eat in the car to avoid the rain or cold. We then attended the regular Sunday morning services.
> —*Edwin and Rosanna Ranck, Christiana, PA*

▼ Plan a special Easter sunrise service as a family. Each family member (regardless of age) can bring something to contribute—a prayer, song, art, or reading.
> —*Nancy Nussbaum, Elkhart, IN*

▼ A highlight of Easter weekend is always the "Family Recital" which we hold at the nursing home where my grandmother resides. Each member of the extended family (with a few exceptions) prepares something for the recital. My older brother used to spend literally months learning a piano piece for this occasion. What I appreciate about the recital is that the emphasis is not upon performance, but on participation. Adults and children are thus put on an equal level.
—*Jane-Ellen and Gerry Grunau, Winnipeg, MB*

Easter Eggs

▼ Coloring, hiding, and hunting Easter eggs is such fun, but we didn't like it detracting from the meaning of Jesus' joyous resurrection on Easter Sunday, so we found an alternative. On Palm Sunday we invite several families to join us for a potluck, bringing with them some eggs they have colored, as well as some plastic eggs filled with surprises for the children. After lunch and an egg hunt for the children, the adults each hunt a plastic egg that was hidden for them. Prior to hiding these eggs, each adult made a coupon for something that they would do for another, then placed these coupons in the eggs to be hidden. Coupons include such things as one car wash and cleaning, a loaf of freshly baked bread, three hours of babysitting, two hours of window washing or yard mowing, etc.

The most memorable egg hunt was the year my husband found $200 in cash in an envelope in the trunk of the car he was cleaning in payment of the coupon he had given. The young couple were as shocked and surprised as my husband, and to this day have no idea how the money got there!
—*Herb and Sarah Myers and daughters,*
Mount Joy, PA

▼ At Eastertime Mom and the children make peanut butter eggs to give as gifts to teachers, family, and friends.
—*Mike and Kim Pellman, Matt and Brooke,*
Bird-in-Hand, PA

▼ At Easter as our children were growing up, we usually colored eggs with another family and had great fun together.
—*Arlene S. Longenecker, Oxford, PA*

▼ We've had alot of fun decorating blown-out eggs for Easter. This year I dyed some with onion skins. I added a little vinegar to the water, laid a leaf or flower against each egg, wrapped each in discarded nylon hose, and tied them in a knot, then boiled them in the onion-skin water. Results were variable, but sometimes beautiful.

—*Rod and Martha (Yoder) Maust,*
Indianapolis, IN

▼ To help the children count the days until Easter, the Sunday before (Palm Sunday), I give them each a little basket filled with seven eggs. Each day they eat an egg. On Easter morning when they lift out the "grass," there's a note underneath that says, "Jesus is risen! Spread the good news!"

—*Sue Aeschliman Groff, Kinzer, PA*

▼ We dyed Easter eggs the day before Easter. Then on Easter morning we hid them around the house. As the children kept finding them and returning them to their baskets, we kept hiding them again!

—*Joan and Arnold Lange, New Oxford, PA*

▼ At Eastertime we decorated Easter eggs with markers. Then we hid them and had a family egg hunt following our Easter Sunday meal.

—*Roy and Hope Brubaker, Mifflintown, PA*

▼ Our children invited their cousins to join them for the annual Easter egg hunt in our backyard Easter Sunday afternoon.

—*Robert and Miriam Martin, East Earl, PA*

▼ We've had an Easter tradition of hiding and hunting Easter baskets. To lessen sugar consumption for our grandchildren, we replaced candy in the Easter baskets with T-shirts when the children were younger, and more recently with other gifts or money, also hidden and waiting to be found.

—*Richard and Betty Pellman, Millersville, PA*

▼ At Easter we hide symbols of the Easter story in plastic eggs. When the children find the eggs, we discuss the symbols. These conversations are becoming more intriguing and complicated as the children get older.

—*Mark and Leone Wagner, Lititz, PA*

Pentecost

▼ We know a family who always wears yellow, orange, or red on Pentecost Sunday to celebrate the flame of new life.
—*Lois and Jim Kaufmann, New Paris, IN*

Halloween

▼ We were never comfortable with the idea of trick or treating at Halloween—too much candy, going to homes of people we didn't know, etc. Yet we wanted to do something special for the children. So each year through their grade school years I planned a treasure hunt for them on Halloween. We purchased small items—balls, crayons, scissors, bubble blowers, favorite cereal, etc. I then hid those items (one for each child at each location) and made a "treasure map" with clues that led them from one location to another. With three children, each child read and deciphered every third clue.
—*R. Wayne and Donella Clemens, Souderton, PA*

▼ "Don't beg for things," we tell our children, but one night a year we disguise them and send them out to collect as much loot as possible. When we were children, we were forbidden to go halloweening, but we were given no alternatives. We have experimented with and enjoyed several other ideas which have come to be known and celebrated as our Alternative Halloween. We invite two or three other families and/or singles to join us for an evening of fun. We bob for apples, eat powdery homemade doughnuts dangling from a string, and play Bible Charades. The climax of the evening for the children comes when the adults hide somewhere in the house. Upon finding one of the adults, the children receive a piece of candy or some other small nonedible treat. The hunt continues till each child has as many treats in his or her bag as there are hidden adults.
—*Herb and Sarah Myers and daughters, Mount Joy, PA*

▼ We skip celebrating Halloween, and instead start putting up Christmas items then, to make the season less hectic later. The children have a tree of their own with unbreakable and homemade ornaments and a train underneath. (That way Mom can have her own color-coordinated tree in peace!)
—*Scott and Sue Steffy, Leola, PA*

Thanksgiving

▼ We have found value in developing food traditions. At one time I thought all the work at Thanksgiving wasn't worth the effort, but now I realize that it can be worthwhile in building positive associations and memories, something I value for myself and my children. We don't abstain from all sweets and fats, but we do include basic healthy foods, too: turkey instead of ham, sweet potatoes and pumpkin pie rather than other fluffy sweet desserts, homemade whole wheat bread or rolls. The process is as important as the product.
—Lois and Jim Kaufmann, New Paris, IN

Child Dedication

▼ A special moment in our becoming grandparents was when we participated in our grandson's dedication. Our daughter and her husband helped plan the personalized service with the minister and church leaders. They picked favorite songs, Scripture, and a litany to be read by the parents, grandparents, and congregation. The Sunday school pupils prepared a tree with spiritual fruits on it and gave those fruits to members of the congregation. We grandparents were given the spiritual gifts of joy and peace.

▼ For the dinner that followed, our daughter used her finest china and invited their closest friends to join in the celebration.
—Sam and Joyce Hofer, Morton, IL

Baptism

▼ On or near the day of their spiritual birthday, each child receives a card about that. Each also gets to choose a meal they'd like Mom to fix for them!
—Ann James Van Hooser, Princeton, KY

▼ My husband is a pastor and began the tradition of inviting parents to assist in the baptism of their child. The child kneels, the father pours water from a pitcher into the pastor's hands, and the mother wipes the child's face.
—Jim and Nancy Roynon, Brad, Taryn, Drew, and Colin, Archbold, OH

▼ My grandparents gave all their grandchildren a Bible with helps at the time they became members of the church. I am doing this for our grandchildren.
—*Erma Kauffman, Cochranville, PA*

▼ To celebrate the children's baptisms, we invited their grandparents to attend the church service and come for the noon meal. We gave the child a well-bound Bible with cross-references to commemorate the occasion.
—*Stan and Susan Godshall, Mt. Joy, PA*

▼ At the time of our children's baptisms we highlighted the occasions with a favorite, festive meal and invited a special friend and grandparents to join us.
—*Ernest and Lois Hess, Lancaster, PA*

▼ When our older daughter was preparing for baptism, we asked each other why the biggest celebrations families traditionally give their children are graduation parties and/or wedding receptions. Doesn't a child's faith decision and entry into the church merit a celebration? (Besides, they may never marry or graduate.)

And so we had a celebration for each daughter on the evenings before their baptisms. We invited grandparents, aunts, uncles, and cousins, our pastor and a few friends from church. We began with a get-acquainted quiz (guests had to recall details from their own baptisms), followed that with a feast, lots of visiting, and finally, singing, inviting everyone to offer their choice from the hymnal. We decorated the house with flowers and balloons, and asked two uncles to take photos throughout the events.

Then we provided each daughter with a photo album for her to fill with her choice of pictures from her party. The solemn occasion took on real joy and a swell of support from each child's closest acquaintances.
—*Merle and Phyllis Good, Lancaster, PA*

Special Season

▼ Our favorite Special-Seasons traditions are an annual wildflower trip (sometimes two or three a season) to West Virginia mountain areas, backroads, and woods to find rare flowering plants. Each fall we have "color trips," again to mountain areas with picnics, walks, and photo-taking times.
—*Shirley Kirkwood, Mt. Solon, VA*

▼ Since Mother's Day usually falls during morel mushroom season, my traditional Mother's Day breakfast is a morel omelette.
—*Tom and Lois Marshall, Naomi, Christine, and Jonathan, Spruce, MI*

▼ When the men in our extended family are at the mountains hunting for deer in November, the women and children get together to make graham cracker houses. The oldest grandchildren are now 13 and they still look forward to it.
—*Jay and Linda Ebersole, Rosalyn, Randy, and Ryan, Lancaster, PA*

▼ Phyllis, Kate, and Rebecca were in a very serious accident several years ago. A drunk driver hit our car head-on one Friday morning when the three of them were shopping. All three were taken to the emergency room and admitted. It was very traumatic for all of us. Rebecca was released on the second day and Phyllis on the third. But Kate had a compressed vertebrae in her back and a messed-up jaw. Two weeks later she came home to a hospital bed in which she lay for another month.

All three are now fully recovered. And as an annual ritual of gratefulness and celebration, we return to the hospital for a meal in their cafeteria. We reminisce, and the girls are permitted unlimited desserts. It's a fun way to keep processing a near tragedy.
—*Phyllis and Merle Good, Kate and Rebecca, Lancaster, PA*

▼ A fun exercise at mealtime when I was a child had to do with seasonal candy and how it was allocated. Just how many pieces of candy may your children have when there are 10 children?! Once or twice a year Mother and Dad would purchase a large brown bag of red cinnamon hearts. Each family member was entitled to as many as she or he could get on a single teaspoon. So the bag was passed around the large kitchen table and we would each dip and dig deeply into the hearts. Then, slowly, each of us lifted the spoon out of the bag. If we heard a piece fall from the spoon, we would dump the load and dig again.

It then became important for each of us to count the number of hearts we received to see who fared the best. You can imagine the enthusiasm such a process generated among 10 children by the time the bag made its circle around the table!

Jelly beans provided even greater fun for us. Again we had a large brown bag, this time filled with multi-colored jelly beans. Each

family member could reach into the bag and remove one bean at a time. The agreement was that you could continue this process until you received two of the same color. Some were blessed with five or six pieces, while others had to settle for two!
—*Melvin Thomas, Lancaster, PA*

▼ Although we enjoy traditional holiday meals, more often we select a special menu from an ethnic cookbook or another book we're reading. One year our Christmas breakfast came from a Laura Ingalls Wilder cookbook. Another year our recipes came from *Monet's Table.*

▼ On the Saturday nearest Valentine's Day, Stan and I prepare a special brunch for our children. Some years we've given them handmade Valentines. Each year at the brunch we go around the table and say something we like or appreciate about each other. Now the children laugh about the years when they were younger and had to think very hard to find something good to say about each other—but they always did!

▼ In Oregon we always eagerly anticipated the June strawberry harvest. Each year we went to the fields to pick our own berries (even taking the children along in backpacks when they were very small). Then came the best part—a meal of strawberry shortcake with plate-sized biscuit-type shortcake, heaps of fresh strawberries, and sweet cream. Even after we moved to Indiana we continued our tradition of the strawberry shortcake meal.
—*Marlene and Stanley Kropf, Elkhart, IN*

▼ For Jesse, losing his first tooth was a very exciting time. He called his grandparents and aunts and uncles. We told him about the tooth fairy and explained that it's not real, but sometimes it's fun to pretend. With the quarter he found under his pillow, he also discovered a letter from the tooth fairy. He's lost two teeth now and seems as excited about the letters as the quarters. "Thanks Mom" was his reply, and then he winked.
—*Anita and Randy Landis-Eigsti, Lakewood, CO*

▼ Between the ages of 11 and 16 each son gets to take two trips with Dad: a service trip (most recently Ben went with me to Romania for two weeks), and an adventure trip (Joshua and I floated the Middle Fork Salmon River in Idaho in June).
—*David and Cynthia Shank, Joshua, Benjamin, Nathaniel, and Caleb, Mt. Crawford, VA*

▼ When each of our parents were in their early 70s, we arranged a cross-Canada train journey for the six of us from Niles, Michigan to Vancouver, British Columbia. The fortnight was a memory indeed. The investment in first class rail travel, dining car meals, and rental car intervals at stops enroute combined to provide a very special cross-generational experience.
—*Alice and Willard Roth, Elkhart, IN*

▼ During the 1990 Gulf War, we kept a candle, either real or electric, burning in our front window. We worked as a family at making black armbands which we made available to anyone at our church.
—*Lois and Jim Kaufmann, New Paris, IN*

▼ One year, to give our girls some sense of their spiritual heritage, we explained a bit of Anabaptist history to them on January 21 (the date on which the movement began in 1525).

Each of us took our Bibles and went somewhere in the house alone to read, thinking about the ways in which we can each be Jesus' disciple. We have not repeated this practice as often as we'd like to, but we found it meaningful.
—*Phyllis and Merle Good, Lancaster, PA*

Anniversaries

▼ We usually celebrated our wedding anniversary with our children by having hoagies and sodas in the park in June.
—*Luke and Miriam Stoltzfus, Philadelphia, PA*

▼ We made June 15, our wedding anniversary, Family Day. It was the day our family began. It became a one-day celebration when we exchanged gifts (instead of at Christmas) and memories. Last year, for example, one daughter entertained us all by recounting in vivid detail what a typical washday on the farm had been like.
—*Omar A. and Delphia Kurtz, Morgantown, PA*

▼ On one of our wedding anniversaries our four children gave us a scrapbook that they had made and gathered. They gave blank pages to their aunts, uncles, and neighbors, and had them fill both sides with pictures, special memories, or anything they wanted to put on it. We were given 100 pages of pictures and memories, a gift we will long treasure.
—*Janet Roggie, Lowville, NY*

▼ We send a check to the married children in the amount of the wedding anniversary they are celebrating—yes, it increases every year!
>—*Roger and Rachel (Graber) Wyse,*
>*Wayland, IA*

▼ On our children's anniversaries we take them out to a special dinner. On their fifth anniversary we take them to dinner and a show or movie.
>—*John and Marilyn Burkhart, Mount Joy, PA*

School Celebrations

▼ We always had a special prayer for the children on the first day of a new school year.
>—*Robert and Miriam Martin, East Earl, PA*

▼ I (Mom) gather the children's school papers together when they bring them from school and put them at the dinner table. Then both Dad and I look them over during dinner. It gives us some table talk subjects (what they're learning, not how they're doing), and they see us both paying attention to their work.
>—*The Baker-Smiths, Stanfield, OR*

▼ When one gets an honor award at school for good behavior, we go out to eat as a family at the restaurant of that child's choice in his/her honor.
>—*Ann James Van Hooser, Princeton, KY*

▼ The last day of school is usually a half day, so we go out for lunch to celebrate.
>—*Nancy and Clair Sauder, Tim and Michael, Lancaster, PA*

▼ We've had a School's Out Party. We cook the children's favorite foods for dinner, watch a video together, or play games and stay up late! We all sleep in one room in sleeping bags.
>—*Wayne and Mary Nitzsche, Wooster, OH*

▼ We went out to dinner (usually to an inexpensive restaurant) at the end of the school year to celebrate its end and the girls' good report cards.
>—*Clive and Margaret LeMasurier, Plainville, CT*

▼ My mother wanted to go to high school when she was a teenager, but didn't have the opportunity. In 1980, the year I started high school, she began correspondence courses at home. When she received her diploma, we had a graduation party for her, including family, friends, and one of her grade-school teachers.
—*Dawn J. Ranck, Strasburg, PA*

▼ We try to make report card time an opportunity for affirming their efforts, regardless of their actual grades. Our emphasis is on doing your very best. Pizza is the food treat.
—*Mark and Leone Wagner, Lititz, PA*

▼ We never made a big thing about achieving A's at report-card-time. Our attitude was, "Do the best you can, and that is good enough," especially when there was sibling competitiveness among the children. Some achieved more easily than others. Why celebrate the child who tries little and brings home the A, while a sibling may put forth much more effort and bring home a lower grade?
—*John and Trula Zimmerly, Jackson, OH*

▼ We have a tradition of "report card meals." Regardless of the grades, we go out twice a year to celebrate the milestone of finishing another half year of school. The girls take turns choosing the restaurant (within reason).
—*Phyllis and Merle Good, Kate and Rebecca, Lancaster, PA*

▼ We don't make a big deal about report cards, except "That's terrific." All four children are "gifted" and we expect them to do well. That's their job, just like we do well in our jobs.
—*Marvin and Rachel Miller, Indianapolis, IN*

Death

▼ The children's mother died of cancer, and on the anniversary of her death, my husband recounts the events of her illness and death for the children, to keep her memory alive.
—*Marian J. Bauman, Harrisonburg, VA*

▼ Thankfully, funerals are becoming celebrations of lives lived—not hush-hush somber, hold still, don't move around events!
—*Orpah and Elam S. Kurtz, Jefferson, NC*

▼ We have experienced several miscarriages. We've planted some perennial flowers as a way to mark that loss and to remind us annually of God's gift of life.
—*Jim and Carol Spicher, Jonathan, Mountville, PA*

▼ Our oldest grandchild was killed in a freak tractor accident six years ago. We always remember that anniversary with his parents.
—*Milton and Ella Rohrer, Orrville, OH*

▼ On the July 6 anniversary of our 12-year-old Bruce's death, we talk about him and do something he would have enjoyed, like make a trip to the Dairyette or hike at the Wilderness Center, a camp used for sixth grade outdoor education.
—*Clayton and Ruth Steiner, Dalton, OH*

Moving

▼ As we left one home for another, we loaded our memory banks by going from room to room, and from the garden to other favorite outdoor spots, soaking up all the wonderful associations with each.
—*Ernest and Lois Hess, Lancaster, PA*

6.

Extended Family
and Friends

Staying in Touch _____

▼ LETTERS! LETTERS! LETTERS! Phone calls are quick, easy,
and, at off hours, not overly expensive. But what do you have to
show for them after the phone clicks? Letters last. They can be
read and reread, savored and saved. Years later they bring back
many memories. Sunday afternoon each week we write to our
parents.
—Herb and Sarah Myers and daughters, Mount Joy, PA

▼ The telephone is an excellent way to communicate with absent
family members. "We'll call this week. You call us next week." This
applies to a daughter across town (who calls daily), to a son in
another state, and a sister-in-law living alone.
—Wiley and Esther McDowell, Goshen, IN

▼ We love to camp, go to the beach with extended family, have picnics,
just allow the cousins to play together.
—Jim and Carol Spicher, Jonathan, Mountville, PA

▼ We have alternated summer visits for same-age cousins. We
regularly pray for family members at our evening meal.
—Jim and Janalee Croegaert and family, Evanston, IL

▼ Over the years we often babysat nieces and nephews for weekends.
This gave their parents some time on their own, allowed us to learn
to know the children better, and provided playmates for our boys.
When our boys were teenagers and the visiting nieces and nephews
were pre-schoolers, it added an interesting dimension to our family
life.
—Arlene Kehl, Kitchener, ON

▼ Our son's favorite uncle took an assignment overseas for three years. To help him remember this special uncle, we began compiling a scrapbook just about this person. In it we arrange photos, articles about him, his art and letters, and anything else which seems relevant to the child.
　　　　—Kelli Burkholder and John King, Goshen, IN

▼ The Thomas family gathers each summer at my sister's house for a fishing party and hot dog roast. We visit while we fish. Later in the summer there is an annual picnic in the park and we rally in a whole-family softball game.
　　　　—Kenny and Rachel Pellman, Nathaniel and Jesse,
　　　　Lancaster, PA

▼ Since Bonita's mother has Alzheimers, Bonita takes care of her at our house one day a week. On those evenings, we have both her mother and father for supper if they care to stay. It has been a way for our children to observe aging and caring. We have also grown much closer to Bonita's parents.

▼ Four times a year (at least) we have family gatherings with Bonita's parents and siblings. Once a year, we attend family reunions (with uncles, aunts, cousins) on each side of Bonita's family. Also, for the last 15 years, I have been in a circle letter with my five siblings. It comes around five to six times a year, and keeps us in touch.
　　　　—Ervin and Bonita Stutzman, Mount Joy, PA

▼ My brothers, sister and I live in four different states, so we take turns hosting an annual family gathering, providing the place and activities. The first year we took campers and tents to a lake in Iowa. This was followed by Lake of the Woods in Ontario, the mountains in Idaho and, recently, a state park in Ohio.

　　We try to have an activity for every age. (One that the younger children really remembered was the arranged appearance of Marko, the Magician.) It is important to have varied activities, but planning too much can destroy the relaxation of the vacation!

　　Families provide and prepare one meal. (Those from Idaho bring potatoes, the Lake of the Wood's brother brings walleye, etc.)
　　　　—John and Trula Zimmerly, Jackson, OH

▼ Our extended family gets together three times a year, at least as many of the clan as can conveniently do so.
(1) Our summertime retreat is the first weekend of August on the Chesapeake Bay. Swimming, boating, visiting together, eating, and

just lounging around keep us occupied. Several couples or persons are assigned to bring food for one meal per group. This schedule is worked out well ahead of time and includes the dishwasing for that meal. Highlights of the weekend are telling about and showing slides/movies of travel, new grandchildren, etc. We take hymnals along and spend a lot of time singing, especially during our Sunday morning worship service.

▼ (2) The autumn outing is to Brandywine State Park, just over the state line in West Virginia. We try to plan this for the Sunday when the leaves will be at the height of their color and beauty and, more often than not, we have a gorgeous day. Two nephews always race up the hill to be sure two picnic tables that we enjoy using have not been claimed by some other group! (In the 25 years we have been going to Brandywine, we have *always* been able to eat at those tables!) Other family traditions include Ruby's porcupine meat balls, Miriam's scalloped potatoes, Judy's coffee, Kathie and Wayne's hot cider, Jim and Julie's little tarts, Esther's apples, and on and on. Then we go down the hill, hike around the lake and up the huge earth dam, from which place we can see the panorama of colored leaves on the hills and the Shenandoah mountain. We sing from memory and reluctantly go down the hill and back home, usually stopping at Esther's house for more coffee, cookies, ice cream and talking and laughing.

One delightful feature of this day is "upsetting the fruit basket" in making up the loads for the cars, so as to be with family members we do not see on a regular basis.

▼ (3) The oldest tradition of all is Christmas Eve at "Grandpa's," but now that both Grandpa and Grandma are gone, things are not the same. While one or both of them were living, we always got together at their house. Grandpa would welcome us with some of his favorite Christmas records playing. We added our gifts to the stack already under the tree, then sat down to oyster stew, celery, apples and grapefruit, and mincepie.

While some of us washed dishes, others filled the candy boxes which were lined up around the table. One person doled out miniature Hershey bars; another, peanut brittle; and four or five others divided the rest of the candy into individual boxes. Last of all an orange was placed precariously on top.

Finally we all gathered into the living room where Grandpa read the Christmas story from the big family Bible, after we had sung many Christmas carols.

—*Miriam L. Weaver, Harrisonburg, VA*

▼ We were able to have Rod's grandmother (who was 99 at the time) live with us for most of a year before she moved to a nursing home.
—*Rod and Martha (Yoder) Maust, Indianapolis, IN*

▼ When Grandpa Naylor died in Florida, it was impossible for our children and the seven great-grandchildren to make the trip to attend the memorial service. Pop had joined the Cremation Society several years prior to his death, and it was decided that the whole family would get together later when we buried his cremains in Indiana where Grandma had been buried years before. Since this was to be a private burial, we tried to plan a little service which would be meaningful to our great-grandchildren. They have had little experience with death and had not had many opportunities to know their great-grandfather.

We bought a sweetheart rose for each member of the family to hold as we showed portraits of Grandpa: in one he was a small boy standing beside his twin brother; in another he was with the grandmother whom they'd never met but whose genes they carry. We looked for family resemblances among those of us who were standing in a semi-circle around the grave. There was a wedding picture of Grandpa and the woman they had learned to call Grandma Zola. In that picture, the great-grandchildren scrambled to see their own parents who had still been children when Grandpa remarried. And then there was a picture of Grandpa and Grandma Zola as the children had seen them a couple of years before.

Asked if they wanted to see the ashes stored inside the urn, the children eagerly gathered close around. We told them about how both their grandpa and grandma had died. We read the reassuring words of Jesus from the Gospel of John: "Let not your hearts be troubled, in my Father's house are many rooms. I go to prepare a place for you...that where I am, there you may be also."

After the urn was placed in the opened grave, Grandpa's elder son took the shovel and began to replace the soil, then offered the shovel to anyone who wanted to help. One small grandson stepped forward immediately to take his turn, and then each of the others followed, reverently giving themselves to the task. When all was finished, we read Psalm 100, and through sentimental tears we tried to sing "Praise God From Whom All Blessings Flow." Each person then laid their rose upon the grave.

We took time to look at the gravestones and talk about others we know who are buried in that lovely, simple graveyard. We breathed

deeply of the country air. Finally, we drove back into town for our evening meal where we continued our "celebration of family."
—*Ruth Naylor, Bluffton, Ohio*

▼   We have family get-togethers to celebrate same-month birthdays.
—*Paul and Elaine Jantzen, Hillsboro, KS*

▼   We do a lot of singing by ourselves and with other families, especially with our extended family. Mother used to say, "If you all want to talk at once you have to sing. Then you'll be in agreement."

My mother's descendants and spouses number nearly 150 so a niece compiled a date book, listing all their birthdays and anniversaries. It's like a perpetual calendar which we use as a prayer diary.

Whoever is with Mother on anyone's birthday, phones the birthday person and all sing "Happy Birthday."
—*LaVerna and Lawrence Klippenstein, Winnipeg, MB*

▼   Besides gatherings for birthdays and holidays, we try to see my parents weekly. Anita's family is scattered. We've made yearly family gatherings with her family a priority.

Some recent favorite activities with friends and family—fondue party, hikes, picnics, "Up-Jenkins" and Pictionary.
—*Anita and Randy Landis-Eigsti, Lakewood, CO*

▼   We live in the Chicago area, far from extended families. We make an effort to maintain ties with family members through occasional visits, but we also make lots of phone calls, send cards and letters, and use videos for some special events. We feel it is an investment to spend money on travel in order to maintain these family ties and for the children to know their roots.

▼   Our high-school-aged son spent one summer living with his grandparents and farming for his uncle. The most important benefit was the chance to learn to know his grandparents and other relatives better.

▼   When we do visit family, we also like to take small gifts for cousins and give them personally rather than send the usual packages at Christmas and birthdays. It is much more fun to be present when you give a gift. Even though we spend our vacation times visiting family, we usually combine sightseeing with our travel and that is an added benefit.
—*Karen Martin, Evanston, IL*

▼ We do not live close to either of our families, but we do live within one city block of a group of people who have become our intentional community. These people have been very important in the lives of our two children, Dagan and Yovana, who relate closely to all the other adults in the group. They are delighted to see each one. When Dagan, who is six, got a new bicycle, his first thought was, "I'm going to call Kathy and tell her." He knows that Kathy is interested in bicycling.

It has become important to us to have a group of people around to share our family with. In many ways they have taken the place of the traditional extended family.
—*Daryl and Marlisa Yoder-Bontrager,*
Lancaster, PA

▼ Family reunions don't happen after the parents are gone, unless one makes a plan to continue to come together. We are widely scattered, so we have one every five years. T-shirts with our family name are a popular item for such occasions.
—*Marie K. Wiens, Hillsboro, KS*

▼ Sometimes we have an informal family reunion at our annual church conference.
—*Phyllis Eller, La Verne, CA*

▼ We and a cousin of mine and her family have, for the last four winters, met halfway (a distance of about 200 miles for each) at a motel for the weekend. Our children have become well acquainted now through this.
—*Harvey and Lavonne Dyck, Christina and*
Colleen, Viborg, SD

▼ Family get-togethers at Christmas and summer are mainly ways of keeping extended family relations warm. My sister's family and our family get together at Thanksgiving, taking turns hosting.

▼ We try to spend every other Friday with my parents, helping with household jobs and taking time to learn from each other. My dad's interest in genealogy gives me much information and lots of stories of his past. Mom and I are learning that life's experiences help us to be more and more alike!
—*Millard and Pris Garrett, Kimmi and Krissie, Lancaster, PA*

▼ My extended family (Harnishes) goes to New Jersey for one week in August. We stay in a rented house and play cards, eat together, and play at the beach.
> —*Marie and Ned Geiser Harnish, Hannah and Nathan, Indianapolis, IN*

▼ Our extended family usually camps together or rents a house in Cape Hatteras, North Carolina.
> —*Tom and Lois Marshall, Naomi, Christine, and Jonathan, Spruce, MI*

▼ With each generation, the family expands and we no longer fit into one house at holiday time. Thus, we celebrate most special days with only part of the larger family. But because our grown children and their families don't often get to see their grandmother, aunts, uncles, and cousins who live in various places, we have a standing August weekend reservation at Quaker Haven—a centrally located camp in Indiana.

We rent the retreat house and have a wonderful time playing games, swapping stories, swimming, and cooking the meals which our daughter plans and everybody helps to fix. Bunk beds and sleeping bags add to the fun. On Sunday morning we attend worship services together.

My husband and I gladly pick up the tab for our children and their young families because we want them to know and enjoy the extended family. Admittedly, we sometimes wonder how long we'll continue to do this, but then each summer the grandchildren eagerly ask, "Are we going to Quaker Haven again this summer?" And we know the answer needs to be "Yes."
> —*Ruth Naylor, Bluffton, Ohio*

▼ Share and accumulate family stories. Tape recorders are great for this especially as people get older. Your family may choose to write some of these stories one day.
> —*Nancy Nussbaum, Elkhart, IN*

▼ Dave's family have settled far and wide; one sister's in California; one brother lives in Florida. Another brother is in San Salvador. Two years ago we had an "Ohio Christmas." Two years from now, we will all be in Florida for Thanksgiving. California comes next...but we're unsure about San Salvador! These are very special times.
> —*Jenny and Dave Moser, Bluffton, OH*

▼ Our daughter and her husband take both their parents on a summer trip. Being with our son-in-law's parents has established a beautiful relationship for us and our children. We have been to such places as Nova Scotia, eastern Canada, and Stone Harbor, New Jersey.
—*H. Howard and Miriam Witmer, Manheim, PA*

▼ We are part of a family business where two brothers, a brother-in-law, and a sister-in-law work together. Respect is the key! Sometimes the six adults go out for an evening of fun. These times are important to keeping a good work relationship.
—*Heidi and Shirley Hochstetler, Kidron, OH*

Singles

▼ We sometimes invite single and married friends for a music evening or poetry time. Presently we're in the process of having each single person from our congregation over for a meal.
—*LaVerna and Lawrence Klippenstein, Winnipeg, MB*

▼ Whenever we have a family for dinner, we also try to invite a single person. We find that singles enjoy the interchange of children and adults and add to our lives by being our friends. Often they can come for dinner on short notice.

I remember one time at the last minute my husband invited a new person who just started attending our church. That night I wondered if he really enjoyed the evening because he was so quiet and didn't seem interested in anything. Surprisingly our paths continued to cross and we were even invited over to his home. Through the years he has become one of our best friends.
—*Sam and Joyce Hofer, Morton, IL*

▼ Living overseas and relating to single missionary women made our family feel blessed to have extra "aunts." Since we came back to the States, we have continued to try to include in our family times people who do not have family.
—*Roy and Hope Brubaker, Mifflintown, PA*

▼ My husband invites international students to hike with him and we have them in for meals and evenings.
—*Shirley Kirkwood, Mt. Solon, VA*

▼ For over 15 years we introduced our family to other nationalities and cultures by entertaining Fresh Air children from New York City. Over the years we also entertained some 40 international students—a good experience for all ages.
>—*Omar A. and Delphia Kurtz, Morgantown, PA*

▼ We have frequently opened our home to singles for both long-term and short-term living arrangements. It has always been mutually beneficial—they have enjoyed having children to relate to closely, as well as other adults to share with on a daily basis; and we have welcomed the gifts and skills they have shared with us and our children. These persons have been from different countries, as well as our own, and from different races, as well as our own, but each has enriched our lives and challenged our growth.
>—*Herb and Sarah Myers and daughters, Mount Joy, PA*

▼ We have sometimes had a single person (a student usually) living with us for awhile. Some of them have stayed in touch and feel free to come by whenever they like.
>—*Rod and Martha (Yoder) Maust, Indianapolis, IN*

▼ We almost always have a young single person (or two) in our household and find they are a help with managing things and contribute in helping the children to relate to others outside the family.
>—*David and Louisa Mow, Farmington, PA*

▼ We share our home with a single friend who has become a very important part of our son's homelife. We share suppers together and the main floor living area.
>—*Ann and Byron Weber Becker, Luke, Kitchener, ON,*

Activities with Friends _____

▼ My husband and I do not have children at the present time. Sometimes we feel quite lonely and "childless." I've heard things like: "Oh, we can't come over for lunch after church because the little one needs a nap and you don't have a crib." So——guess what we bought for five dollars at an auction? Yep! I now preface invitations to our home for Sunday afternoon with: "We have a crib if ____ needs to nap."
>—*Nancy Nussbaum, Elkhart, IN*

▼ When the children were very small, we organized an exchange with four families for Monday nights. One set of parents kept all seven children and planned a special project for them. The other three sets of parents were free to do something together or alone every Monday evening from 7:00 to 10:00. The children developed special relationships, as well as all parents with each other's children.
—*Linda and Ron Gunden, Lisa and Angela, Elkhart, IN*

▼ We have a babysitting co-op of sorts. We exchange one to two hours of babysitting with another couple every few weeks. The parents take turns going out as a couple while the children play together. We have gotten close to the other children this way, as well as getting time out as a couple.
—*Bob and Jeanne Horst, Harrisonburg, VA*

▼ Our family and another family took day-long train trips. We went to parks for the day and then boarded the train to head home.

▼ Our extended family now gets together often for a fish fry, weekend camping, or a ride down the Mississippi on a riverboat cruise.
—*L. Glen and Allie Guengerich, Kalona, IA*

▼ We have enjoyed tent camping with another family on adjacent sites.
—*Ernest and Lois Hess, Lancaster, PA*

▼ We camped with another family on several occasions. We also co-owned a boat with this same family.
—*Bob and Doris Ebersole, Archbold, OH*

▼ We enjoy camping with other families. As our children were growing up, we spent many enjoyable weekends camping with church friends on Skyline Drive. Our children have good memories of those weekends, riding bicycles, roasting marshmallows at the campfire, and playing and eating with the other children of the group.
—*Ken and June Marie Weaver, Harrisonburg, VA*

▼ We have adopted an annual tradition with another family. When our children were young, we would see people around us packing up their families and heading down to a nearby city for a long weekend by the pool. Our two families felt we could not afford this, nor did we see much benefit in stuffing our six children into two small hotel rooms, so we planned a "big city" weekend in another part of our own home town!

Our friends moved into our home for the weekend, and we settled into theirs. We did not answer the phone. We cancelled all our commitments. We spent the weekend swimming, tobogganing, renting a movie, playing games, etc. Our meals were simple. We had such a good time that we have, with a few exceptions, continued this practice every year. It has become a little more difficult to cancel all commitments as the children have gotten older, but we all enjoy the weekends.
        —*Jane-Ellen and Gerry Grunau, Winnipeg, MB*

▼ One thing we do on a *regular* basis with several other families is bowling. After bowling we meet at one of our homes for fellowship.

▼ Aneta had 10 brothers and sisters. Now that their families are grown up, those of us who live near each other, go out to eat together every other week.
        —*Aneta Kalb Gardner and Charles V. Gardner, Goshen, IN*

▼ When our family visited with friends or extended family, we often chose teams or divided evenly and did Bible story skits.

▼ We especially try to include singles when we entertain. We like to have six or eight guests for Sunday dinner or for an evening meal. It does take energy but it is rewarding.
        —*Harold and Florence Bucher, Scottdale, PA*

▼ A fun activity to do with guests (especially an inter-generational group) is to divide them into groups of three or four, mixing the ages, and giving them all the same word to pantomime. Each group heads to private corners throughout the house to plan their presentation. Then each returns, acts out their wordless "drama," while the rest try to guess how they are using the word they've all been given. (Words like "star," "peace," and "spring" allow a lot of imagination to be expressed.)
        —*Merle and Phyllis Good, Kate and Rebecca,*
        Lancaster, PA

▼ We like to make and eat homemade ice cream together.
        —*Robert and Miriam Martin, East Earl, PA*

▼ Mountville has an original soda fountain "gramps corner grocer." It's a favorite place to walk to, get a snack, and relax in the evening.

▼ Our small group from church and neighbor families keep us in touch with others from various backgrounds.
—*Jim and Carol Spicher, Jonathan, Mountville, PA*

▼ Every year we go to a beautiful lake in northern Michigan and stay with two other families for one or two weeks.

▼ Every Sunday our children play with the children of another couple, alternating between the two homes.

▼ I want to invite about six to eight older women for a visit with Kate and me (Shirley).
—*Shirley H. and Stuart W. Showalter, Goshen, IN*

▼ Several families like to take a picnic lunch to a nearby farm pond where we fish for bluegill and bass. Sometimes the men don't get to fish very much, they are so busy baiting the children's fishing hooks.
—*Heidi and Shirley Hochstetler, Kidron, OH*

▼ We enjoy taking weekend trips with other families. We've gone to the mountains, the ocean, and nearby cities.

▼ Brooke is a swimmer, and so we enjoy getting to know other swim team families by going out to eat after meets.
—*Mike and Kim Pellman, Matt and Brooke, Bird-in-Hand, PA*

▼ When our children were ages nine and 11, we bought a little cabin (45 minutes away) with three other families. We spent most of our weekends the next several years working and playing there together. That was a good way to get away from phone and business at home.
—*Linda and Ron Gunden, Lisa and Angela, Elkhart, IN*

▼ We find families (particularly urban ones) who have done special activities like rocket-launching, kite-flying, nature hikes, etc. and then invite them to our house in the country to share these special childhood activities with us.
—*Lorna Chr. Stoltzfus, New Holland, PA*

▼ We like to follow our summer backyard picnics with a downtown scavenger hunt. We've found it a way to introduce guests to the city's loveliness, its architectural secrets, its history. We split up into two teams and give each a list of questions to answer. (The questions are the same for both teams, but they are listed in reverse order, so that each group follows its own route, but passes the other team at midpoint.) The idea is to answer all questions correctly and be the first team to return to our house. It's good exercise, it's gently educational, it's possible for inter-generational groups, and it's worn away some skeptics' prejudices about living in the city.

—Merle and Phyllis Good, Kate and Rebecca,
Lancaster, PA

▼ Living overseas while our children were middle-schoolers gave us the opportunity to maintain an awareness of and appreciation of our own country, while we were cultivating cross-cultural gratitude. One way we did this was by joining four other North American families for a traveling buffet. Each family prepared and served a food specialty as we went from house to house for the meal.

—Alice and Willard Roth, Elkhart, IN

▼ Traveling and hosting with Mennonite-Your-Way has brought us special and valuable opportunities. It's been good for our children to learn other families share similar concerns, and that God's people are everywhere.

—The Baker-Smiths, Stanfield, OR

▼ Before we had children, we puzzled long on how we could both continue our work together, and not feel guilty about the child care provided for our children. This was a bit complicated by living in the center city.

We found a most fortunate solution. Since they've been very young, our girls have stayed with an Amish family out in the country. Over a 15-year period, we have related to five different families, all within a mile's radius of each other.

We have liked their sense of family and values, the absence of television, videos and radio, the closeness to nature and animals, and the opportunity for the girls to learn many basic skills in the gardens and kitchens of these families. Many times the girls stayed overnight. Their Amish playmates became good friends. And most of all, our daughters possess a healthy appreciation of their religious cousins, the Amish, just as they've come to appreciate the racial and ethnic diversity of the city, too.

Staying with an Amish family calls for many adjustments—there are no phones to communicate change of schedules; sometimes a funeral or a wedding will make it impossible for them to accommodate us; and discipline and self-understanding may be approached differently. But we've usually found a way to work with this. In fact, our girls became so attached that they've often invited the Amish family to their birthday parties, along with their own grandparents.

—*Phyllis and Merle Good, Kate and Rebecca,*
Lancaster, PA

▼ I'm a serious letter writer and buy cards by the dozen.

▼ We have had our name in the *Mennonite-Your-Way Directory* for many years, and have had the opportunity to host families with children, since we have four of our own.

▼ We have had two Mennonite Central Committee exchange trainees, which has been a wonderful on-going experience. We shared our home for eight years with other couples and single adults—sharing kitchen and also child care—until we had three children. We now have a small bedroom we keep open for short-term students and friends, or people who have family in hospitals here in town. I have learned to not "entertain" but to enjoy our company. I don't "fix" breakfast; I set out bagels, fresh fruit, cereal, and coffee, bowls and cups. I may or may not get up, depending on guests' schedules. I keep a regular bedtime schedule, except for very special friends. I also figure if our family dirt bothers people, that is their problem and not mine, although I struggle with that all the time!

Having frequent guests is something we all enjoy. Our children enjoy it but don't put their activities aside for guests. This practice has helped make them outgoing and friendly, and they can't wait to visit friends in other countries.

—*Marvin and Rachel Miller, Indianapolis, IN*

▼ Clair and I lived outside of our home community for the first five years of our marriage. When we moved back home, it took a while to find our social niche. Then we started to spend time with some high school friends who had also moved away from home and back again. We developed an intentional kind of event, when we would talk about things that mattered to us and support each other in our early parenting experiences.

We took turns meeting in our homes for supper. The host family provided the main entree and one family brought salad, the other a dessert. We intentionally kept the menu simple so the event would not be a burden for anyone.

All three families remained involved with their own circle of friends and church family, but we always set the date for our next dinner

before the evening was over. We met about six times each year for
more than 10 years.
— *Nancy and Clair Sauder, Tim and Michael, Lancaster, PA*

▼ It is easy to feel lost and alone so far from family. However, when
we moved here the church was in the process of purchasing a
six-flat apartment building to be rented to church members. We
moved into the building with one child. Four of the other
apartments also had preschool children and we soon became one
large extended family with "cousins," "aunts," and "uncles." We
shared babysitting, chores, meals, shopping, transportation,
squabbles, colds, and illnesses, like any other family. We also
"adopted" a single male from the church, and he became a special
"uncle" for our son and shared many meals and events with us.
Though our children are older now, and we no longer live in the
apartment building, the family feeling remains. Sometimes we feel
closer ties to our "family" in the city, than our relatives.
— *Karen Martin, Evanston, IL*

▼ Almost all of our family is out-of-state, so our church is an
important part of our extended family—particularly our small group.
Our small group is made up of two families and three or four
singles. We deliberately keep our size to 11-12 people so that we
can fit around a table each week for a meal. We keep the meals
simple (one-dish meals with bread) and the singles in our group
take turns bringing bread or dessert.
Eating together is important to us. The once-a-week ritual of
preparing the food, setting the big table and being an important part
of this event is very significant for our children.
— *John and Ruth Miller Roth, Sarah, Leah, Hannah, and
Mary, Goshen, IN*

▼ We have chosen to live in a neighborhood with over 100 other of our
church members. We have shared meals and work. In fact, it is a
kind of urban version of the traditional Amish or Mennonite barn
raising.
— *Jim and Janalee Croegaert and family, Evanston, IL*

▼ We have a small number of neighbors who live in a sort of
community. We share child care, some equipment, and *work days*.
This sure makes less than favorite tasks become pleasant.
— *Tom and Karen Lehman, Corbett, OR*

▼ Because I (Merle) grew up in a large family, and loved it, it was difficult for me to adjust to the idea of a smaller family as we planned our own. One way to extend our family and to experience a greater sense of community in the city was to live as "intentional neighbors" with another family. For a while this meant together owning a house with three apartments, two of which we occupied as families. Later, we bought rowhouses side by side, broke a door between our basements so the kids could play together—and on the second floor so we could listen for each other's kids if one couple wanted to go out for a late supper after the kids were tucked in. We also joined our yards and shared our tools. It wasn't perfect, but it enlarged our family for our girls, it made the city less lonely, and it taught us to be willing to depend on others.

—Phyllis and Merle Good, Kate and Rebecca,
Lancaster, PA

▼ We have begun inviting our local friends (especially friends with children who usually need to leave early in the evening to get their children to bed) to stay overnight so we can have good conversation after the children go to sleep. Usually we get together on a Friday night for supper and are together through brunch on Saturday, either made at home or eaten in a family restaurant. We (parents) feel a lot more satisfied with the amount and quality of time we have with our adult friends, and the children enjoy the excitement of a sleepover, as they share their rooms with our guests.

—Mary Alice and Gerald Ressler, Lititz, PA

▼ As a single, mobile woman, I found moving to be a time when community was critical, and so was a pickup truck. I eventually bought my own pickup. Even though I am now married, the pickup continues to be useful to our family. What's more, I've discovered that being able to offer a pickup is a quick link to persons in need.

—Janice Miller and David Polley, Ann Arbor, MI

▼ We are very good friends with three other families. We have camped together, gone swimming together, and have had days of play together. We four couples always get together to celebrate our anniversaries. Each couple chooses a place to eat. This practice alone gets us together four times a year.

—John and Marilyn Burkhart, Mount Joy, PA

Activities With Grandparents _____

▼ We're all busy, and with school activities and homework, we don't visit grandparents as much as we'd like to. One partial solution occasionally is to meet at a restaurant for supper. No one has to cook, clean, or miss an evening meeting at church or elsewhere. We can sit and visit for an hour or two and still get home in time to finish homework.
—*Phyllis and Merle Good, Kate and Rebecca, Lancaster, PA*

▼ During our children's growing up years, we lived within 20 miles of one set of grandparents. We took advantage of this by often visiting them. We played games we all could be part of, such as croquet and table games.
We discovered that traveling together in the same car and staying in the same motel room gave the grandparents, as well as the children, new and different exposure to each other. I remember one occasion when we were all examining a new motel room for the first time, Grandpa said to Grandma, "Wow, this is pretty foxy, isn't it!" Our children kidded their grandparents for a long time about the "foxy" room!
—*Glen and Thelma Horner, Morton, IL*

▼ The grandparents usually take the children for outings to see different places, attractions and theme parks or even to go Christmas shopping. They also plan special events for the teenagers, taking them to dinner theater, a passion play or Christmas program, tractor pulls, and day trips to historical places.
—*Anne Long, Mount Joy, PA*

▼ The girls' grandparents planted a tree for each grandchild in the lot behind their house. Our girls enjoyed helping to plant the tree (when they were three or four), and it gives them a sense of owning part of Grandpa's and Grandma's place!
—*Phyllis and Merle Good, Kate and Rebecca, Lancaster, PA*

▼ For our parents' 75th and 80th birthdays we've had family gatherings or dinners which included slide presentations chronicling theirs and their families' lives during the previous 25-30 years. The grandchildren especially enjoyed this activity—noting the changes in their relatives.

▼ For our parents' 50th wedding anniversary our families planned an open house and family dinner. In addition, we gave them a photo album in which each of their children had filled several pages. These included photos of their family involved in activities they enjoyed and often included the grandparents with their grandchildren.

▼ My husband's mother has made many quilts over the years. Each of her children received several when they were married and she has also given one or more to each of her 19 grandchildren. For her 86th birthday we presented her with a photo album showing a current picture of each of her grandchildren with his/her quilt, plus her children with one of their quilts. On the cover of the album was a cross-stitched picture with the words, "Those who sleep under a quilt sleep under a blanket of love."
—*Arlene Kehl, Kitchener, ON*

▼ Some enjoyable times that our family has had with extended family have been our trips to the places where the grandparents (our parents) grew up. We take the better part of a day, charter a vehicle, visit the home, the school, and other important sites of that grandparent's childhood and youth. Children are involved with their cousins in experiencing the sights, smells, and sounds—we often provide a quiz for the kids. And we foster storytelling by the grandparents, including a sister or brother of theirs who can help flesh out the stories. Old memories create new memories.
—*Phyllis and Merle Good, Kate and Rebecca,*
Lancaster, PA

Family Letters

▼ Our family now lives on both coasts and in the Midwest and Canada. The cousins don't have many opportunities to learn to know each other, so I (Grandma) collect family member photos, and on their birthdays, each grandchild gets a few pages to add to her/his "Birthday Book." This keeps the cousins all current on each other's activities and progress.
—*Helen G. Kennell, Eureka, IL*

▼ Keith's family has had a circle letter for at least 12 years. (There are seven families, living in various states/countries.) We each write no more than one full page and must send it off to the next household within three days of receiving it. By the time it gets around to us

again, about one to one-and-a-half months have passed. Before we send our next letter, we take out our old one and file it. This collection will be a wonderful   diary for our own family in the future.
—*Keith and Brenda Blank, Rebekah, Laura, and Matthew, Philadelphia, PA*

▼ We only see some of our family once a year. I keep updated pictures of my children's cousins close by in small photo albums. We talk about these cousins quite often. I have my daughter draw pictures and send them in the mail to these extended family members.
—*Brenda Augsburger Yoder, Lancaster, PA*

▼ Years ago a family letter was begun among my father's brothers and sisters. Now grandchildren and some great-grandchildren are a part of it. Pictures are sent around with the letters. The pack makes a circle approximately once each year.
  Another family letter was started years ago by my mother and is circulated among my brothers and sisters. It takes about a month to make the circle and it keeps the family closely in touch.
—*Laurence and Marian Horst, Goshen, IN*

Food with Extended Family _____

▼ We have created traditions around visits with my nieces. One favorite tradition is the Cousins' Meal. The meal is prepared by the four cousins with some help from me. The complexity of the meal has increased as the cousins have matured. We started with French bread pizza and have progressed to lasagna, salad, and brownies.
—*Suzann Shafer Bauman, Lima, OH*

▼ For Thanksgiving one year my extended family had "brunch" and omelettes made to order!

▼ Since our children's grandparents live close by, we try to see them at least twice a month, sometimes as often as three or four times.
—*Scott and Sue Steffy, Leola, PA*

▼ My husband's side of our family always held a rabbit pie supper every November after small game season. (There were several hunters in the family.)

▼ My husband and his two brothers (ages 74, 67 and 58) have breakfast together every Thursday morning at 6:00 a.m. And we have an "aunts and cousins" luncheon once each year.
—*Iona S. Weaver, Lansdale, PA*

Food with Friends

▼ Almost all our get-togethers are potlucks so the work load is shared.
—*Miki and Tim Hill, Woodstock, MD*

▼ We (Ned and I and our kids) eat supper with another couple and child every other week, taking turns hosting the meal. We have been doing this for almost two years. This builds a relationship with another family with similar interests.
—*Marie and Ned Geiser Harnish, Hannah and Nathan, Indianapolis, IN*

▼ We have a potluck group that meets every other week in the winter and rotates among our homes. In the summer we move to the park and have a volleyball game following our dinner. We always celebrate birthdays at the potluck gathering closest to the date. Anyone is free to bring visiting friends or new acquaintances. The group tends to grow in the summer and dwindle to a core of about five families in the winter.
—*Gretchen Hostetter Maust and Robert Maust, Adam and Amanda, Keezletown, VA*

▼ Five years ago we formed a dinner group with three other households. The group provides fellowship, stimulating dinner conversation, and an opportunity for our children to interact regularly with other adults. It also relieves the burden of meal preparation. It is understood that meals are to be simple (often soup, salad, and bread). The setting is very informal. The soup pot goes directly from the stove to the table. There are not expectations to remain beyond the 6:00-7:00 dinner time. People often "eat and run."

We meet for dinner two evenings each week, rotating among the four households. When we meet at our house, we are responsible for meal preparation and cleanup. The others simply come and relax. The other three evenings we're the ones to just go and relax. We've

maintained our commitment to this type of a small group longer than any other because it doesn't require extra time (we would eat meals anyway) and it involves our whole family.
—*Martha and Rich Sider, Lancaster, PA*

▼ Weekly we invite other families, couples, or singles, to our home for a meal or dessert.
—*Kelli Burkholder and John King, Goshen, IN*

▼ We used to have an "extended family meal" each Thursday evening. It was a special meal and we always included a nearby aunt, a nearby single woman from church and sometimes "visitors." We experimented with different foods, eating styles and "our extras" often had great ideas and helped provide food. We found it worked best before our kids reached the teen years and became super busy.
—*Bylers, Williamsport, PA*

▼ In the summer, on almost every Sunday afternoon, we have a barbecue for a neighbor or whoever happens to stop by. We always have extra food, expecting someone to stop over.
—*Cemlyn Nelson, North Pole, AK*

▼ We have met with a group of people from church for the past 15 years on every other Sunday evening. Families have come and gone. The group size changes. Our only agenda is to have a potluck together in one of our homes. Over the years we have found that giving everyone a schedule at the beginning of the year keeps us going. We have encouraged people to come only when they want to and when it works into their schedule. If they are not available when their turn for hosting is scheduled, it is their responsibility to trade with someone and notify the rest of the group.
—*Donna M. Froese and Don E. Schrag, Samuel and Joseph, Wichita, KS*

▼ Entertaining has become a regular family event. Each member of the family has jobs to do to prepare for "company." We try to do it with an attitude that makes entertaining an important and special part of our family life. We often mix generations and have an older "grandparent" type with a younger family or singles.
—*Chuck and Robyn Nordell, Fullerton, CA*

▼ This may sound crazy, but our dinner guests are often subjected to a game of hide-and-seek in the yard. It gives us all a little exercise and the enthusiasm of the children (ours are aged four and eight) is infectious.

▼ One young father in our congregation says he has a periodic need for a campfire (don't we all?). So three to five families, mostly with elementary-age children, bring simple picnic and campfire snacks, and we meet at a park or somebody's farm, build a fire, play, chat, eat, and sing 'til the embers burn low. It's easy, informal, and lots of fun.
—*Laura and Steve Draper, Winfield, IA*

▼ Sometimes for fun, when we host a meal for family or for friends, we ask that each person be called by their unused name (which is usually their middle name, but sometimes a first name). If a person uses both names, as in Mary Ellen, then we use that person's mother's maiden name. Anyone calling persons by their regular names rather than their less used name is threatened with the loss of dessert. It's great fun. Children love it.
—*Phyllis and Merle Good, Kate and Rebecca, Lancaster, PA*

▼ Although we have no children of our own, children seem to enjoy coming to our home. I started a tradition when children come for a meal. I put a white sheet on the table (as a tablecloth) and have several boxes of fabric crayons on hand. Each child is invited to make a beautiful work of art on the sheet. Their parents help them write their names and the date. Each time they come, the children look to see not only where their pictures are, but who else has been to our home since their last visit! This gives children something to do while they are waiting for the last minute preparations (or after the meal) and also gives them a strong message that they are important in our lives.

This technique works with regular crayons, too. You simply need to put a paper bag between a hot iron and the drawing for a few seconds to fuse the crayon into the fabric before washing. It makes a lovely tablecloth which I will cherish for years to come!
—*Nancy Nussbaum, Elkhart, IN*

▼ I (Donella) am part of a group of five women who meet together monthly—more or less. Twice each year we gather as families for a summer picnic and for dinner during the Christmas holidays. These get-togethers have become important for our children as well as for the adults. We have been meeting for at least 14 years.
—*R. Wayne and Donella Clemens, Souderton, PA*

▼ We developed a friendship with a neighbor family and got together to celebrate two birthdays which are close together. Even when both families were in Africa (one in Tanzania and the other in Kenya), we were able to continue the tradition while we were on sabbaticals.
—*Daniel and Erma Wenger, Lancaster, PA*

▼ We always have potlucks for Passover, New Year's Eve, and sometimes July 4, Labor and Memorial Days. That way no one is exhausted from doing all the cooking, and we all get to be together.
—*Evie Talmus and Rich Schlachman, Jake,*
San Francisco, CA

▼ Our neighborhood has an annual picnic. This is fun and keeps good relations with neighbors. We even have a "business" meeting for recording new and old business and scheduling the next year's picnic and location!
—*Galen and Jeanette Miller, Clymer, NY*

▼ We've had a neighborhood ice cream supper every summer after grain harvest.
—*Monroe L. Beachy, Sugarcreek, OH*

▼ Every summer we have a picnic with four other families who were friends of ours before we were married. That event is the only time we see most of them.
—*Jay and Linda Ebersole, Rosalyn, Randy, and Ryan,*
Lancaster, PA

Activities with Church Friends

▼ The first Sunday of every month is a fellowship meal at church. Everyone brings a dish to pass. It's good food and fellowship.
—*Janet Roggie, Lowville, NY*

▼ We enjoy once-a-month Sunday potlucks at our church with our Sunday School class members. Last summer our six families took a day trip to the Ft. Wayne Zoo. Another summer day was spent at one of the family's lakeside cottage.
—*Jenny and Dave Moser, Bluffton, OH*

▼ We are members of a small group consisting of four to six families. We have various activities for the children, study times for the adults, and just fun times for everyone once or twice each month.
　　　　—Mark and Maxine Hershberger, Aaron and Stefan, Dalton, OH

▼ We belonged to a small church, so the whole church family was involved in picnics, weekend retreats at campgrounds with swimming, boating, games, eating together, and hiking.
　　　　—Marvin and Violet Jantzi, Phoenix, AZ

▼ Every Saturday or Sunday evening (when we first were married) we invited a different family to our house for a "game night" or meal.

▼ Once a month many friends from church gather in a home for music night. With our pastor on the banjo, and the choir director on a washtub bass, we add the fiddles, guitars, mandolin, hammer dulcimer, maracas, spoons, or anything else.
　　　　—Joan Schrock Woodward and Don Woodward, Elizabethton, TN

▼ We invited a lot of our church family to our house, often for an evening of music. We had guitars, autochords, violin, vocal, and an autoharp or electronic full-pedal organ.

▼ As a pastor and wife we had to do a lot of visiting, and very often took our children with us. That built good relationships, that, after all these years, still exist.
　　　　—Helen and Jack Wiebe, Selkirk, MB

▼ We exchange a spicy Christmas letter, summarizing the past year.
　　　　—Orpah and Elam S. Kurtz, Jefferson, NC

Holiday Activities with Friends

▼ *All* of our extended family lives at least 3,000 miles away from us. Holidays are times when we include singles, internationals, and other families "in orbit." It's a different group every time.
　　　　—Joan and Larry Litman, Hoboken, NJ

▼ During holidays we invite neighbors or friends who would be alone to share our holiday dinners and fellowship.
　　　　—Rachel Tamm, Allentown, PA

▼ We invite people with no or limited family connections to our home on New Year's Eve. Everyone brings finger food. We play games all evening, especially enjoying a homemade form of Pictionary using a large chalkboard so many can see/participate. We have a short devotional at midnight, including singing around the piano. Many bring sleeping bags and stay overnight. Anyone who has come in past years is automatically invited the next year. This has combined church friends, neighbors, and relatives.
—*H. Kenneth and Audrey J. Brubaker, York, PA*

▼ Some years we celebrated New Year's Eve with several other families with school-age children. It was special for the children to stay up until midnight and participate in games with the adults. The Dictionary Game (recently manufactured as Balderdash) was a favorite.
—*Arlene Kehl, Kitchener, ON*

▼ We have close friends whose children are the same ages as ours. At Christmastime we try to do special things together when our kids all come home. One year we rented a cabin at Oglebay Park and spent the weekend playing games, eating together, hiking, and talking. All of us *still* talk about that special year when we chose to forego giving presents and spend time together instead.
—*Jim and Dee Nussbaum, Kidron, OH*

Holiday Activities with Extended Family

▼ The extended Rutt family (three generations) gets together at a campground every Memorial Day weekend. Relatives come from near and far to cook, eat, play, and share together under a pavilion and around a campfire for three days. Annual events include volleyball games, blanket toss, and a Sunday morning sharing service around a campfire.
—*Roger and Pamela Rutt, Lancaster, PA*

▼ We have *always* gone to the mountains with the Burkholder family over the 4th of July. Everyone knows to reserve that weekend for the extended family.
—*Galen and Marie Burkholder, Jed, Kara, and Gina, Landisville, PA*

▼ At Christmas our family always gets together. We take turns hosting the event, starting with the oldest sibling in the family, so you know when it will be your turn to organize it.
—*Janet Roggie, Lowville, NY*

▼ We take turns hosting Thanksgiving and Christmas with our children's in-laws' families, making it fair for everyone.
—*J. Herbert and Cleo Friesen, Mt. Lake, MN*

▼ For years, we have hosted a Christmas get-together for my husband's family the Saturday or Sunday before Christmas. We serve just appetizers and hors d'oeuvres, and the cousins exchange Christmas gifts. The event is our Christmas gift to the family and our contribution to keeping in touch, especially now that the grandparents are deceased.
—*Clive and Margaret LeMasurier, Plainville, CT*

▼ The five weddings of our grandchildren have meant meaningful reunions, since our family is now scattered in three states and one foreign country.
—*Edna Mast, Cochranville, PA*

7.

Giving
Individual Attention

Preschoolers _____

▼ I nursed my babies—that is individual! While nursing, I could read or sing to the "kneebaby" who cuddled up on the other side. At later times, we did special hobbies—raising guppies, for example—to keep a close touch with one child at a time.
—*Luke and Miriam Stoltzfus, Philadelphia, PA*

▼ We read separately to each child when they were young.
—*Ernest and Lois Hess, Lancaster, PA*

▼ We split the kids; each of us takes one and plays, goes for a walk, reads a book, or plays games.
—*Phil and Penny Blosser, Beavercreek, OH*

▼ We tell "Luke stories." "Luke stories" consist of cuddling into a comfortable chair and always beginning with "Once upon a time there was a little boy called Luke..." The stories are short, involving special people, interests, and activities in his life. We find that five or six Luke stories can transform a fussy, demanding 18-month-old into the contented baby he usually is.
—*Ann Becker and Byron Weber, Kitchener, ON*

▼ My mother told stories to her children. Each child had a special animal that always played a central role in those stories. Mine was a rabbit. All the stories my mother told that were just for me centered on my adventures with my rabbit. Of course, I also listened to the stories that were told for my siblings, but I felt special when the story was about my rabbit and me.
—*Cheryl and Jerry Wyble, Salunga, PA*

Grandkids

▼ Dean took granddaughter Erika, a two-year-old, to the hog market. She got to choose a soda. She loved it and is ready to go again. We like to invite our grandchildren to spend time at our home without their parents. At chore time Dean has found it special to take one child with him.
—*Laverne and Eldon Dean Nafziger, Hopedale, IL*

▼ On birthdays Grandma and Grandpa Roth take each child (alone) out to eat. These grandparents live out-of-state but always manage to set up a time at least close to the special day. It's an event our children look forward to, even if it's a month after their birthday!

On birthdays Grandma Mattie bakes a homemade pie for each of her 23 grandchildren (and eight children), and the birthday person chooses the kind. She, too, lives out-of-state but always manages to get the pie to the birthday person, at least close to the day. Whenever it arrives, early or late, it's always a treat!
—*John and Ruth Miller Roth, Sarah, Leah, Hannah, and Mary, Goshen, IN*

▼ We give our grandchildren individual attention by taking them out separately to a restaurant for a meal at their birthday times.
—*Elmer S. and Esther J. Yoder, Hartville, OH*

▼ For grandchildren: take them shopping for their birthdays (let them pick a gift in a designated price range), eat out and maybe take them to see a family movie.
—*Bob and Doris Ebersole, Archbold, OH*

▼ Sometimes we take individual grandchildren on outings, to the park, to a restaurant, or shopping.
—*LaVerna and Lawrence Klippenstein, Winnipeg, MB*

▼ When our children were small, we took each one separately to a symphony concert. Now I am having each grandchild come for a day and overnight. Just the two of us do something special, like take a train ride or go to the "hands-on-house" or a museum or doll store, and then have lunch at the restaurant of his or her choice.
—*Arlene S. Longenecker, Oxford, PA*

▼ We like to have our grandchildren stay a few days or a week at our house *without parents.* Those are the times when we really get to know them—and have such special times together.
> —*J. Herbert and Cleo Friesen, Mt. Lake, MN*

▼ As a grandparent I try to sit with them and listen to them and also share about my struggles. I also pray for and write letters to each one to encourage them.
> —*Erma Kauffman, Cochranville, PA*

Finding Natural Ways _____

▼ While I was growing up, my parents made a real effort to spend time with each of us alone. Often this was done in conjunction with everyday tasks. Some of the best conversations I've ever had with my father took place during Saturday morning trips to get milk or gasoline. Each of us was also occasionally treated to dinner out without the other siblings.
> —*Kristine Platt Griswold, Falls Church, VA*

▼ While our six-year-old is at school (morning kindergarten), I take time with our two-year-old. When the young one is taking an afternoon nap, our six-year-old knows that "my time" is "her time." She has many suggestions for how we can spend our time together. My husband also takes one daughter at a time with him when he goes for machinery parts or visits the local grain elevator. Both girls have adult friends I've never met. Dave takes advantage of these drives by having some interesting talks with our six-year-old. And, the girls are learning about farming.
> —*Jenny and Dave Moser, Bluffton, OH*

▼ Martha often had one of the children dry the dishes while she washed them. At those informal times, the most unpredictable discussions would emerge. This was much better than scheduling a set time for the discussion of heavy subjects. One needs to talk about subjects when they arise—whether one feels he/she has time for it or not.
> —*Russell and Martha Krabill, Elkhart, IN*

▼ We gave individual attention incidentally, but naturally. I would take one child along to town, or to run errands, or work one-on-one around the house and farm.
> —*Edwin Miller, Wellman, IA*

▼ We help each of them with special projects or homework. I ask
them to help me with special tasks so we have time to be alone. We
also take different ones along on shopping trips at different times.
—*Roy and Hope Brubaker, Mifflintown, PA*

▼ Whenever one of us needs to do an errand on evenings or weekends,
we try to take one child along, for some one-on-one time with them.
—*Richard Harris and Caprice Becker, Manhattan, KS*

▼ Sometimes I ask myself, is this task chaff or wheat? Often the most
urgent demands of the day, like dishes, phone calls, and errands
are like chaff. But "wheat time"—small bits of loving moments with
my child—is the kind of thing that will accumulate over time to
make a lasting difference. What are some wheat time events?
Reading a book together at an unexpected time, going on a night
walk right after supper, enjoying each other's company while
changing a diaper or brushing hair, letting your child help with a
task you could do much more quickly yourself, listening to her
story, or watching her "trick" on the swing set.
—*Susan and Scott Sernau, South Bend, IN*

▼ I help at the school a couple afternoons each week. Walking home
with my son gives us a good time to talk.
—*The Baker-Smiths, Stanfield, OR*

▼ When the children came home from school, I tried to have a snack
ready or easily available, and made time to sit down and talk. When
they got home at different times, it was easier to manage. I tried to
get to know each of their teachers and many of their classmates and
families in elementary school. I also was available to talk when they
went to bed.
—*Phyllis Eller, La Verne, CA*

▼ Now and then we eat a meal out with one child, plan day outings,
and even occasionally take a child with one or both of us on a trip.
After our children reached high school and college age, it became
even more necessary to plan times *and* be on the lookout for times
when they were available to do something on the spur of the moment.
—*Jim and Janalee Croegaert, Evanston, IL*

▼ I tried to allow for individual choices in that each child could select
a book for bedtime (a total of three) and each child selected a record
to be put on the player (again a total of three) each night. They

loved this ritual and learned to appreciate each other's choices as well as their own.
—*Ken and Eloise Plank, Hagerstown, MD*

▼ Our daughter has three girls; two are twins. To avoid competition she looks for activities in which each child can excel. One is taking piano lessons, another violin lessons, and another aerobic exercise.
—*H. Howard and Miriam Witmer, Manheim, PA*

▼ Tell each one every day that he/she is special in some way. When they were small, we talked with each one individually at bedtime. We also looked for opportunities for each to do something special alone with parent(s). We made every attempt to respect their individual concerns, feelings, and ideas.
—*R. Wayne and Donella Clemens, Souderton, PA*

▼ There is no substitute for love. No matter what comes up we let our children know we dearly love them. This builds relations so that they feel free to share their cares as well as joys.
—*L. Glen and Allie Guengerich, Kalona, IA*

Photo Albums

▼ We are trying to keep detailed records of their childhoods—scrapbooks, journals, slides, video, audio recordings. Reading stories collected from earlier years and listening to baby sounds is fun to do together now.
—*Shirley and Stuart Showalter, Goshen, IN*

▼ For each of our three children I have made complete photo albums from their births to the present. I write the dates and events on the back of each photo, then place them in albums, chronologically, so that each photo can be easily removed to see the writing on back and then replaced. The children love to look at their personal albums and each others. Because of the cost and time invested in these, I keep them on a high shelf in a closet where they can be gotten down only with adult assistance. This serves two purposes: (1) to protect them, with some adult supervision, (2) they're "out of sight, out of mind" so the children don't think about them as readily as their things they see and reach. If the children are bored, I periodically suggest getting their photo albums down, and that's always a big hit.
—*Pamela and Roger Rutt, Lancaster, PA*

▼ I have kept a journal for each one. I intended the books to be for them when they are older, but the stories have already become favorite reading.
>   —*Mattie Miller, Sugarcreek, OH*

▼ I took "first day of school" pictures every year of each of our daughters. What a record to look at, from a very worried kindergartner to a confident senior in high school!
>   —*Clive and Margaret LeMasurier, Plainville, CT*

▼ When our first child graduated from high school, her picture was framed and hung on the stairway wall. Eventually all four children's graduation photos were there. When one married, the high school picture was replaced with the wedding photo, and so on. When a grandchild was born, the wedding picture was replaced or the baby picture was inserted alongside the wedding one. It's become a documentary wall marking our times; it's also a place for grandchildren to look and ponder.

▼ When one of our children (or grandchildren) has a birthday, our gift is always a book, appropriately autographed by us parents/grandparents.

▼ Our family's story history is documented. Earlier we did it by slides; now it is on home video, with the earlier slides now also placed on video. Periodically, one or more of those videos is shown (often at Christmas) as we relive and recall. Yes, we have more than one copy: the grown children have their own duplicates.
>   —*Leroy and Pauline Kennel, Schaumburg, IL*

Working Together

▼ Our children are far enough apart in age so that we were often alone with one while cleaning house together, washing the car or picking beans. These were good opportunities for fellowship, as well as times in the car on our way to and from their activities.

   Now that three are on their own we chat on the phone or have them in for meals separately, on occasion.
>   —*LaVerna and Lawrence Klippenstein, Winnipeg, MB*

▼ Our third son enjoyed making six individual salads for dinner each night while Mother fixed the main meal.
>   —*Emmet and Elsie Buhle, Media, PA*

▼ The children take turns drying dishes while I wash. This provides an opportunity for us to talk about whatever is on their minds.
—*Louise Longenecker, Oxford, PA*

▼ Our children were assigned turns to help with evening dishes with a parent. While closely working together with one of us, the child shared his/her day's experiences and concerns. For this reason, our getting a dishwasher was delayed for later years.
—*Marvin and Violet Jantzi, Medina, NY*

▼ I take turns taking each child to get groceries or go shopping with me. It's also a good way for me to have one-on-one conversations and get to know them individually. Having them help me bake bread or cookies is fun too.
—*Keith and Brenda Blank, Rebekah, Laura, and Matthew, Philadelphia, PA*

▼ When our children were between two and six years old, I went grocery shopping in the evening and took only one child with me at a time. They loved the attention and were expected to help me find the groceries.
—*Marvin and Rachel Miller, Indianapolis, IN*

▼ My mother never discussed the "facts of life" with me. I had to learn elsewhere. I resolved that my daughters would be better informed. After supper when we did the kitchen work, after my husband and the boys went to the barn, they learned about that part of life at the kitchen sink.
—*Edna Mast, Cochranville, PA*

▼ We have a family auto repair business. From the time he was a toddler, our older son, Richard, went to the shop to "help" his dad. As Richard's clothes absorbed grease from the shop, his mind and spirit absorbed knowledge and attention from his dad. By the time he was in first grade, Richard could name every make of car. (There weren't as many then as now.) I guess we shouldn't be surprised that Richard today, as a young adult, is a skilled auto mechanic with a close relationship with his dad.
—*Dick and Nancy Witmer, Manheim, PA*

▼ One child would go along when Daddy delivered or went for things. Our business was at home and involved frequent short and longer trips. Children took turns or earned the right to "help."
—*Harold and Rachel Ruhl, Ronks, PA*

▼ Our children were in 4-H and Scouts. I was a leader in both and we worked together on some projects.
—*Rachel Tamm, Allentown, PA*

▼ I like to share my hobbies with them.
—*Lorna Chr. Stoltzfus, New Holland, PA*

Driving Together

▼ Driving time is one of the best settings for talking—forced togetherness, no danger of a sibling overhearing, and you don't have to look at each other!
—*Lois and Jim Kaufmann, New Paris, IN*

▼ After dinner my husband reads to the younger boys to relax them and to teach them as well. He also drives them to their music lessons, giving them special attention and praise if warranted. Our second son attended a school some distance away from our home for grades six through 12. Emmet drove him there each morning on his way to work; a good chance to talk.
—*Emmet and Elsie Buhle, Media, PA*

▼ Chauffeuring is a Number One way to have personal time with children. I found out all sorts of things about their lives while I drove. I mourned them turning 16, only because it took my "alone" time with them away. Now I make a special effort to just "visit" with each child at least once a week. Their schedules are very busy.
—*Marvin and Rachel Miller, Indianapolis, IN*

▼ On occasion when we're driving here or there, one of us parents rides in the back seat with one of the girls while the other daughter rides up front beside the driver. The conversation in the car is remarkably different, often happier.
—*Phyllis and Merle Good, Kate and Rebecca, Lancaster, PA*

Showing Support _____

▼ We attend as many of our sons' sports events as possible, to the exclusion sometimes of adult activities.
  —*David and Cynthia Shank, Mt. Crawford, VA*

▼ Our 10-year-old son likes when we attend his sports events or take time to listen about the latest baseball cards he has acquired.
  —*Elizabeth Weaver, Thorndale, ON*

▼ We faithfully attended programs each child was in: from tag football games to band concerts to FFA (Future Farmers of America) activities. I helped-watched-directed-assisted in a lot of craft constructions. I also taught each boy to make cakes, cook meals, sew on buttons, etc. Dad taught farm chores: from hay baling to helping with corn.
  —*Glenn A. and Hazel Miller, Hudson, IL*

▼ When one of the children had a public performance—music, drama, speaking—we celebrated by going for ice cream afterwards. It was a time to unwind and for us to say "good job, we're proud of you."
  —*R. Wayne and Donella Clemens, Souderton, PA*

▼ Declare a day that person's Special Day. Get them a flower, take them out for a float, go through their scrapbook, talk about their feelings, etc. This is not their birthday.
  —*Bylers, Williamsport, PA*

▼ Sometimes we took each one out for a special meal but most often we gave special attention by shopping or going to their games when they were in sports. Now, as adults, we visit them in their homes.
  —*Jim and Dee Nussbaum, Kidron, OH*

▼ Family council time, held each Monday evening, was helpful. This was a time when everyone had equal time to speak whatever was on their minds and to learn to listen to the others. It reduced complaining and arguing because we guaranteed a fair hearing in council time. Most problems and issues were able to wait; occasionally we parents had to work one-on-one apart from Monday evening, but not often.
  —*Mark and Pauline Lehman, St. Anne, IL*

▼ On New Year's Eve each of us wrote a resolution for ourselves which we could share with the family if we wished. We had developed a

habit of being late for church, and we all felt badly about it. One year someone made a resolution that the family be on time every Sunday. It worked!
> —*Dietrich and Mary Rempel, Hesston, KS*

▼ When our daughters or daughters-in-law are expecting babies, we try to send them a small gift each month of their pregnancies. We share prayer requests and we pray together over the telephone.
> —*Stephen and Sadie Yoder, Quarryville, PA*

Special Meals

▼ Because it seemed easier for Mom to find time throughout the day for each child, Dad developed some *specific* activities. Because he works Saturday, he takes Wednesday off. Each Wednesday morning one of our three children has breakfast out with Dad. Even during school, because the practice is so special, the children have no trouble getting up that half hour or so earlier.
> —*Don Kraybill and Elizabeth Loux, Matthew, Micah, and Ashley, Harleysville, PA*

▼ I (David) plan specific activities with our sons, put those events on my calendar and refuse to let others (church, work, etc.) have that time, since I already have an appointment. I take each son out by himself once every month for breakfast. I start at age three and I intend to go through age 18. That will be 180 breakfasts with each boy, one-on-one.
> —*David and Cynthia Shank, Mt. Crawford, VA*

▼ About once a month Dad takes each child out for breakfast at a restaurant that they can walk to or ride bike to. They each look forward to it eagerly.
> —*Judy Stoltzfus, Colorado Springs, CO*

▼ I make it a practice to take one child out each week. They take turns, moving from the oldest to the youngest. When it is a child's "special time," that child chooses where we will eat and what we will do together. Our four-year-old usually chooses to eat at a fast-food restaurant with a playground and then to stop at the library and the park. Our twelve-year-old son loves to go to the baseball card shop and an all-you-can-eat restaurant. Our ten-year-old daughter likes to shop.

These "special times" have become real important to the kids. We don't postpone "special times" casually. I am often asked, "Whose special time is next?" and "When do I get a special time with Dad?" It is not acceptable to go with Dad instead of Mom. Dad's times must come in addition to Mom's times!
—*Melody Hall, Goessel, KS*

▼ Once every month Dad takes out one of his daughters on a date to the restaurant of their choice. It makes them feel very special and is important for developing an open relationship (the girls are six and eight).
—*Mary Hochstedler and Ruth Andrews,*
Kokomo, IN

▼ My husband was able to be free at noon, so occasionally he would arrange to take one child out to eat for lunch.
—*Ann Martin Kauffman, Goshen, IN*

▼ Over the years we have looked for opportunities to take them out for an ice cream cone or snack, either both parents or one. Often a lunch at Hardees or McDonald's with one parent was very special. Because we rarely ate out as a family, these were seen as quite special times when the children were young.
—*Linda and Ron Gunden, Elkhart, IN*

▼ When our children were in the elementary grades, Friday nights were set aside for eating out. Our two oldest children are only 16 months apart. One night Mother ate with Son while Father ate with Daughter. The next Friday night Mom ate with Daughter while Dad ate with Son. The next Friday all four of us ate out together. On the fourth Friday night it was Mom and Dad's night out "solo." One night while Mother and Daughter were eating in a restaurant, Dad and Son arrived at the same place. When Son saw Mom and Daughter were already in the restaurant, he wanted to go to another restaurant and be with Dad alone.

This was one way to give them our undivided attention, and it didn't cost very much because we usually ate at fast food restaurants. As they got older, this practice faded because it didn't fit into the children's schedules.
—*Fred and Faye Litwiller, Goshen, IN*

▼ We have monthly date night. My husband and I each take one child out for a date. (We also have a "date night budget" which they know about or else it could get quite expensive!) We have the best time on our dates because we are out as friends, giving one-on-one attention. We've been doing this since the kids were about five and eight. I also try to have a semi-regular "child of the day" once or twice a month. That child chooses dinner, gets served first, says the blessing, and is just made to feel extra special.

  —*Patrick and Gina Glennon, Turnersville, NJ*

▼ My sister and I are several years apart, so we attend different schools. Because of this, every once in a while one of us has a day off from school, while the other does not. On these days, Mom often takes the one at home to her choice of a restaurant for lunch. Not only does it give us a needed break from our sibling, it makes us feel special to get all of Mom's attention.

  —*Heidi and Shirley Hochstetler, Kidron, OH*

▼ Dad takes the boys out for breakfast at the place of their choice for their birthdays.

  —*Nancy and Clair Sauder, Lancaster, PA*

▼ The birthday person was sometimes given the opportunity to choose the birthday dinner menu. Other times, that person's favorite dishes were prepared as a surprise.

  —*Richard and Betty Pellman, Millersville, PA*

▼ When the children were between the ages of six and 12, Mom took each child on his/her birthday into the city (Lancaster) on the town bus. We had lunch together and then came home on the bus.

  —*John and Marilyn Burkhart, Mt. Joy, PA*

▼ If birthdays fall on a school day, one parent takes time off work to go to school and eat in the cafeteria with our celebrant. This is a big deal in elementary school, but may not be "cool" later on.

  —*Gretchen Hostetter Maust and Robert Maust, Adam and Amanda, Keezletown, VA*

One-on-One

▼ Even though we're a small family, we've sensed a need to spend some stretches of time alone with each child. We instituted One-on-One Days soon after both girls began school and we had less time at home with them.

On a One-on-One Day, each parent takes one child on a special excursion, planned in secret by just the two of them. (These have been mostly to local destinations, although a few times we've gone to some nearby cities to a special art show or attraction.) The emphasis is on doing what the child enjoys and having plenty of time to visit together. Then we all meet for supper together at a prearranged time and place to disclose to each other what we did for the day.

Our modest goal has been to have at least two One-on-One Days each year (often in the summer) so that each parent and each child have a day together in the course of a year.

> —*Phyllis and Merle Good, Kate and Rebecca,*
> *Lancaster, PA*

▼ We consciously work at one-on-one activities. These have included shopping trips, eating out, sports (usually Dad and one child)—particular activities that allow times for talking.

> —*Lois and Jim Kaufmann, New Paris, IN*

▼ We read and play games with individual kids. Helping them with their music lessons is valuable too; we use the Suzuki method which calls for a parent's involvement.

> —*Tom and Lois Marshall, Spruce, MI*

▼ The Suzuki violin method with its Mother-tongue learning concept has structured daily one-on-one time for us. Opportunities to perform, both informal and formal, bring more of the same, plus affirmation from family and friends.

> —*Laura and Steve Draper, Winfield, IA*

▼ Occasionally we pair off and each parent takes a child to breakfast, for a walk, or to play some ball. Having both parents spend time together with one child is more difficult and usually occurs when the other child is away (sort of by default).

> —*Phil and Sandy Chabot, Becky and PV, Cromwell, CT*

▼ We've done the following activities: take them on a camping/fishing trip, one parent and one child at a time. Eat a special dinner in a restaurant every other month, one parent and one child. Mom and Daughter work in Self-Help one-half day a month. (It's a small store, so we have plenty of time alone.)

> —*Virginia Buckwalter, Scarborough, ON*

▼ Dad took them to ball games, one at a time. And some years ago he worked at a small control tower which had very little activity on the mid-watch. He took them along one at a time on a midnight watch, allowing them to see what he had to do and be alone with him. They still say that meant a lot to them.
                    —*Rachel Tamm, Allentown, PA*

▼ We take our children, alone, for half a day about once a month to do whatever they would like. Usually it includes a meal, then a canoe ride or a visit to the library, airport, etc.
                    —*Tom and Karen Lehman, Corbett, OR*

▼ When they were younger, their father would go with one (taking turns) for an all afternoon bike ride.
                    —*Mr. and Mrs. Nelson Schwartzentruber, Lowville, NY*

▼ The best present Clayton ever gave was the year he scheduled Saturday morning dates with our individual children.
                    —*Clayton and Ruth Steiner, Dalton, OH*

▼ Time alone with my dad, when I was a boy, was rare (I have five brothers and four sisters.). I recall feeling deprived in not having quality time alone with my parents, of not having my own drawer space for my clothes, or a desk for my books and papers. I often compared myself with my closest friend and first cousin who could eat an entire candy bar himself; who had his own bicycle and his own bedroom; who could put as much ham in his sandwich as he wanted. He did not inherit his older brother's shirts, shoes, socks, and dark-blue suit that did not fit nicely at the collar.

But on certain occasions, I was called into Dad's study—alone—and the door was closed. Actually, the first time it happened, it was shared with my older brother. Dad asked us if we knew what our rabbits were doing when the one was on top of the other. And then, in a manner that would have made most bishops blush and Dobson beam, Dad carefully and simply shared with us the anatomy of our biological beginnings. And suddenly the world was a bigger place.

I was eleven the second time I was called into the study alone with Dad. Clearly and concisely, Dad shared with me what it meant to become a Christian—to accept Christ as my personal Savior. Soon thereafter, I "stood" in church, during one of Dad's revival meetings, and made that most important decision.

But it was the third time that I remember most vividly. I was approaching dating age. Alone with Dad in his study, he said, "Mel,

I have three deep desires for all my children. First, that each of you choose to accept Christ and make him Lord of your lives. That's a decision you must make—no one can make it for you. Second, I want you to have a pure courtship." And I knew what he meant. "And third, I hope you find as good a wife as you have a mother." He concluded, "There are few things in life that bring greater pain than a broken home, and there are few things in life that bring greater joy than a happy home." I know now what Dad knew then. That he made the effort to talk to me privately and alone impressed me. I realized he loved *me* (even though I was one of 10), and, consequently, I took his words more seriously.

—*Melvin Thomas, Lancaster, PA*

▼ For our six-year-old daughter who is deaf, we write about the day's activities in a special notebook each evening before bedtime. She needs the extra language and one-on-one attention. We now have four years worth of "diaries" that she enjoys reviewing.

—*Roger and Pamela Rutt, Lancaster, PA*

▼ When the girls were little and I was busy during the day, I decided to institute "an hour with Mother" on an individual basis in the evenings. This did not happen very often, so it remained a special treat. On the evening for Kathie, the other two would go to bed at their regular time, but Kathie could stay up and we would do whatever she most wanted to do (within limits of course). It might be making candy or popcorn; doing some sewing project; reading a story or whatever, but it was just for her and me. Carol and Jeanie each had their turns as well. This did not require a great deal of time, but brought pleasure and a sense of belonging and importance to each girl.

—*Miriam L. Weaver, Harrisonburg, VA*

▼ Our oldest, Leah (five), has her special individual time with Mom and Dad after her twin siblings (age two) go to bed. We take turns reading books to her. (It's especially fun to read to her the same stories I remember my mother reading to me.)

▼ It's a bit more difficult giving individual attention to twins. We try to read books of their choice or help one at a time with a project they're working on.

—*Tom and Sue Ruth, Lancaster, PA*

▼ Having "art class" with a child has been a great success in our family. Adult and child begin with any size paper. Directions are given simply and slowly at first, until your child becomes familiar with this exercise. "Class" could begin something like this: (1) Make three circles anywhere on your paper. (2) Draw a line through one of the circles. (3) Fill in one of the circles with a marker. (4) Make a line beginning at the top of your paper down to the bottom. (5) Now make a dot anywhere on that line. Continue as desired. Directions should match your child's level.

It's very important to stop when your child loses interest. More important is to give your child a turn to be "in charge" and give directions. It gives them "leadership" over an adult in a positive setting. It also gives them a chance to make choices and decisions.

P.S. You are not to be "drawing" anything in particular but just having fun. Papers will be quite different even though both followed the same directions!

> —*Lois and Randy Zook, Lancaster, PA*

▼ Even now at ages 17 and 19, our daughters like individual attention. When they are both home, if I'm doing something with one, my husband will do something with the other. We may go out to eat (the local diner is a favorite) or tag sale poking, or maybe run errands or do something at home for them that we haven't gotten to before.

> —*Clive and Margaret LeMasurier, Plainville, CT*

▼ Jim takes our oldest son golfing. There they have several hours of time alone. (Incidentally our son is better at golf!)

> —*Jim and Nancy Roynon, Brad, Taryn, Drew, and Colin, Archbold, OH*

Bedtime _____

▼ Bedtime has always been a special time. We each put a child to bed (alternating each night) and try to have an unhurried time of reading books and talking about the day.

> —*Anita and Randy Landis-Eigsti, Lakewood, CO*

▼ Before bedtime, our children like to read. We often pull out a book, lie down beside them, and read, too.

> —*Jane-Ellen and Gerry Grunau, Winnipeg, MB*

▼ When our children were young, we tried to give individual attention at bedtime when they liked to talk or vent their feelings. Their

bedrooms somehow became the place to "sound off," get advice, or just chat.
> —*Jim and Dee Nussbaum, Kidron, OH*

▼ Each night John and I spend time (five to 15 minutes) with each child before tucking them in, rubbing each one's back, and talking about her day.

▼ John takes one child with him to his office for an hour or so each week. They take along "quiet play" and enjoy being a part of his life at work. Our children consider this a special treat and are on their best behavior.
> —*John and Ruth Miller Roth, Sarah, Leah, Hannah, and Mary, Goshen, IN*

▼ Our younger son (age six) loves the individual attention he gets at bedtime: storytime is followed by lighting a candle, then each of us (parent and child) tells what we are thankful for on that particular day. We end by praying together and finally snuffing out the candle.
> —*Elizabeth Weaver, Thorndale, ON*

▼ At one stage, our children took turns staying up one-half hour longer than the usual early-to-bed-time.
> —*Richard and Betty Pellman, Millersville, PA*

▼ The hour after our younger two go to bed is the special time for our oldest. He has a snack/dessert with us parents before reading his bedtime stories.
> —*Richard Harris and Caprice Becker, Manhattan, KS*

▼ Sometimes we go to the child's room and talk, or we wait up for whoever is out and, when they get home from events, talk while things are still fresh in their minds.
> —*Richard and Jewel Showalter, Chad, Rhoda Jane, and Matthew, Irwin, OH*

Trips Together _____

▼ Take a child along on shorter or longer trips, even if it is just a business trip. It may mean extra bother and make you more inefficient, but it is easily worth the investment. Children remember these times for the rest of their lives.
> —*David and Louisa Mow, Farmington, PA*

▼ Dad travels as part of his work and, usually once a year, takes one of the children with him for a few days on one of his trips. (He chooses conferences in Seattle where an uncle, aunt, and cousins live.) As the children have gotten older, they've gained a growing understanding of what he does on his trips away.
> *—Elizabeth Loux and Don Kraybill, Matthew, Micah, and Ashley, Harleysville, PA*

▼ We've taken trips with each child—one was with Dad to Haiti for two weeks as volunteers. Another went with Mom and Dad to Haiti to work for one week. A third motorcycled with Dad to Nova Scotia. The fourth took a 15-day motorcycle trip to Yellowstone National Park.
> *—Orpah and Elam Kurtz, Jefferson, NC*

Letters

▼ When each of our children were born, I wrote "A letter to my son/daughter," telling them the details surrounding their birth. I tried to be specific, without being too graphic. I expressed how much we wanted them, how we loved them even before they were born, and how precious it was to count their tiny fingers and toes. And of course I added the funny things like when Daddy ran up over an eight-inch curb trying to park in the hospital parking lot or when our daughter talked non-stop for an hour when she first held her brother. It has preserved their birth days much more than my memory ever could have!
> *—Miles and Dawnell Yoder, Lancaster, PA*

▼ I write each of our three children a letter every week. I also send clippings from newspapers and the church bulletin. Sometimes I hear "Mom, your letter came one day late!"
> *—Ralph and Mary Martin, Goshen, IN*

One-on-One Shopping

▼ My husband often took one of the children out for "a date." They would go shopping, eat out, or do something that child wanted to do. The other child and I stayed home, which gave us the chance to do something special together, too.
> *—Mim and Roger Eberly, Milford, IN*

▼ Every August each child got his/her own special day to go school shopping with Mom. It always included lunch at a restaurant of his/her choice and lots of time to talk about the coming school year.
—*Larry and Evie Hershey, Atglen, PA*

▼ By the time Number Three joined the group that needed to shop for a new school year, it took only one shopping excursion with all three to know a better way had to be found. Thus, another tradition was formed. Sometime in August each child had a special day with Mom in the city. Not only were new clothes acquired, but the child of the day had lunch in her/his choice of restaurant with Mom's full attention. Topics were how that child had changed in the past year, what her/his aspirations and dreams were, what kinds of problems or concerns she/he was facing, etc. It became an important time of evaluation and strengthening of bonds for both Mom and child that lasted even after school clothes were no longer needed. That full day each year helped establish trust and open communication throughout the year.
—*Norman and Ruth Smith, Ailsa Craig, ON*

▼ I like to take one child shopping with his/her birthday money.
—*Christine Certain, Fresno, CA*

One-on-One Special Interest Activities

▼ We try to cultivate special interests/abilities by working on projects together. Benjamin and I do things together in the garden and shop. Daniel and I work together at the computer. Bonita works individually with the children in the kitchen. Bonita and/or I may have private talks with the children in the bedroom at night—their room or ours.
Bonita often sings together with Emma, who is developing a singing voice. They also go shopping—a favorite for Emma.
We took Ben with us to his teacher's wedding.
—*Ervin and Bonita Stutzman, Mt. Joy, PA*

▼ Take advantage of their different interests. Christina wanted to join 4H; Colleen didn't. So that created a special time for me to work with Christina.
—*Harvey and Lavonne Dyck, Christina and Colleen, Viborg, SD*

▼ When the boys reached third grade, they and Dad spent many hours building model cars and trucks together in our basement workroom. Thom recalls the first car he built was an Indy car. Today Thom photographs car races as often as possible. Both sons as young adults still include models they can build in their Christmas wish lists.

—*Charlotte H. Croyle, Archbold, OH*

▼ For a Senior Project Lisa chose to make a crazy quilt. We shopped all over Los Angeles together to find antique fabrics, wrote to her great-aunts and grandmothers for samples, researched quilting and various stitches. It took all the hours the school allotted to the project (6 weeks) and Mom's help.

—*Frieda Barkman, Twentynine Palms, CA*

8.

Keeping Children Creatively Occupied

Boredom

▼ From the time the children were little, we decided not to accept the complaint, "I'm bored." I usually answered, "That is your choice, but remember all the different things there are to do," and I would remind them of some ideas and activities. If they chose none of them, they were not to bug me about being bored.
—*Linda and Ron Gunden, Elkhart, IN*

▼ We begin with this statement: You may not say "I'm bored." Boredom is your responsibility because there are unending opportunities to read and discover new things, so if you are feeling bored find something new to discover.
—*Mark and Leone Wagner, Lititz, PA*

Limiting Activities

▼ The biggest challenge we face now that our children are teenagers is not how to keep them active, but how to slow them down and help them set priorities with their time. Our children constantly comment about how fast time goes.
—*Marvin and Rachel Miller, Indianapolis, IN*

Preschool Activities

▼ Our best investment for our children when they were preschoolers was a set of wooden building blocks built by the Hutterian Brethren in their Community Playthings line of toys.
—*Mr. and Mrs. Nelson Schwartzentruber, Lowville, NY*

▼ We placed our large rectangular sandbox on an embankment so that it shed water and got morning sunshine and afternoon shade. It was a great source of enjoyment for the neighborhood children.

They built roads and towns, added twigs and branches, drove cars and trucks, added water and built houses.

▼ We had a large chalkboard on one wall in the house and each child had a section to use when they were quite young.
—*Enos and Erma Shirk, Thornton, PA*

▼ Painting with water on a sidewalk porch has been a great activity for our preschool-aged son.

▼ We have fish as pets. He feeds them, talks with them, and is anxious to introduce his friends to the "creatures" in the tank.
—*Jim and Carol Spicher, Mountville, PA*

▼ Our preschoolers' favorite activities include "helping" Mama or Papa, reading library books, listening to tapes (often from the library as well), and playing outdoors. One idea I learned from a friend—buckets of water, paintbrushes, and a cement driveway or sidewalk make for lots of fun "painting."
—*Rod and Martha Maust, Indianapolis, IN*

▼ We try to buy toys that can be used in many different ways and that encourage creativity: dramatic play clothes, playdough, clay, blocks, Duplos, Legos, large train set with houses and people, farm set, dollhouse.
—*John and Ruth Miller Roth, Sarah, Leah, Hannah, and Mary, Goshen, IN*

▼ When we lived overseas, we didn't have a lot of options for creative activities. I made playdough, and sometimes as a family we each created something and then guessed what the others had made.
—*Roy and Hope Brubaker, Mifflintown, PA*

▼ Two-year-old Jake likes to make tents out of sheets over chairs in the dining room, then play hide-and-seek. I make wands out of paper towel tubes and ribbons, then we march around the house or put on reggae and dance with our wands.
—*Evie Talmus and Rich Schlachman, Jake, San Francisco, CA*

▼ Our son walked at an early age and could be destructive when we visited in homes which were not child-proofed. Our friends assured us that "He can't hurt a thing," while he proceeded to wreck things with his curiosity. We partially solved the problem by supplying

him with construction blocks and puzzles which were of high interest to him. He was only permitted to use them when we were "company" and visiting away from home. To this day we refer to them as the "company" blocks.
—*John and Trula Zimmerly, Jackson, OH*

▼ Our children had lively imaginations, so they often played "olden days" because we read through the Little House books by Laura Ingalls Wilder several times. John made a barn and dollhouse (which I helped decorate) when our children were small. That gave them lots of creative play ideas.
—*Joyce Rutt Eby, Goshen, IN*

▼ I involve my children in running the household to the best of their abilities. One of our five-year-old's jobs is to feed the goldfish. Our five-year-old stirs pancake batter for me and the two-year-old gets the syrup from the fridge! Sure, it takes *forever*, but they are learning that helping is important and that a family works *together*.

They are part of work in other ways, too. I include them whenever possible, presenting chores in as positive a light as I can! Then we share a "fun" thing when a specific task is done, like going outside on a short bike ride. I have a box of "art" supplies—lots of ribbons and lace, colored pencils, paper, stick glue, macaroni, silk flowers. "Make me a card from our art box," I'll say.
—*Scott and Sue Steffy, Leola, PA*

Elementary-Age Activities

▼ We encouraged our children's grandparents to give them gifts of books, paper, glue, crayons, and tape. This supplied the children, when they were in early elementary school and younger, with endless hours of fun. Out of all the gifts they've received their "cut stuff" was the most celebrated. We let them put on art shows—displaying their work or giving it to someone special. We let them make a mess. They often moved half their bedroom into the living room to play house, but it was quickly cleaned up afterwards.

▼ It's important to provide children with simple toys that can be used in many ways, such as boxes, buckets, marbles, purses, blankets, shovels, and silverware. It all encourages creative play.
—*Ellen Herr Vogts, Newton, KS*

▼ Buy a frame from the store and put your chidren's artwork in it. If you have several children, you can highlight one child each month, etc. Display it in a visible place and celebrate your child's artistic talents. Your children will spend a great deal of time making new works of art to place in the frame. Be sure to date and attribute each piece. It will be a nice keepsake for you—and might be a lovely gift—a collection of one's own artwork upon the birth of the "artist's" first child.
   —*Nancy Nussbaum, Elkhart, IN*

▼ In one room of our house are boxes of collections which can be used in art activities. Our children enjoy having time to go through the boxes and make things. They are responsible for all birthday cards which go out from our family. Some of the cards they have created have been wonderful!
   —*Jane-Ellen and Gerry Grunau, Winnipeg, MB*

▼ Playdough is messy, but it is helpful in developing fine motor skills. If you have a child in elementary school, who is having difficulty with writing neatly and other fine motor activities, give him/her a lump of modeling clay (available at any craft store) to sculpt things with each day. Let them sculpt while you read to them at night.

▼ You can make a placemat for use with clay and playdough out of magazine pages or construction paper. Cover with clear contact paper, or just place the sticky sides of two pieces of contact paper together for an easy and lovely placemat. Roll up and place it in a bag with the clay.
   —*Nancy Nussbaum, Elkhart, IN*

▼ Since I (Joan) was an elementary schoolteacher, I often brought ideas home from school for educational games—cards with word meanings, spelling, math, etc.
   —*Joan and Arnold Lange, New Oxford, PA*

▼ When I (Joan) was about nine years old, my father encouraged me to begin a diary/journal, which I continue to the present. He also taught and encouraged all us kids to write haiku poetry, which we still do periodically.

▼ I feel too often we try to "program" our kids' creative time. Imagination is a wonderful thing. As a child I spent *hours* playing house, climbing trees, riding bike, wading in water, all in my own little world. Kids need to know how to play by themselves.
   —*Joan Schrock Woodward and Don Woodward,*
   Elizabethton, TN

▼ We try not to just supervise, but to participate with the kids in their projects. If they are painting a picture, then one of us may be able to paint our own picture. Marlisa recently took a watercolor class. The children have done interesting things by being able to use her good brushes and paints. Marlisa's father has a studio where he paints. The children have enjoyed painting in the place where he paints.

▼ Halloween is a good time to let kids have fun with creativity. We ask them what they want to be, then go to the thrift shop and find some fabric or old shirt or whatever, and begin cutting and sewing. They have turned into some very charming bats and rabbits.
            —*Daryl and Marlisa Yoder-Bontrager, Lancaster, PA*

▼ I often looked out my kitchen window to see the washline or swing set transformed into "tents" with the help of blankets. Two or more little people dressed up in costumes from a box which held a variety of interesting clothes emerged from time to time from under the blankets. Sometimes the basement became a store or hospital. If all else failed, they could always be found reading. (Sometimes this mother has gotten frustrated when household chores were and are left undone because someone is deep in a book.) We are grateful, however, that our children enjoy reading so much.
            —*Loretta and Roy Kaufman, Sterling, IL*

▼ When our sons were in elementary school, they and their friends played endless games of baseball and kickball in our backyard. One day when I was grumbling about the bald spots in the grass marking homeplate and the bases, my husband said, "Don't worry about the grass. We're growing boys now. There'll be plenty of time to grow grass later."
            —*Henry and Edna Brunk, Upper Marlboro, MD*

Reading _____

▼ Take lots of time to read to your preschoolers to develop their love for books. Buy good books and use the church or public libraries so a wide range of reading material is always available.
            —*Lois Dagen, Lancaster, PA*

▼ We got each of our children cards for the public library when they were quite young. And we made a point to talk about what *we* have learned through reading.
            —*R. Wayne and Donella Clemens, Souderton, PA*

134

▼ We had no television when the children were small so I read to them a
lot. Now each of them enjoys reading more than watching television.
    —*Grace Brenneman, Elida, OH*

Quiet Time

▼ We find it important that children have one time in the day, even
just a half hour, when they do something quiet by themselves. It
helps them cope with life better.
    —*David and Louisa Mow, Farmington, PA*

▼ When the children were small, but no longer taking naps, we
regularly had an hour of quiet time after lunch. Each child could
look at books or read or do a quiet activity in a room by him- or
herself. This gave everyone a rest. It was an especially useful
practice during the summer when there were few routines.
    —*Stan and Susan Godshall, Mt. Joy, PA*

▼ In the long summer months, each afternoon that it's possible, I have
the children lie down and read or look at books for 30 minutes.
They usually protest loudly but always enjoy the time. I read to the
ones who haven't learned to read yet.
    —*Sue Aeschliman Groff, Kinzer, PA*

▼ I feel it is important to teach our children to like themselves and to
know how to be alone. We have replaced afternoon naps with an
hour of quiet time now that they are older. (We do this during the
summer months.) The children retreat to their rooms or another
quiet place to read, rest, or play quietly, alone. They don't complain
about this and sometimes it lasts longer than an hour.
    —*Jim and Nancy Roynon, Brad, Taryn, Drew, and Colin,
    Archbold, OH*

Activities For Many Ages

▼ I decided early on in my parenting that I wouldn't make myself
indispensable to our children's play. I'd encourage creativity, but I
would *not* entertain them all day, every day. Perhaps I
accomplished this by accepting the mess creative play entails;
messes were cleaned up, but during play the mess was acceptable.
Clutter, rather than order and boredom.

Our babysitters were instructed to allow clutter, rather than watching TV. One favorite sitter regularly brought with her a fresh batch of homemade playdough.

▼ One year I invited all of our neighborhood children to attend an Art Show at our house. Each child was invited to a bring a piece of original artwork—drawing, clay, anything. All art was displayed and easily seen—on the clothesline and on tables. After viewing together, each child was given a homemade award of some sort. No one was left out of the awards ceremony. Then we served simple refreshments.

Why didn't I make this Art Show an annual affair? Perhaps I didn't realize the lasting influence and fun of such events. Perhaps it took too much time and energy at that time in my life!
—*Charlotte H. Croyle, Archbold, OH*

▼ I try to keep art supplies on hand. We try not to be wasteful, but I keep scissors, construction paper, glue, crayons, and colored pencils available. When the children were two to five years old, they spent a lot of time cutting pictures out of old magazines and catalogs to make collages.

▼ We often have a large 500-1500 piece jigsaw puzzle in progress for anyone to work on.

▼ The children learned at an early age to do cross-stitch and embroidery and usually have a project in the works. My boxes of fabric scraps are available to them. They come up with ideas, do the cutting and pinning, and I usually do the sewing on the machine so that their creations stay together.

▼ They've learned to use the typewriter and enjoy pecking out their messages.

▼ We have a garden in the summer and they each have a small section that they are responsible for keeping clean.
—*Louise Longenecker, Oxford, PA*

▼ Battery-operated toys are outlawed in our home (a few have slipped in over the years). Birthday and Christmas gifts always include basic, but hopefully somewhat unique, items such as neon paper, markers or colored pencils, chalk, cutting tools, and how-to books (origami, drawing cartoons/animals, pressing flowers, etc.).

▼ We try to limit our children to one outside involvement of their choice, besides music lessons or choir.

▼ Both of us are firm believers in the importance of children entertaining themselves. Because we live on a farm that we own in common with five other families, there is always something to do with 13 children around. We have lots of sports equipment (tetherball, badminton, volleyball) and encourage the children to initiate games, creek and pond fun and general free play. One of the major reasons for the existence of our farm partnership is to establish a healthy environment for our children and their friends. We encourage our children to bring friends to our home.
　　　　—Gretchen Hostetter Maust and Robert Maust,
　　　　Keezletown, VA

▼ We keep creative supplies accessible and bring home new ones occasionally. Fabrics, good scissors, paints, an easel, construction paper, watercolor paper, newsprint, balsa wood, wood blocks in all shapes and sizes from a cabinetmaker friend, bags of buttons, glitter, beads. We keep track of the small stuff in a plastic chest designed for nuts and bolts and screws. Neighbor friends come up with fresh ideas, too, when they see this collection. I visit thrift shops during the month of October when they bring out all their weird and exotic stuff (before Halloween). From these visits we've developed a very complete and diverse dress-up closet at scant expense. There seems to be no end to the fun kids can have with wigs and interesting old clothes.
　　　　—Laura and Steve Draper, Winfield, IA

▼ The children have a large assortment of dress-up clothes. All manner of hats, capes, robes, and shoes are within easy reach. It's amazing to see the combinations of clothing they come up with and the many uses one article in the collection can have. This activity can absorb *many* hours of play time.
　　　　—Virginia Froese, Springstein, MB

▼ We had old school desks in the attic for coloring and reading on rainy days. There was also a mini-schoolroom set up with desks and chalkboard in the basement.
　　　　—Richard and Betty Pellman, Millersville, PA

▼ A broken window blind made a wonderful "banner" to spread out on the family room floor. The children colored and painted on it to their heart's content. Sometimes it occupied them for a large part of a rainy day.
　　　　—Ken and Eloise Plank, Hagerstown, MD

▼ Our sons played with large furniture packing boxes. At first Dad would go to a nearby furniture store and bring the boxes home. Later the children dragged them home themselves.

There are many uses for boxes: private places to hide and to store personal things in. With a collapsed side, a box becomes a slippery slide. Create kitchen stoves, refrigerators, and cupboards, or beautiful trains.

One Halloween the boys made a haunted house in our basement with boxes. They put two or three boxes in a T-formation. Children crawled in one end and brushed against rubber gloves painted red and filled with water. There were holes in the boxes where our sons could reach in and grab kids, and make weird sounds to scare them. They had several box "stations" of scary activities. One box was a coffin with somebody in it. They charged neighborhood kids one cent admission each: a real moneymaker!

▼ Our one daughter constantly played nurse and hospital. She made nurses' uniforms out of old sheets, and later bought an old white uniform from a local thrift shop, using her own money. She'd make many charts of the body systems and, with her sister and friends, memorized her charts and spent hours bandaging and caring for her dolls. Her favorite childhood gift was an old nurses' patient chartcover and a working stethoscope.

▼ Our other daughter more often initiated school and library play. She and her sister spent many a dreary-outside day with books and papers spread out over our basement, making all of their personal books into a Croyle Library. Many of our books still have the library envelopes and tabs they put inside each book cover.
—*Charlotte H. Croyle, Archbold, OH*

▼ When several of our boys wanted a greenhouse, they put up plastic and planted seeds. Another time they wanted their own garden, and they faithfully weeded and watered it. (They grew big heads of lettuce and good sized pumpkins.) At another stage they built a tree house out of old used lumber. Another time they moved a little shed into the woods, made trails and bridges to it and actually slept in it.

▼ On rainy days they stretched the dining room table out and played ping-pong on it. They also collected old boxes and jars and played store.
—*David M. and Rhonda L. King, Cochranville, PA*

▼ When the children were older, and after school was out, they each were required to houseclean their bedrooms. They'd take everything out, rearrange or add things, and usually have a good time. Each summer they each learned to do one or more new things like doing laundry, making a cake, or mowing the yard. Eventually, the older children had a lawn mowing business for a number of summers, with the help of Dad.

—*Ben and Lorraine Myers, Dillsburg, PA*

▼ 4-H is good—both the children and I learned a lot. They had animal projects, sewing, and cooking.

—*Wilma Schmidt, Walton, KS*

▼ I enjoy crafts, so we usually had many projects going. One year we made puppets for our Sunday school department. Another year I volunteered for Story Hour at the library and our older children helped prepare the material and present it.

—*Laverne and Eldon Dean Nafziger, Hopedale, IL*

▼ Children's magazines make wonderful birthday and Christmas gifts. Children get issues monthly throughout the year, providing them with ongoing reading and activities.

—*Nancy Nussbaum, Elkhart, IN*

▼ We made lots of trips to the library for story hour, films, and checking out armfuls of books. We shelled peas and lima beans together and picked potato bugs on a small-pay scale. Our pool table and basketball were shared with neighborhood children.

—*Ernest and Lois Hess, Lancaster, PA*

▼ Our family walks to playgrounds in parks or schoolyards. We purposely purchased a home near those places so all of us, or the children alone, could do this.

—*Richard Harris and Caprice Becker, Manhattan, KS*

▼ On the farm our children created their own entertainment. Little Anna would line up her dolls on the stairs and "teach them." (She became a teacher.) In her teens Verda volunteered to make supper all by herself every Monday, "no leftovers." (She still loves cooking and entertaining.)

—*Edna Mast, Cochranville, PA*

▼ Make provision for them to help with what you are doing. Children will gladly fill your jars with peaches or tomatoes for a small reward. They will enjoy cleaning strawberries for a few cents per quart. They

also love to hang wash on the line if you provide a line they can reach. They will do a good job of dusting so you will have time to take them miniature golfing or to see some llamas or ostriches in the community.
—*Mattie Miller, Sugarcreek, OH*

▼ When our children were growing up, we had a half-acre truckpatch behind our house. We farmed vegetables and the children peddled them. Martha would pick the beans, tomatoes, etc. I dug the potatoes—one year we raised 60 bushels. Martha would bag them up and the children, six to eight years of age, would put them on a coaster wagon. Mary Ann would pull; James would push, and they would go from door to door in the neighborhood, "selling." When they got older, they used their bicycles (with baskets) to sell.
—*Russell and Martha Krabill, Elkhart, IN*

▼ We invite the boys to help when we're cooking, baking, mowing, sweeping, and cleaning.
—*Kenny and Rachel Pellman, Nathaniel and Jesse, Lancaster, PA*

▼ Our oldest children were in their teens before we had a TV, so they spent a lot of time in the public library. One enjoyed doing science experiments and another liked to make things, and all took music lessons which involved a lot of time in individual practice. Because we lived far from relatives, they spent time writing letters (or drawing pictures).

They've done a wide variety of tasks, depending on their ages. Dusting the leaves of many plants, dusting furniture, the old treadle sewing machine and coils of bedsprings. They sorted cards or nails or washed their toys. Their father and the boys spent many seasons keeping the neighborhood alleys and ditches clean and mowed. When they were bored, I sent them on errands, taking a bit of baking to elderly neighbors or simply visiting them. We made up songs and poems and riddles and read a lot.
—*LaVerna and Lawrence Klippenstein, Winnipeg, MB*

▼ We live on five acres and have made an effort to provide play equipment, such as bikes, trampoline, and swings for the children's use. We have also home-schooled all of the kids for part of their elementary years, partly to give them adequate free time. We have not felt a need to entertain them. They have trees, a field, enough junk (cement block and boards), old sheds, and time to develop

many self-motivated activities. Several are avid bird-watchers and experts. We have provided piano lessons for all our kids. Some have had additional instrument lessons or child's choir. Music is important to our family.
    —*Lois and Jim Kaufmann, New Paris, IN*

▼ Music lessons, building a tree house or clubhouse, and 4-H projects, like raising goats and rabbits, kept our children busy.
    —*Robert and Miriam Martin, East Earl, PA*

▼ We try to focus on the idea of projects. Some of the projects they have worked on are learning piano, learning tennis, learning swimming, becoming an expert on maps, Kansas geography, Kansas history, manners, phone etiquette, facing fears and developing courage, practicing honor, pet training. I am able to arrange my work schedule so I can be available to supervise the children after school and in the summer.
    —*Donna M. Froese and Don E. Schrag, Samuel and Joseph, Wichita, KS*

▼ In summertime we require three hours of work in each child's schedule. It can be away from home (volunteering at a hospital, helping another Mom, library assistant, etc.), but if there is no "outside the home" work, Mom arranges work and a record is kept on the fridge! They complain but it keeps them busy, helps Mom (although it is work to keep four constructively working), and makes them feel accomplished!
    —*Bylers, Williamsport, PA*

▼ When the kids were young, we encouraged them to make up their own games. They had their own variation of baseball using baseball cards. They spent hours playing whiffle ball, soccer, football, and table games with their friends and cousins. At one point our kids were preoccupied with building tree houses and spent long hours constructing them. Leaf- and grass-raking were also game time—jumping into huge mounds of leaves or making "grass houses," outlining rooms with the clippings. All the kids in our neighborhood played hide-and-seek after dark on summer evenings.

▼ During their elementary school days our children began creating their own plays. When they felt ready to present one, they called aunts, uncles, cousins, and friends and invited them to come. They charged one cent each and were delighted with the income and fun of presenting their own production. They even used their toddler

brother in a variety of ways and coached him to say a few lines at
the appropriate time.

▼ For a number of years the two eldest boys tinkered and learned to
repair engines, so old engines were scattered around the house and
garage during that time.

▼ All the boys enjoyed trapping during the winter months and learned
to do their own skinning before selling the pelts. An older man
down the street spent a lot of time telling trapping stories and
showing them how to skin their catches. (He ran a sporting goods
shop and was an expert trapper himself.)

▼ When our daughter became interested in doing macrame, we went
shopping for supplies so she could make plant hangers. She did so
well we encouraged her to sell some to relatives, which was her own
way of earning some money on her own, since her brothers took
control of the paper route.

▼ While in Nigeria our children all learned to make things money
couldn't buy. They learned from the Nigerian kids how to make
things out of wire, string, and grasses. They collected butterflies
and learned how to mount them. One collected foreign stamps and
another collected interesting stones.

▼ Music lessons were disastrous at our house. Practices became
battlegrounds, so they didn't last more than two years.
—*Jim and Dee Nussbaum, Kidron, OH*

▼ We encourage reading, sports, music lessons, trying to follow their
interests, but also encouraging them to take risks. Our 16-year-old
son discovered stunt kites and has spent hours flying them. His
friend also bought one, so now they can have kite fights and chases.
—*Richard and Jewel Showalter, Irwin, OH*

▼ Have children over to play with them; do craft projects together.
When our daughter was in junior high, several friends came to bake
and decorate cookies, which they then took to a neighbor and sang
for her.
—*Bob and Doris Ebersole, Archbold, OH*

▼ When my granddaughters come to visit, we bake cookies together.
We began this tradition before they were three years old. Now two of
them are 13 years old and they still want to do that! We also bake
Zwieback or rolls together. Grandpa sometimes takes them to his

workshop and they create something out of wood to take home. They love that too!
—*J. Herbert and Cleo Friesen, Mt. Lake, MN*

▼ When the grandchildren come to visit, we usually have a fun work project waiting which requires a longer attention span than is needed for watching TV. Some projects we preplan and partially complete, particularly the more difficult and complicated parts.

▼ Example: How would you like to match wits with a gang of squirrels? What about making a three-ring squirrel circus just outside the kitchen window? To start, suspend a long flimsy piece of band iron from the fence with a corn ear wired to the end. Do you suppose a squirrel will be daring enough to try being an acrobat? What do you suppose will happen when he inches his way nearly to the springy end of the band iron and the kitchen door slams?

What about drilling a hole in the end of a corn ear and slipping it on a pole stuck in the ground? Will the squirrels get braver when four or five begin chasing around?

Will they shinny up the poles to the feeding platforms? Is it possible to replenish the sunflower seeds on the feeding platforms with a tin can nailed to the end of a long stick? Should the feeding platforms be tall and wave in the wind? How about locating them within a few feet of a window at eye-level and keeping a loaded camera nearby?

By using scraps of wood and discarded furniture pieces might one be able to assemble an interesting bird feeder which squirrels cannot resist exploring? What about teaching squirrels to run an obstacle course, or learn to do a sequence of activities in order to feed? Who minds working in the kitchen when there is a front row seat at the squirrel circus?

▼ Another project is making an exciting, yet cozy, place for kittens to play. We need large cardboard tubes, wood strips, carpet scraps, a stapler, sheetrock, screws, and a little imagination. Do you think kittens would enjoy carpet-lined tubes with holes? How about carpeted ramps? With all those materials, and a little imagination, a litter of growing kittens will have an exciting place to romp and play.
—*Cornelia and Arlie J. Regier, Overland Park, KS*

▼ We invite our younger grandchildren to plant our garden with us. We talk about the seeds and how they grow. Together we watch the budding of trees and flowers; we look for insects and birds and talk about how God takes care of all things.
—*Erma Kauffman, Cochranville, PA*

▼ We've always tried to allow them to be interested in what we parents are doing. Christina and Colleen paint faces at some of the art fairs I attend.

> —*Harvey and Lavonne Dyck, Christina and Colleen,*
> *Viborg, SD*

▼ Let kids make what you would call a "mess." They need room to be creative. They can also learn to clean up when they are finished.

> —*Brenda Augsburger Yoder, Lancaster, PA*

▼ We have put together a long list of things to do when it seems like there is nothing to do. We work on this list from time to time and add to it. It's kept in the "Things To Do" file.

> —*Chuck and Robyn Nordell, Fullerton, CA*

Hobbies

▼ Our son recently began collecting stones, shells, bugs, etc. Instead of just putting them away, we're beginning to set up a "science corner" in our home. We'll add the pet turtle, the goldfish and their plants.

> —*Kelli Burkholder King and John King, Jacob Hans and*
> *Suzanne, Goshen, IN*

▼ Every child should at one time or another have a pet or a plant to care for.

> —*Nancy Nussbaum, Elkhart, IN*

▼ Pets were a valued part of our family and we taught responsibility in caring for them. We bought our son two pigeons which eventually developed into a flock—and a hobby for him. We discovered that pigeons are excellent models of family life—the parents bond for life and share in the raising and feeding of their young.

Another hobby our son became involved in was raising earthworms. Together we built worm bins out of plywood. We filled them with soil, compost, manure, ground walnut shells, and a touch of lime to hold moisture. We learned that rabbit manure was an excellent food and watermelon rinds were gourmet treats, resulting in big, fat worms! Our son became a supplier to bait stores, packaging and delivering the worms and keeping the stock fresh. It taught him responsibility, reliability, elementary finances, bookkeeping, and how to deal with store managers.

> —*Ken and Eloise Plank, Hagerstown, MD*

▼ Stamp collecting was a hobby we all enjoyed while overseas. It seems we have less time to work on that here in the States.
—*Roy and Hope Brubaker, Mifflintown, PA*

▼ We've found that through encouraging hobbies, our children have discovered their "gifts."
—*David and Louisa Mow, Farmington, PA*

Friendships

▼ The children's grandmother and two bachelor uncles live next door to us. Our children are always welcome there. One uncle takes them fishing several times a year, and every summer they go camping for three days at his camp where they help to gather firewood.
—*Mr. and Mrs. Nelson Schwartzentruber, Lowville, NY*

Sports

▼ We encourage sports involvement. It keeps them too busy and tired to get into trouble.
—*Larry and Evie Hershey, Atglen, PA*

Music, Lessons, Practice

▼ I've started a sing/dance play group with our five-year-old. It's not formal music lessons, but the kids have fun and are learning at the same time. Three other children join us weekly for an hour of singing children's songs, moving to music, and playing rhythm instruments.
—*Anita and Randy Landis-Eigsti, Lakewood, CO*

▼ We asked all our children to take piano lessons for one year. One of them continues with great interest.
—*Ervin and Bonita Stutzman, Mt. Joy, PA*

▼ We asked the children to take music lessons through junior high. After that they got to choose whether or not to continue.
—*Stan and Susan Godshall, Mt. Joy, PA*

▼ We encouraged reading and music lessons. Some responded to music with more grace than others. The least enthused took guitar lessons when he was 26!
—*Laverne and Eldon Dean Nafziger, Hopedale, IL*

▼ When our oldest son was eight, he begged to learn to play the piano. He was talented and a good example to his other brothers who not only learned to play piano but to play the clarinet, cello, and viola. They practiced before breakfast, after school, and in the early evening.
—*Emmet and Elsie Buhle, Media, PA*

▼ Learning an instrument teaches a child self-discipline, in addition to teaching music skills.
—*David and Louisa Mow, Farmington, PA*

Chores

▼ The summer when James and John (twins and our oldest children) were 14 years old and I worked in a hospital full-time, they kept begging for home-baked bread. I told them that I was too busy to bake bread, but they could do so if they liked. One week, on my day off, I baked bread and they watched me and asked questions. The next week, on my day off, they baked bread and I watched them and gave suggestions. They baked bread each week for the rest of that summer. It did not always turn out perfectly, but the whole family felt a sense of pride and pleasure in their achievement. All of our four sons, as adults, are happy and comfortable cooking and baking. The "summer of the bread-bakers" was a creative confidence-builder.
—*Wilma Beachy Gingerich, Harrisonburg, VA*

Volunteering

▼ Two of our children did volunteer work in a retirement home and hospital in their early teenage years before they could be employed. It was good experience for them and helped to occupy their time.
—*Marian Bauman, Harrisonburg, VA*

Jobs

▼ One summer our children, then 15, 13, 11, and nine had a weekly bake sale. Some things they baked ahead and froze, like bread and cookies. Pies required their getting up early and baking them fresh on sale day. Mother bought all the ingredients. The kids researched the cost of ingredients for each item sold, then subtracted the cost before sharing out the profits. They learned bookwork, persistence, cooperation, and how to bake, although they made very little money!
—*David and Martha Clymer, Shirleysburg, PA*

▼ We've encouraged our children taking part-time jobs in restaurants and working for farmers or on carpentry crews as soon as possible. Hard work is a good discipline.
—*Richard and Jewel Showalter, Irwin, OH*

Pets

▼ We tried to provide for our children's pet interests with animals that we could accommodate—gerbils, hamsters, hermit crabs, fish, kittens, and a puppy. In lieu of our daughter's own horse (which we couldn't adequately handle on our one-half acre lot), she attended horse camp for several summers.
—*Ernest and Lois Hess, Lancaster, PA*

▼ Some children do well with pets. Animals bring out a tenderness and love for other creatures, and pets that reproduce have other important lessons of life to teach. We have always had a guinea pig in the family and, at times, gerbils, fish, cat, turtles, or rats. (Parents do have to reckon that much of the pet care is going to fall to them.)
—*David and Louisa Mow, Farmington, PA*

▼ Our daughters were 10 and 12 and wishing for a pet when friends of ours went away for two weeks and asked the girls to take care of their two puppies. They and Dad went to feed, water, and clean them daily. The puppies barked, snapped at them, and made a smelly mess. They were so much work and nuisance that at the end of two weeks the last thing they wanted were dogs. They were happy to settle for a rabbit outside in a cage, which was more our style!
—*Sam and Joyce Hofer, Morton, IL*

▼ When I (Merle) realized that in years to come, our daughters were likely to blame me for their not having a dog as a pet when they were growing up, I presented them with a challenge. "I'm in favor of a dog," I said. "In fact, I'm disappointed that you haven't been able to solve the probable problems so we can get a dog!" What problems? So we made a list of all the possible problems (who would feed the dog, who would clean up after the dog, where the dog would stay when we're away, etc.), and the girls came up with solutions for every problem. So we got Jorg, and we've never been sorry!
　　　　—Phyllis and Merle Good, Kate and Rebecca,
　　　　Lancaster, PA

▼ We had numerous pets which each child helped care for. Caring for the dog who lived outside in her own house created the most friction until we marked the calendar every day with "C" or "E," which ended any question about which child's turn it was.
　　　　—Mary and Nelson Steffy, East Petersburg, PA

▼ We have a pet schnauzer that each child takes a turn feeding and watering for one week at a time.
　　　　—Judy Stoltzfus, Colorado Springs, CO

▼ Our pet menagerie at present includes 10 tadpoles, two mice, one guinea pig, one dog, and one cat. The children have learned about metamorphosis, death, mating, and birth.
　　　　—Mark and Leone Wagner, Lititz, PA

▼ Our family always had pets. Some were better choices than others. When our sons were very young, we fell in love with a Saint Bernard, disguised as a cuddly ball of puppy fluff. Although the puppy grew into a gentle dog, it was too big for toddlers. When the dog tried to play with the boys, it pushed them over. Much later we got a golden retriever who both loves children and is very gentle with them. Cats, too, have been a part of our family. Tiger provided our sons with a lesson on birth when she had kittens in a box in the laundry room.
　　　　—Dick and Nancy Witmer, Manheim, PA

9.

What About Television?

No TV—With Exceptions

▼ We have chosen to live without TV because we feel our time is spent more wisely without that to lure us from reading books, playing games, etc. I'm glad I don't need to supervise TV watching; there is too much violence and trash to sort through. At times we wish we had it for news coverage or special features, but we have gracious friends who allow us to come view the special features whenever we care to.

—*Roy and Hope Brubaker, Mifflintown, PA*

Compensation For No TV

▼ I still enjoy the freedom of living without television. During a recent summer when a six-year-old grandson was vacationing at our home, it was the fifth day when he suddenly left the table in the dining room, went to the doorway of the living room and glanced all around. "You don't have a TV," he said. On visits since that time we stay involved with games, puzzles, and other activities so that TV is not our entertainer.

—*Lois Dagen, Lancaster, PA*

▼ When our oldest child became a teenager and television watching really became a problem, we took the drastic step of getting rid of the TV. We were without it for over five years. It was then that my husband and I learned to love word puzzles. The children were very upset at first but learned to accept it. Now the oldest child is very strict with her children in TV watching and uses videotapes a lot instead, with which she can use more control.

—*Norman and Dorothy Kreider, Harrisonburg, VA*

▼ After our TV broke, we went without for several years. People kept trying to give one to us, and finally someone succeeded. We use no antenna or cable and can only get channel 12 (public television) and occasionally one other channel. Late in the summer and around the Christmas holidays, we like to borrow Steve's parents' VCR for

several weeks. It's fun to have it for awhile, and it's also good to return it to them.
—Laura and Steve Draper, Winfield, IA

▼ We gave our son this alternative to watching TV: if you actively help restore an antique car you will: (1) be able to tell your grandchildren that you learned to drive on a 60-year-old car; (2) we will join the local antique car club and participate in activities; and (3) when you are ready, we will sell the car and give you half the profits. He agreed and soon was involved in setting goals, solving problems, learning mechanical skills, and experiencing hard work—drudgery as well as success with his father.
—Cornelia and Arlie J. Regier, Overland Park, KS

Preschool Strategy

▼ We did not have television when the children were little. When we did get one, we watched programs with them and were very selective.
—Jim and Shirley Hershey, Bloomingdale, NJ

▼ We only watch PBS and even that has to be monitored. Primarily we watch educational children's shows.
—Miki and Tim Hill, Woodstock, MD

▼ We try to limit TV to the educational channel as much as possible. To earn extra TV time, the kids read books and help around the house.
—Phil and Penny Blosser, Beavercreek, OH

▼ We didn't have a TV until about two years ago. The rule is one hour a day. Until recently our kids didn't know anything existed besides PBS. As they get older, I'm sure it will be an issue we'll have to deal with. My husband and I don't watch TV, except when we join the children in watching their hour. We try to watch with them.

▼ An exception to the one hour rule—when I cut their hair they can watch an extra PBS show. They sit still and look forward a little more to haircuts!
—Anita and Randy Landis-Eigsti, Lakewood, CO

▼ Our preschool children watch one-half hour program a day: children's education programs on weekday afternoons and National Geographic on Sundays. We keep our TV upstairs in our bedroom, away from our normal day's activities. Instead of watching TV, we live with a messier house, visits from neighborhood friends, and the assumption that our children will need guidance and encouragement from us throughout the day, and our suggestions for better alternatives.

> —*John and Ruth Miller Roth, Sarah, Leah, Hannah, and Mary, Goshen, IN*

Junior High and Senior High Strategy _____

▼ When the children were young, we limited the amount of time they watched TV and the shows they could watch. As they grew older, their involvement in school events, sports teams, and music lessons took the majority of their time. TV watching came to be generally limited to sports events on weekends.

> —*R. Wayne and Donella Clemens, Souderton, PA*

▼ As our children's outside interests increased, the TV time went down. Cultivating other activities seems antidotal.

> —*Orpah and Elam Kurtz, Jefferson, NC*

▼ Our antidote to TV: make life more interesting than the tube. We chose a school with high scholastic standards where studies were interesting and demanding. With regular homework, there was little time for TV.

> —*Frieda Barkman, Twentynine Palms, CA*

Timing of Watching _____

▼ We did not permit TV watching right after school, because the children needed physical activity. They also had to have their homework done before they could see TV, and then they had to choose shows with discretion.

> —*Bob and Doris Ebersole, Archbold, OH*

▼ When alcohol commercials come on, we change channels. The children now do this on their own. During the school year, they are allowed to watch one hour after school (they're home at 2:45), depending on the homework load and/or plans for the evening.

> —*Jay and Linda Ebersole, Rosalyn, Randy, and Ryan, Lancaster, PA*

▼ We were firm about no TV during meals. When the TV was on, I kept an ear tuned to what was being watched so I could monitor it. Our after-school pattern was for the children to have a snack and talk with me and each other about their day. Then they had playtime or TV, followed by supper, and doing homework.
—*Ellen Peachey, Harpers Ferry, WV*

Placement of TV

▼ We've moved the TV to the basement and we listen to the radio a lot. I also get records from the library to listen to. My parents had the TV in a non-central location while we were growing up, and so it wasn't in a natural gathering place.
—*Marie and Ned Geiser Harnish, Indianapolis, IN*

▼ We have a small black and white TV which we keep unplugged and put away, getting it out only when we have a specific program in mind, such as a news show or special movie. We get most of our news from radio and newspapers, as we find the ads (especially for upcoming TV shows) offensive, even if we choose programs carefully.
—*Rod and Martha Maust, Indianapolis, IN*

▼ The more readily accessible a TV is, the harder it is to limit its use and the more likely it will be chosen over other activities. Our small portable TV is in the bedroom closet unless we decide to watch something. Beside that, having a TV that isn't very high quality and that gets only a few channels cuts down on its invasion of our family life.
—*Herb and Sarah Myers, Mt. Joy, PA*

▼ The TV is in the room off the kitchen where we can see what the kids are watching. We mostly watch sports and news together.
—*Jay and Linda Ebersole, Rosalyn, Randy, and Ryan, Lancaster, PA*

▼ We don't keep the television in the center of the living room with all chairs pointed to it. We have a small TV placed on the floor in the dining room. If we want to watch it, we lie on the floor.
—*Daryl and Marlisa Yoder-Bontrager, Lancaster, PA*

▼ As teachers we stress the need for "TV free" space, so that children have an appropriate study environment. That seems so obvious, yet

many families have the TV on all the time. It's part of the
omnipresent noise in our lives.
—*Joan and Larry Litman, Hoboken, NJ*

Guidelines For Use

▼ We have tried to keep TV a very low-key part of our life. The
preschoolers watch one hour of children's programming on
weekdays. The school-age children watch two hours of TV on
Saturday mornings. We rarely watch as a family. We find that
there are so many other activities we'd rather be doing.
—*Virginia Froese, Springstein, MB*

▼ We live with television by limiting it to one hour, three days a week.
I guess most people would say we live without it.
—*Donna M. Froese and Don E. Schrag, Samuel and
Joseph, Wichita, KS*

▼ Limit it to approved (by parents) shows. Keep it a treat.
—*Harold and Rachel Ruhl, Ronks, PA*

▼ Our children (ages eight, six, and two) are allowed one hour of TV
each day. They may choose when to watch approved shows, either
in the morning after they are ready for school or in the afternoon or
evening after their homework and chores are done around the
house. This eliminates constant begging to watch TV and permits
parental control. The children have some choice and usually turn it
off themselves when their hour is finished. So far they are content to
watch the same shows at the same time. TV hours may not
accumulate if they are not used each day. Interestingly, there are
many more days they do not watch their "quota," than days they do.
—*Roger and Pamela Rutt, Lancaster, PA*

▼ We had the policy that any toys advertised on TV were off limits for
purchase.
—*Mr. and Mrs. Nelson Schwartzentruber, Lowville, NY*

▼ TV is limited during the school year and may not be turned on until
music practice, chores, and homework are complete.
—*Tom and Lois Marshall, Spruce, MI*

▼   Our school-age kids are limited to one hour per school day; one-and-a-half hours on Saturdays. Our lives are too busy and TV offers so little good, that it is seldom on in the evenings. The exceptions are one family show and sports. We also watch part of the morning news shows. Our teenager sometimes watches a program late on Saturday night, although we discourage that becoming a weekly habit.
—*Lois and Jim Kaufmann, New Paris, IN*

▼   When the children were preteens, we gave each one a jar of marbles. Each marble was worth one-half hour of TV time. When the marbles were all gone, they had to find other things to do the rest of the week. At the beginning of the week, we discussed which programs they would watch in their allotted time.
—*Robert and Miriam Martin, East Earl, PA*

▼   Our first television entered our home when the oldest was in grade five. We intentionally bought a not-too-good used black and white, with the understanding that when it wore out we would go a full year without a set before buying another. We went through three like that before finally purchasing a better one. Incidently, there was no antenna so we could get only one channel. We looked at the TV guide carefully each week and decided which programs were suitable. We didn't necessarily watch all of those, but we did not watch the unapproved ones.
—*Norman and Ruth Smith, Ailsa Craig, ON*

▼   When the children were young, they earned television privileges based on time spent practicing music lessons. For every 10 minutes of practice, they could watch 30 minutes of television. From junior high through high school graduation we did not have TV, for which both children have expressed deep appreciation.
—*Mary and Nelson Steffy, East Petersburg, PA*

▼   Only 30 minutes per day is our standard. No violent shows may be watched. We do expand the 30-minute time limit for special shows or on rainy non-school days, sometimes.
—*Ellen Herr Vogts, Newton, KS*

▼   We monitored television closely, allowing the children to watch only programs we approved, and then we limited the time for those. Homework came first. The TV was turned off at mealtime.
—*Marvin and Violet Jantzi, Medina, NY*

▼ We purposely didn't own a TV until our oldest child turned 12. Before the purchase, each of us, children and parents, wrote guidelines which we incorporated into one list, giving each one a sense of ownership in our understanding.
—Ernest and Lois Hess, Lancaster, PA

▼ Fortunately our older children were teens before we had a TV. Initially we set a limit to the number of hours and the programs watched. Our youngest is addicted to it, and we have deprived him of it for up to a month as a disciplinary measure. Because we seldom watch TV, that's been no problem for the rest of us. He surprised us when he volunteered to do without TV for a year if we, like another family, would give him a sum of money. He, and we, kept the bargain.

▼ Until six months ago our only TV was an old black and white set given our children by their grandparents. It needed pliers to change channels and brought us only a couple of stations, and these, often poorly. So it was no big temptation. It was in the basement and, with frequent overnight guests, often out-of-bounds.
—LaVerna and Lawrence Klippenstein, Winnipeg, MB

▼ Our approach to television and movies has been very restrictive. Our daughters are teenagers now, and are making more decisions on their own. We've evolved from no movies and only an hour or so of television a week during their early years to an occasional movie, a video for a special reason, and four and a half hours (apart from news) of TV a week. We still seem restrictive, but we know they'll soon be on their own and are giving them more freedom to decide by themselves.
—Phyllis and Merle Good, Kate and Rebecca,
Lancaster, PA

▼ We often watch TV as a family on Friday nights. There are several programs that the children routinely watch during the week. Our basic understanding is no more than one program per day during the school year. During the summer months, the children must "buy" one hour of TV time by first reading one hour. Quite often, after an hour of reading, they opt for playing outside with friends and TV is forgotten.
—Gretchen Hostetter Maust and Robert Maust,
Keezletown, VA

▼ During the summer, the boys can select one program per day. If they turn the TV on without permission, they lose all TV privileges for one week. Exceptions are made with special permission.
—Nancy and Clair Sauder, Lancaster, PA

▼ At our house, the family gets up each morning to no television, no radio, no stereo. The quiet encourages reading and softer, less stressful conversation. Hey, we have our share of loud talking, but it's always much more tense if there's artificial sound invading our quiet. We prefer a less frantic, more peaceful atmosphere.
—Phyllis and Merle Good, Kate and Rebecca, Lancaster, PA

▼ We keep it off during meals. If it doesn't interfere with school work, church activities, sports, socializing, and family chores, then we don't shut it off. We see TV much like reading—as a way to relax and wind down, so if I see our children sprawled too long in front of it, we look for other fun activities or invite friends over to play.
—Marvin and Rachel Miller, Indianapolis, IN

▼ We had a TV part of the time our children were growing up. When they were smaller, and until the time they went to and graduated from high school, we watched certain programs together, then discussed what we saw and read "between the lines."
—Enos and Erma Shirk, Thornton, PA

▼ A VCR allows us to tape educational shows or classics to enjoy together at a special time.
—Katherine Hogue, Springstein, MB

▼ When the kids were young, violent cartoons and movies were taboo. We prohibited adult TV until they were in high school, when we talked about what they could watch. Most TV that they watched was some kind of ball game, endorsed by their dad and tolerated by their mother! Now that the children are gone, we watch very little TV—the news, weather, an occasional movie, one religious program. When the kids come home (none are married as yet), they often get a movie to watch, or if special games are on they'll watch that. (The TV is on more when the kids are home because they say they don't know what else to do.)
—Jim and Dee Nussbaum, Kidron, OH

▼ TV is available, but no one sits down to watch without permission. We started with half an hour per person per day, but we never needed to monitor that closely. TV news is watched without questions asked; we used to watch one show together as a family activity and special movies if it suited. That was it!
—Millard and Pris Garrett, Kimmi and Krissie, Lancaster, PA

Expose, But Carefully _____

▼ I had cousins who came to my house and didn't want to do anything but watch TV, so I would like our children to be somewhat exposed to it.
—*Carl and Audrey Landis, Ronks, PA*

▼ We believe that sheltering our son completely from television is doing him an injustice. After all, television is a wonderful source of information and current events. Instead, we carefully choose the shows we feel he can watch, and then watch with him, trying to explain any questions he has or discrepancies he observes between our chosen lifestyle and what he sees on TV (as best a five-year-old can understand!). We seldom approve cartoons. Even though some are cute and make-believe, many more tend to be violent and/or unchristian.

▼ Commercials are another important reason to watch television with your children. Many glamorize the immoral or try to "educate" our youth in ways our family deems inappropriate.
—*Jeffrey and Jessica Summers, Jared, Narvon, PA*

▼ We have a VCR which helps us to be more selective in what Michael watches. When we watch TV, we generally watch it together. We got cable for one month and decided that for us it made TV too tempting, so we discontinued it.
—*Bob and Jeanne Horst, Harrisonburg, VA*

▼ For many years we chose to not have a TV. When we became involved in homeschooling, we decided to use TV as an educational tool and have found it to be mostly an enriching experience in our home. Our children now attend a local public school, and we find that with school, and our many work and play activities, we don't have much time to sit in front of the TV. We have worked at helping our children develop interests and hobbies at a young age, offered some involvement in sports and classes of one sort or another, but most of all have just given them time and materials to be at home and keep busy and happy. Watching TV for us is kind of special and very educational, but we do need to pick and choose. So far, so good!
—*Samuel C. and Margaret Wenger Johnson, Bart and Hannah, Keezletown, VA*

▼ Television is a wonderful tool. It becomes a demon when we view it as building material. Our television is not on during the day. We select programs to watch ahead of time. The anticipation is just like looking forward to seeing a movie.
> —*Mark and Leone Wagner, Lititz, PA*

Good Times with TV

▼ Watching TV together can be a good time for physical closeness. My daughter was feeling sorry one day for a friend of hers, because "her mom and dad didn't have time to hold her and watch TV together."
> —*Harvey and Lavonne Dyck, Christina and Colleen, Viborg, SD*

▼ I enjoy sitting down with the family to see a movie that we have rented. That is one time when we are all together.
> —*The Sfrisi family, Lodi, NJ*

10.

What About Chores?

Age-Appropriate Jobs

▼ I've enlisted our two children, at 19 months old, to help with setting the table, wiping their high chairs, and wiping the dirt on the floor. They enjoy being given special new tasks at this early age. They help me plant seeds in the garden and dig up weeds with their own tools. They love to have their own watering cans to water the veggies.

—Marie and Ned Geiser Harnish, Indianapolis, IN

▼ Jacob loves to vacuum and almost daily requests the vacuum cleaner. He doesn't know it's a chore, but our floors have been cleaner with his new interest. Jesse takes care of the trash.

—Anita and Randy Landis-Eigsti, Lakewood, CO

▼ From three years of age on, each child is responsible for making her/his bed, getting dressed, picking up her/his room, tidying the bathroom, and being present for morning prayers. In addition, each day I set the timer for 20 minutes and we all work hard. What doesn't get done waits till the next day. Having a finite time for chores makes it more acceptable to the children.

—Miki and Tim Hill, Woodstock, MD

▼ All four of our sons had chores to do starting at age three. The youngest emptied the wastebaskets in each room. The older sons polished all the shoes on Saturday, mowed the lawn, set the table, took out the trash and put their toys away in the house or garage. They were praised but not paid for doing a good job.

—Emmet and Elsie Buhle, Media, PA

▼ As our daughters get older more is expected of them. At four they began helping to make their beds. Mom folds sheet/blankets back and the child is expected to finish making the bed. By six, they are expected to make their beds by themselves before leaving for school. Both four- and six-year-olds put clean clothes in their drawers, rinse the dishes, and put them in the drainer as Mom washes the

dishes (gives us time to talk) one night a week, set the table one night each week, and keep their rooms picked up.
—*Wayne and Mary Nitzsche, Wooster, OH*

Lists Of Jobs

▼ Making a written list has always worked better for us than verbal requests. Crossing things off the list gives the worker a sense of progress, and it reduces the amount of parental reminding. It also takes some forethought and seems less like making work for work's sake.
—*Stan and Susan Godshall, Mt. Joy, PA*

▼ I keep small wipe-off magnetic memo boards on our refrigerator doors on which I write each morning that day's list of chores. The children may do the chores any time during the day but they must be finished before bedtime, before watching TV, and before playing with friends.
—*Roger and Pamela Rutt, Lancaster, PA*

▼ I believe in lists. A list of the chores children are expected to complete on a certain day or within a certain time frame gives them freedom in choosing how and when to do those jobs. Lists give them the pleasure of crossing finished things off their lists.

▼ Another way to get the house cleaned is to put each individual job that is part of that on a separate slip of paper. (For example, dust the living room, clean the sink and tub in the bathroom, sweep the bedroom, wash the kitchen floor.) Each person pulls a slip and does what it says. Slips are pulled till all the jobs are done and the house is cleaned.
—*Herb and Sarah Myers, Mt. Joy, PA*

▼ Since I work part-time, I found it goes best if I write the children's summertime chores on a list. It takes the argument out of job assignments; the children can usually choose what part of the day to do their jobs, as long as they get them done.
—*Marian Bauman, Harrisonburg, VA*

▼ When Mom left for work, a list of chores was posted on the refrigerator for each child. As they did the chores, they checked them off the list. All the chores on the list were expected to be checked off by the time Mom came home from work. If they were not, there were no TV privileges until the chores were done.
—*Robert and Miriam Martin, East Earl, PA*

▼ I write their jobs on cards (3x5 cards cut in half) and put them in the pockets of their job charts. (I tape six pockets, each made of a 3x5 card cut in half lengthwise, to a 12x5 piece of cardboard.) When the jobs are completed, the cards are moved to the "Jobs Finished" pocket.

▼ Toys must be put away before evening snack time. Anyone who doesn't help forfeits her or his snack.

▼ I think it is important for me as a parent to do my work well and cheerfully, and to let the children know when I feel good about what I've done. They can also see that I sometimes get frustrated or don't like a particular job, but that I still need to do it.
—*Louise Longenecker, Oxford, PA*

▼ Each child got a list of Saturday chores. They liked it best if I made a treasure hunt, with each note telling them what chore to do next. There was a treasure at the end, too—usually a small treat.
—*Ellen Peachey, Harpers Ferry, WV*

▼ A regular schedule for chores seems to help—rooms must be cleaned by noon Saturday, setting the table at certain times, washing dishes at certain times. There is a small reward in the week's allowance for doing these things without complaining and on time.
—*Laura and Steve Draper, Winfield, IA*

▼ Daily chores are posted on the wall. Usually we spend about a month focusing on a particular task, both teaching and encouraging the children. After a month they usually have incorporated the chore into their daily routine.

▼ Weekly chores are done as a family activity. We all seem to work better with someone else working beside us on household chores. We set a goal of getting the house cleaned or the yard attended to. I make a list of tasks that are included in cleaning the house and divide the list up.

  The children wanted to change jobs every week for a while. However, we found that sticking with the same task every week gave them a sense of competency and we all seemed to be happier.
—*Donna M. Froese and Don E. Schrag, Samuel and Joseph, Wichita, KS*

▼ We discuss, revise, and assign chores each January. Most of these are "Saturday" chores.

▼ The children wash dishes on weekends and during all school
vacations.
—*Mr. and Mrs. Nelson Schwartzentruber, Lowville, NY*

List Jobs, Rotate Jobs

▼ In the summertime when our children were growing up, we had a
daily chore assignment sheet on the bulletin board. We rotated
their assignments, and as they finished they checked them off.
When they were done, they could read, play, or do whatever they
chose. As parents we thought of work as a challenge instead of
drudgery. This seemed to be caught instead of taught.
—*Harold and Florence Bucher, Scottdale, PA*

▼ We kept dishwashing and drying on a rotating schedule among our
five children so no one always worked with the same sibling. Ours
was a blended family and some of their best "talk times" were in
pairs at the kitchen sink.
—*Shirley Kirkwood, Mt. Solon, VA*

▼ None of us likes the rigidity of lists with assignments. We wanted to
instill in the children a sense of freewill responsibility to do one's
share of household work. We did discuss who would do what on a
regular basis.
   When our two daughters were in grade school and junior high, they
devised their own system to keep each other's dishwashing turns in
check, to avoid disputes over fairness. Every time one of them had
completed this chore, they would mark the little graph chart with
their name, which they had fastened on the refrigerator door. The
unexpected fun of this was that instead of just making a check
mark, they drew tiny pictures, signs, and symbols, whatever was
foremost on their mind on that day. Between the two this became
nearly a competition in cleverness. For me, these were tiny
revelations and thermometers of their moods.
—*Reinhild K. Janzen, Newton, KS*

▼ Each child should have one responsibility that is his/hers only to
do. Each should be encouraged to choose this responsibility from a
short list of options which you have put together. Children need
responsibility, but they also need choice!
—*Nancy Nussbaum, Elkhart, IN*

▼ We make a chart that lists all the chores, including pet care. Each week each child has a different assignment. A chart lasts five weeks, since we have five children. During the school year, the chart starts over again every five weeks. In the summer, additional chores are added. If a child does his or her chore well, on time, and without complaining, he or she can choose the supper menu for one night the following week.
—*Anne Long, Mt. Joy, PA*

▼ We keep changing our methods with chores and motivation. It just seems to go that way. However, in our experience, rotating the job responsibilities too quickly does not help; it is better to keep a child on "dishes" or "garbage" for a month, at least. As they get older we turn full responsibility for particular jobs over to them.
—*David and Louisa Mow, Farmington, PA*

▼ I make a list with weekly cleaning chores, and the boys and I sign our initials next to the jobs we will do. Sometimes having the privilege to select first is a reward for something else, or we take turns signing, or I sign for my jobs first and the boys divide the rest of them.

I usually try to rotate the tasks so I do each chore every two or three weeks. That way I can accept less than perfect performance on the jobs. I accept an honest effort at a job as "good enough," then I clean the corners the next time around, if necessary. Of course, the boys have improved their vacuuming, dusting, and bathroom cleaning skills over the years.
—*Nancy and Clair Sauder, Lancaster, PA*

▼ Saturday chores are primarily housecleaning. We have a chart in the desk with three basic jobs to do, and we rotate the kids each week. One job is to do the vacuuming; one job is to vacuum the steps with the handheld vacuum, shake the carpets, and dust the furniture. One job is to clean the basement bathroom sink and mop the linoleum floors. Each knows exactly what to do and does it.

We own and manage apartments and our children have helped us clean there. That has helped us teach them how to work, even in unpleasant circumstances.
—*Judy Stoltzfus, Colorado Springs, CO*

Take Turns

▼ Our children take turns feeding pets and doing dishes. At one point I used a chart with stars and stickers.
—*Roy and Hope Brubaker, Mifflintown, PA*

Assigning Chores

▼ During the school year we assigned chores. During the summer I posted a schedule of chores on the refrigerator door with the dates by when they needed to be finished. The children would initial the chores they chose to do each week. Each also helped to plan the menus for the summer meals.
—*R. Wayne and Donella Clemens, Souderton, PA*

▼ We held family meetings where we discussed things to be done. First, the children volunteered for specific tasks; any leftover "undesirable" jobs were then divided up.
—*Ken and Eloise Plank, Hagerstown, MD*

▼ Get children involved as soon as they're old enough in family conferences where decisions about chores and feelings can be expressed. Elect a president and secretary to keep meetings going and record the discussion. Realize Mom and Dad have veto power!
—*Bylers, Williamsport, PA*

The "Random" Approach

▼ We try not to make so many rules that the children feel they have to rebel. Work, such as taking out the trash and helping with dishes, is done randomly, depending on who doesn't have music lessons or sports activities that evening. We close the bedroom doors—I try not to discuss their bedrooms! I don't hassle much about music lessons; their music teachers will discipline them if they aren't doing well.
—*Marvin and Rachel Miller, Indianapolis, IN*

▼ When too much clutter had accumulated, I would put the children's odds and ends on a pile in the middle of the living room. They had 15 minutes to "claim" their items and put them away. Anything left became "my property." All three children quickly put their things away!
—*H. Kenneth and Audrey J. Brubaker, York, PA*

Fun While Working_____

▼ I worked with the children as they did their Saturday morning
chores. It was a good way to teach them, and to remind myself that
they couldn't do things like an adult who had years of experience.
Sometimes I wrote each job on a slip of paper, then had each child
draw a slip for his/her assignments. I would include "extra"
assignments, like standing on a chair or singing a certain song, just
to keep the mood bright. We often had a special snack when chores
were finished.
   —*Bob and Doris Ebersole, Archbold, OH*

▼ Charts with checks that earned something special kept chores
going, along with many reminders. One child, now a mother, had a
very difficult time doing anything alone. She needed a companion
and still does!
   —*Harold and Rachel Ruhl, Ronks, PA*

Working With Children_____

▼ I have often helped the children get started or complete chores
which were tedious, and have even worked alongside them the
whole time if that seemed necessary. Sometimes they could help
themselves to a jelly bean after completing each part of a lengthy
job. I tried to be sure the children overheard me telling their dad, a
grandparent, or a friend about the work they had done. That often
helped them be less reluctant to help next time.
   —*LaVerna and Lawrence Klippenstein, Winnipeg, MB*

Teaching Responsibility_____

▼ I liked to teach our children how to do a variety of jobs, even if at
times it seemed to be more work than it was worth. My goal was
that they would enjoy working and take pride in doing a job well. I
was aware that might take 20 years!
   —*Sam and Joyce Hofer, Morton, IL*

▼ We have tried to teach our children that they benefit from group/family living; therefore they need to contribute to group functioning. The younger ones have daily morning chores, the older ones daily evening chores. Boys and girls are included in all kinds of work.

—*Lois and Jim Kaufmann, New Paris, IN*

▼ We tried to avoid having the children expect to be paid for home duties.

—*Omar and Delphia Kurtz, Morgantown, PA*

▼ We started a campground, primarily so our children would learn a variety of tasks and the value of work. They learned to take pride in their accomplishments.

—*Grace Kaiser, Phoenix, AZ*

▼ We sit down when school begins and work out a chore schedule that we all feel is manageable and helpful to the total family. When school is out, we sit down and plan a new schedule. It has always worked. We do some swapping of chores, but we are each responsible to see that our own particular jobs are covered in some way.

—*Millard and Pris Garrett, Kimmi and Krissie, Lancaster, PA*

▼ If our children complain about doing a job, I usually remind them of what their dad and I do everyday—make meals, go to work, wash the dishes, etc. I explain that we don't do those tasks just for ourselves, but for our family, because "that's what families do." My intention is to help them understand that even though we didn't make the mess, we need to clean it up. We try to build their sense of family community. (I try not to say any of this negatively or to make them feel guilty, but simply as a reminder.)

—*Merv and June Landis, Talmage, PA*

Rewards

▼ When the children were young, we made a chart with chores listed. They would get small rewards for jobs accomplished. As they outgrew the rewards, they still carried on the good work habits which they had learned—making beds daily, cleaning their room, helping in the kitchen, and others.

—*Verna Clemmer, Leola, PA*

▼ We have individual helper charts—at day's end completed tasks are checked off. At week's end a special sticker is put into a special folder. There may be small fanfare—announcing the child's name as they approach to receive their folder along with handshake and hug. Feeling a sense of accomplishment; that is their reward.
—*Katherine Hogue, Springstein, MB*

▼ At one point we had a chart of chores that needed to be done. There were points assigned to each chore and a reward for accumulated points. Each child was expected to do a certain number of jobs each day but was able to choose to do more if she/he wanted to earn their reward more quickly.
—*Norman and Ruth Smith, Ailsa Craig, ON*

▼ Our rewards for completing chart chores?—a family activity like fishing, swimming, playing a game, biking, or playing ball.
—*Mark and Leone Wagner, Lititz, PA*

▼ When our children were between eight and 12 years old, I made a contest out of cleaning their rooms. They loved it and went way beyond the call of duty. I always got something small for the winner's room as the prize, and candy or gum for the others.
—*Linda and Ron Gunden, Elkhart, IN*

▼ My mother hid pennies in places I tended to skip while dusting. She would tell me how many she hid, so if I didn't find them all I'd go over my work until I found them. I got to keep them! We got no other special rewards except commendation and sometimes ice cream or candy.
—*Ruth Burkholder, Bronx, NY*

▼ When our children were elementary school-aged, we operated a large chicken farm. Our weekend schedule included long Sunday afternoons in the egg room. To keep it from becoming a drudgery, I hid little snacks before packing time. The kids had to wait until the digital clock said "2:00 p.m.," then they frantically hunted until they each found their surprise. The treats were things I didn't normally buy—soda, individual packs of crackers, candy bars, etc. It became a much anticipated time and was as much fun for Mom and Dad as for the kids!
—*Larry and Evie Hershey, Atglen, PA*

▼ Summertime on the farm meant chores and work in the forenoon and swimming in the afternoon in the nearby stream.
> —*Stephen and Sadie Yoder, Quarryville, PA*

▼ We assign one chore per year of life: our 10-year-old has 10; our seven-year-old has seven. Our 10-year-old daughter loves to spend the night with friends. If she has to be reminded more than once to do something, she gets a penalty point. If she has 10 points in a month, she loses one of the two overnights she is allowed each month.
> —*The Baker-Smiths, Stanfield, OR*

▼ At one time we designated Friday evening as family night. We all cleaned together for one to two hours, then followed that with an outing or pizza.
> —*Glennis and Mark Yantzi, Kitchener, ON*

▼ We expect routine jobs, such as burning trash, feeding the dog, washing the car, and mowing, to be done without pay.
One-of-a-kind jobs, such as chopping wood, cleaning cupboards, and painting, we reward monetarily.
> —*Mark and Maxine Hershberger, Aaron and Stefan,*
> *Dalton, OH*

▼ We have the increased allowance/increased responsibility rule. Kate (age eight) gets $3.00 week. She has her own envelopes for church and gives 50 cents a week. She is expected to make her bed, clean up her room, help with meals, garden, etc. and run errands. Anthony (age 15) gets $13.00 week. He is expected to buy his own clothes (we help on big items such as coats and shoes), mow the grass, wash and fold laundry, keep his room decent, babysit occasionally, run errands, sometimes help with cooking/kitchen cleanup. We pay him good wages ($5.00 an hour) for special jobs such as washing windows, housecleaning cupboards, etc.
> —*Shirley and Stuart Showalter, Goshen, IN*

11.

What About Money?

Learning Math _____

▼ We allow our preschool children to hand money to the clerk, to teach them that what we buy is exchanged for money. We've begun giving our oldest child a quarter twice a week, contingent upon a clean room, but she doesn't seem to be very motivated to earn it regularly. She accompanies me to garage sales sometimes and spends some of her allowance, which stretches it a lot further.
—*Mary Alice and Gerald Ressler, Lititz, PA*

▼ Sarah is just learning about money. We made a deal with one clerk at the grocery store whom we trust very much. When Sarah buys something, she always checks to see if she's been given the right amount of change. Sometimes the clerk deliberately gives her incorrect change to see if Sarah will catch it. (She is always careful to give her what she is due when she's finished with the transaction!)
—*Phil and Penny Blosser, Beavercreek, OH*

Earnings and Allowances _____

▼ When each of our children reached age four, we began to give them a weekly allowance, not based on work, but as deserving members of the family. We expected them, though, as family members, to help with family tasks. They divided their allowances three ways—10% was for giving, 20% went into their jars labeled "saving," and 70% could be used for spending. At each birthday we increased their allowances by an established amount.

▼ Each child used his/her spending money as he/she wished, which was sometimes difficult for us to stand back and watch. At age four and five they usually blew all of it on gum, but by age eight they had learned to save it, with the help of comments from their older siblings, such as, "You're chewing your money away." The amount of work the child did each week varied, but I found this system more workable than paying them for each job.
—*Sue Aeschliman Groff, Kinzer, PA*

▼ We struggle with whether kids should get an allowance just for being part of the family, or for chores they do.
        —*Mike and Kim Pellman, Matt and Brooke, Bird-in-Hand, PA*

▼ We have given a very modest allowance to the children as soon as they could count money. They always give a tithe or more, spend some for their own interests, and put the rest in savings accounts in their own names at the bank. For some reason, all of them are savers. They have bank savings accounts all out of proportion to their very small allowances. On rare occasions, we pay them for tasks around the house, but have never linked the allowance with chores.
        —*Ervin and Bonita Stutzman, Mt. Joy, PA*

▼ We're not any more creative than each child having a savings account. They are both rather unimpressed with it.
        —*Gretchen Hostetter Maust and Robert Maust,*
        Keezletown, VA

▼ We put our children on an allowance by a formula. The allowance = age x 2¢ x 7 days. (This was given weekly and increased each year.) Their allowance was divided into three parts: 50% spending, 40% savings, 10% tithing. We had them enter those amounts into a small notebook we set up for them.
        —*Millard and Pris Garrett, Kimmi and Krissie, Lancaster, PA*

▼ We grew sweet corn to sell every summer when the children were school-aged. It gave them the opportunity to learn to handle money. We encouraged them to tithe their corn money; each decided where to give his/her own tithe. We also required them to put a percentage in the bank, and they could spend the rest.
        —*Larry and Evie Hershey, Atglen, PA*

▼ I learned about money by growing vegetables (4-H garden) and selling them to my parents and neighbors.
        —*Lorna Chr. Stoltzfus, New Holland, PA*

▼ When our children were too young to be without a babysitter but too old to have a babysitter, we tried this approach for short absences: the three children would be their own babysitters, and we would pay them (one-third each) what we would have paid a babysitter. If they were not cooperative, they would not be paid. Several times when we came home, one child would say, "You may pay the other two, but I didn't cooperate." This taught honesty, independence, and

cooperation, while still giving them an opportunity to earn money. Eventually they all three had many babysitting opportunities from neighbors and friends.
—*H. Kenneth and Audrey J. Brubaker, York, PA*

▼ The only time our children earn money at home is when they are child-sitting themselves. Our oldest, at 12, is able to look after the other two children. We wanted to give each of them an incentive to take responsibility for themselves. So we divide the wage which we would normally pay a babysitter into four equal parts. Because the 12-year-old is technically in charge, she receives two parts of the fee. Each of the younger siblings receives one part of the fee. Before we leave the house, each child must write down and sign what they are responsible for in order to earn their child-care money; for example, tidying up after their snack, being in bed at a certain time, etc.
—*Jane-Ellen and Gerry Grunau, Winnipeg, MB*

▼ Our kids began babysitting at a young age and at that point began paying for their own entertainment. We also gave them a small allowance that increased to $20 per month when they got to junior high. At about junior high age they were able to pay for most expenses related to clothes and entertainment.

They know we expect them to have jobs, and they prefer making their own money. I think job responsibility has given them much satisfaction and has taught them responsibility with money.
—*Linda and Ron Gunden, Elkhart, IN*

▼ Our children learned early that we didn't have a lot of money compared to others. To help them learn how to save, the kids each had a paper route and earned enough to buy their own bikes and some things they wanted that were special. (One was a stamp collector for a while.) It was difficult to teach them to tithe, but each of them are giving persons in many ways, not only financially. They learned that we tithe and that God has continuously blessed us, even through the tough times, so they learned from our example. We never made it mandatory to tithe but encouraged them to.

▼ Each of the children had to help earn the major part of their college tuition, since we couldn't afford to foot the entire bill. Those were lean years, but it has been good for them to be able to pay their own way through school. The boys found Goodwill clothes quite acceptable, and all have learned to live with less money than many of their peers have, and be content.
—*Jim and Dee Nussbaum, Kidron, OH*

▼   Our children received an allowance from when they were quite
young on through high school. They were taught to budget money.
Some went in their savings accounts. In sixth, seventh, and eighth
grades our children shared a paper route. They had to collect
payments monthly from their customers. We taught them tithing,
but let the choice about how much to give up to them. They had to
save at least half of the remaining income.
—Dick and Cathy Boshart, Lebanon, PA

▼   When our children reached age 10, we began giving them a monthly
allowance which corresponded with their age—$10/month, etc.
Then they also became responsible to purchase their own clothes
(with our advice, but they paid for the purchase). They all got
part-time jobs at around age 14. At that point their allowances
stopped, but they continued to be responsible for clothes and other
things they wanted. They tithed their wages from the beginning; it
was assumed. They also opened savings accounts as they began to
earn.
—Richard and Jewel Showalter, Irwin OH

▼   I am acquainted with one family who had the following system:
before the children received their allowances, they needed to show
how they had used the previous week's money. It didn't necessarily
matter what they had done with it, just that they were keeping
track. The children needed to review their records to see where
their money was going! No records—*no* allowance!

▼   The father and the young son took out a loan in the son's name
(with the father as cosigner) when the boy needed to buy a lawn
mower to start his mowing business. He learned all about interest
and repayment schedules—and he repaid the loan in full on his own!
—Nancy Nussbaum, Elkhart, Indiana

▼   Our children grew up on a farm with orchards, so they had seasonal
opportunity to earn money by picking fruit, packing, etc. As they
grew older, some solicited their school friends to take a job in the
orchard. That child was responsible for overseeing those she or he
invited to work. One son built a cider press from a kit and hired
neighbor children to help him run it. He was responsible to pay
them, and the profits from selling cider were his. That money went
into his bank account for future spending. In addition to buying a
bike, he later invested in a more efficient press to earn more profits.
—Marvin and Violet Jantzi, Medina, NY

▼ We gave our children early opportunities to earn their own money, like collecting and selling to recycling centers. All of them had working papers and market jobs by age 14.
—Luke and Miriam Stoltzfus, Philadelphia, PA

▼ We like to teach our daughters the importance of being self-sufficient, of learning skills which are marketable so they have the choice of earning their own living. But we've also tried to emphasize that money should serve us, rather than the other way around. So we've supported our daughters in volunteer work as well. In fact, three summers of volunteer work—gardening for a museum, working at a library and hospital—is not bad preparation for learning responsibility for future earning jobs.
—Phyllis and Merle Good, Kate and Rebecca,
Lancaster, PA

▼ Our goal was to have our children become financially independent by age 18; however, because of college, that was not possible. When they turned 16, they were given a certain sum whenever a parent received a paycheck. From this amount, they put a percentage in a can or envelope for saving; in another they put money for offering. The remainder they were to use for buying clothes and for entertainment, including gas for the car. Exceptions were winter coats and other major expenses, which we parents helped with.
—Robert and Miriam Martin, East Earl, PA

▼ When our children reached high school, we negotiated their allowance amounts monthly to cover all projected needs for gasoline (they had their own car to drive), tournaments, and food while they were away. It seemed like a lot of money at one time, but it saved us in the long run, and they had their month planned financially and even time-wise.
—Irvin and Leona Peters, Winkler, MB

▼ We didn't give our children an allowance nor a reward for individual tasks, but at the end of the summer we paid each of them a lump sum for their summer's work. They put this in a savings account for college. We paid for any needs they had and gave them money for fairs and other entertainment. They knew whatever they didn't spend they could keep. In fact, they made a game of it to see how much they had left. We never insisted that they tithe, but set an example by tithing ourselves.
—Harold and Florence Bucher, Scottdale, PA

▼ Money was scarce when our first two girls were growing up. When we said, no, we couldn't afford something, that was the truth and they did not question it. When our two younger daughters asked for things and we said, no, it was always a hassle. They knew we *could* afford what they wanted, but were choosing not to buy it. Our two older girls have learned to manage money well and satisfactorily for themselves and are generous in their giving to others. Our two younger daughters, by having plenty and being given many things, have a harder time understanding the true use of money and how to use it appropriately.
    —*Sam and Joyce Hofer, Morton, IL*

▼ Our children do not receive an allowance, but are able to earn some money in the summer by helping to shell peas, pick blueberries, etc. From the time they were small, they have liked to count the money they have, separating out the pennies, nickels, dimes, and quarters. We talk about what they might like to buy and whether the purchase would be worthwhile or lasting. If they'd like to spend or give away some of their funds, they may do so after we've talked about it. Perhaps because we do not have television and do not often go shopping, their wants are few.
    —*Louise Longenecker, Oxford, PA*

▼ One year, when our budget was very tight and a vacation seemed unlikely, we explained the situation to the boys, along with a plan we had to make at least one vacation day happen. The children really wanted to visit a nearby amusement park, an outing that would cost our family about $40.00 at the time. We decided we would set aside the money we earned from our backyard strawberry patch and use it to pay for a day at the park.

At the end of the season we had just enough to cover admission to the park, with no money left over for snacks or souvenirs. We packed a lunch and set out for a wonderful day of rides and fun. Although the boys were quite young, they clearly understood that just being at the park was the treat, and they didn't even ask for snacks. An ice cream cone at the end of the day seemed really special that time. They clearly saw the relationship between the work involved in picking the strawberries and selling them to passersby, and having enough money to go to the amusement park.
    —*Nancy and Clair Sauder, Lancaster, PA*

▼ One regret—I wish I had taken our teenage children along (one at a time) when I went grocery shopping. They might have learned from my penny-pinching, although most of them are careful shoppers.
—*Iona S. Weaver, Lansdale, PA*

▼ We wanted our children to learn the difference between a need and a want. One method we used was to write down on paper something that they wanted. If they still were certain they wanted it after a month, it was probably a good choice, and they usually bought it if they could afford it.
—*Mary Hochstedler and Ruth Andrews, Kokomo, IN*

▼ One of our sons had a struggle that whenever he had change, he wanted to spend it. We found him a cash register bank into which he could deposit nickels, dimes, and quarters. But the drawer would not open until a total of $10 was deposited. Whenever he got to $10, he never knew what he wanted to spend it on. So we put it in the bank for him!
—*David M. and Rhonda L. King, Cochranville, PA*

▼ *Consumer Reports'* magazine for kids (now called *Lillions*) is a good resource for ideas about the value of a dollar, what average babysitting charges are, product evaluation, etc.
—*Don Kraybill and Elizabeth Loux, Matthew, Micah, and Ashley, Harleysville, PA*

Clothing Allowance_____

▼ When one of our daughters was in junior high and wanted clothes just like her friends with the right labels, we offered to pay her for her work during the summer. With that money she was to buy her own clothes for the fall, as long as she got everything she needed for the school year. She weighed her choices carefully, agonized over them. In the end she opted for more clothes, rather than a few more expensive ones.

Another daughter chose a few designer clothes, rather than more inexpensive ones when her turn came. Both lived throughout the year with the decisions they made. Both learned something about choices in financial decisions.

Sharing what God gave us was an open topic in our house that was more caught than taught.
—*Norman and Ruth Smith, Ailsa Craig, ON*

▼ As our daughter entered junior high and her desire for "proper clothes" became a major issue—with Mom being the "bad guy" who had to say "no" a lot—we switched to giving her an allowance based on a percentage of our income. If our income was reduced or increased, she realized the effect. Together we decided what her money should be spent for. The clothing then became her issue and not a source of friction between mother and daughter. She learned to sew to help reduce her expenses.

—Ken and Helen Nafziger, Jeremy, Kirsten, and Zachary, Harrisonburg, VA

▼ When each of our daughters (we have four) turns 13, we open a checking account for her in her name and give her $50 a month to be used for clothing and school lunches. Each is free to supplement that with babysitting as she can.

—Leonard and Karen Nolt, Boise, ID

▼ When our children were quite young, they received a small allowance, 90% of which they could spend as they wanted and 10% of which was for church. When our children reached junior high age, we increased the amount so they could purchase their clothing and have some for savings. The amount was adequate so that when they gave 10% to church and put 10% in savings, the rest was more than enough for clothing. They made their own decisons about what to buy and when to buy. We did not have them begging for clothes just because they wanted something new or wanted to keep up with other children who had something new. They appreciated the freedom and the feeling of responsibility.

—Stanley and Arlene Wiens, Newton, KS

▼ When our girls were in middle school and desperately wanted brand-name clothing, we gave them the cash value of good clothing at reasonable prices. They needed to use their own money to supplement it in order to get the brand they wanted.

—Ken and Eloise Plank, Hagerstown, MD

▼ When the children became teenagers, I found it worked well for us to pay for half of an article of clothing and let them pay for half. That way the cost and expense of clothing was a concern of theirs, too, rather than our supplying some of their clothing and having them supplement that.

—Marian Bauman, Harrisonburg, VA

▼ Our teenagers receive a clothing allowance each month. This encourages them to make responsible choices and reduces begging. They also can choose to spend that money for other things, but we have tried to provide other money for basic needs like food and school expenses.
—*Lois and Jim Kaufmann, New Paris, IN*

Budgeting

▼ At the time we began giving allowance money, we also gave a small ledger book with instructions on how to keep records, tithe, and save. We required the children to put half of their income into savings through the age of 16.
—*Ernest and Lois Hess, Lancaster, PA*

▼ We let them handle money and have bank accounts early. When their earnings or allowances were gone, we gave no advances. They could borrow from each other, and this taught them the value of repayment and about other people welshing on loans.
—*Grace Kaiser, Phoenix, AZ*

▼ When our own children were small, we wanted to give them experience in handling money. We helped them set up categories and amounts for savings, tithing, and spending. Envelopes or a discarded purse held the deposits. It was their own decision whether to spend their spending money each week or save it for a larger item. Each year we increased their allowances. Each child needed to record all expenditures and be able to show how he/she spent the money. Each has made wise and unwise decisions and seems to have gained valuable experience in the value of money.
—*Mrs. Robert Sauder, York, PA*

▼ Out of our children's allowances they set aside a tithe for church and savings. They're allowed to spend the remainder on what they want—we may make suggestions but do let them make "foolish" purchases. As a general rule we do not advance money, so they learn to spend only what they have.
—*Phil and Sandy Chabot, Becky and PV, Cromwell, CT*

▼ Our children were allowed to keep the money they earned, but we helped them set up a record book so they could set aside a given percentage for contributing to church or mission related projects. The rest they could divide between saving and spending. We felt this encouraged awareness of world needs, thinking ahead to a college fund, and careful spending.

—*Richard and Betty Pellman, Millersville, PA*

▼ Our approach to allowances has been simple—our daughters were given three containers marked "Savings," "Spending," and "Giving." Our only requirement was that part of their allowance went into each container at least once a year. We didn't want to force them with percentages; we hoped they would work to sort that out themselves over the years, and in so doing make decisions which will shape their attitudes as adults. They know our convictions, but we hope they develop their own.

—*Phyllis and Merle Good, Kate and Rebecca,*
Lancaster, PA

▼ We buy things on sale and secondhand. We are trying to show the children how to save money and encourage them not to pay money for labels. (They don't always take our advice.) We show them how we manage our money as they get old enough to be trusted with confidential information. They feel honored. We use a computer program for our family finances. We bought Anthony an accountant's ledger, like my dad bought me when I was a teenager, and have shown him how to create a budget plan. Now that he has a summer job we will have a special discussion on how we negotiate spending, giving, and saving.

—*Shirley and Stuart Showalter, Goshen, IN*

▼ When our son was in middle school, he became more aware of fashions and what other kids did and wore. At that time he began to want brand-name clothes. Since he had shown responsible behavior in handling money, we decided to increase his allowance, giving him enough to cover clothes and other expenses. We told him what he was to pay (clothing, spending money, haircuts, bus fare, and school supplies) and helped him set up a budget. At various times we have increased the amount, but we have been able to avoid arguments about clothes and events, because he decides what is important without having to ask us for money for those things. We have been pleased to see him make good decisions about spending and saving money. (We also use birthdays and Christmas to supplement clothing items.)

—*Karen Martin, Evanston, IL*

▼ We have encouraged our children to tithe from their allowances, but that doesn't usually happen. To encourage them to save for college, we match any money they put in their savings accounts.
—Lois and Jim Kaufmann, New Paris, IN

▼ Wayne has taught spending, saving, and investing to the children. I remember several extended conversations with the children while we were traveling, about money, stocks, the stock market, and reading the *Wall Street Journal.* The children have each had a small allowance to teach them money management and tithing. They received larger amounts for special tasks. Now, as young adults, they are planning and developing budgets.
—R. Wayne and Donella Clemens, Souderton, PA

▼ We are now urging our adult children to begin retirement accounts and have their wills written.

▼ We give each new grandchild a gift of money to begin a savings account.
—Orpah and Elam Kurtz, Jefferson, NC

Vacations and Entertainment _____

▼ When we were on vacation, we gave the kids a supply of money to cover their gift and junk-food spending, so they would not beg for money at every turn. The amount was negotiated at the start of each day when they were small, and at the beginning of the trip as they got older.
—Irvin and Leona Peters, Winkler, MB

▼ We parents bought our children their first two bikes. For their third one, they had to first earn a third of the cost, and then we supplemented the rest. They were responsible for the total cost of their next bike.
—Dietrich and Mary Rempel, Hesston, KS

Tithing

▼ When I was young I had two banks—a piggy bank for me and a church bank for God. My weekly allowance was 10 cents, which was given to me in pennies. One penny went into the church bank and nine in the piggy bank. (I'm still a tither.) I plan to give David a church bank for his baptismal birthday.
> —*Beth Schlegel and David Stoverschlegel, North Wales, PA*

▼ We model giving by letting our children see the checks we give in the offering. We give above budget and above tithe to special funds and talk to our children about why we do it. We expect them to tithe (10%) both their allowances and paychecks.
> —*Shirley and Stuart Showalter, Goshen, IN*

▼ Our kids' allowance amounts increase with age. We want their giving to be joyful, so we let savings and tithing up to them. Surprisingly, all three tithe more than 10% of their allowance.
> —*Tom and Lois Marshall, Spruce, MI*

▼ We gave the children allowances quite early. Each week they were given money, one-third each for church, spending, and saving. The spending money they used as they wanted. As they earned money, we taught them that the first tenth was the Lord's, but gave them the choice of giving it.
> —*LaVerne and Eldon Dean Nafziger, Hopedale, IL*

▼ When we set up budgets with our children, we always listed items that needed to be paid from each paycheck. We always had the tithe listed at the top; it was the first to come out. Our daughter tells us they do the same thing now in her family.
> —*Rachel Tamm, Allentown, PA*

▼ We were encouraged from little on up to tithe 10% of whatever money we made. It never really seemed like a chore because we learned so young, and we saw the example of my parents doing it.
> —*Mark A. and Marilyn Martin, Manheim, PA*

▼ "Stewardship Education" is *not* going very well. This year we forgot or neglected to put money into our Lenten offering box all during Lent. So on the Saturday night before Easter, we took 40 quarters (40 days of Lent) and put them in, one at a time, each taking turns saying either something we were thankful for or something we

hoped the money would buy. It all was quite meaningful by the time we were done.
—*The Baker-Smiths, Stanfield, OR*

▼ Our children split their allowances this way—50% goes to the bank, 25% to spending, 25% to offering, which doesn't have to go to church. They may give this money where they see a need: for example, to an aunt having financial trouble or a friend who needs medicine.
—*Mary Hochstedler and Ruth Andrews, Kokomo, IN*

▼ We have always stressed helping others, and both our daughters are active in that way. One Christmas the girls pooled their money to take a disadvantaged friend of theirs shopping to buy gifts for her family and herself. Another time they gave me some of their own money to put with ours to buy a gift certificate at a local grocery store. We sent it, secretly, to a friend whose husband had been out of work, with no unemployment compensation.
—*Clive and Margaret LeMasurier, Plainville, CT*

▼ Over a bowl of ice cream every Sunday evening, we put money in our work bank. We collect this money for a year toward a special agreed-upon project. We try to choose a project our children, presently age seven and 10, can relate to. The children count the quarters at our Fall Celebration, and we either send a check to our chosen project or purchase items locally and mail *them* to our project.

Our projects have included a check for famine relief in Ethiopia (where I, Margaret, grew up as a missionary kid); a check for humanitarian aid to Iraq; a check to help provide artificial limbs for war victims in Nicaragua; tennis balls and crayons which we packaged and mailed to Nicaragua; a Push Me-Pull Me toy for refugee children. These are only a few of our ideas—your own imaginations can come up with hundreds of others.
—*Samuel C. and Margaret Wenger Johnson, Bart and Hannah, Keezletown, VA*

▼ Ellis and I purposed to quietly model our giving. Ellis preached from the pulpit the value and necessity of regular giving, never actually mentioning what we give. And we didn't discuss figures or percentages of our private giving with our children.

On Sundays, I sat with our children while Ellis was preaching. My habit was to give our offering envelope to one or the other of the

children, and let that child place it in the offering plate. The child
was free to see the amount written on the envelope and make
his/her own deduction about our giving.

We tried to make it a point *not* to tell our children, "We can't afford
that."   We'd say instead, "We don't choose to spend our money for
that," then explain why.
　　　　　—Charlotte H. Croyle, Archbold, OH

▼　One of the most important—but difficult—values to teach our
children has been an understanding of why we try to cultivate a
standard of living below our income. "But can't we afford it?" needs
to be answered with a reply that takes the emphasis off money and
places it on what counts most in life. In truth, we can't "afford" to
cultivate a feeling of arrogance or superiority if we wish to respect all
persons. We've tried to teach our daughters and ourselves that we
should live in such a way that anyone feels comfortable in our
home, and anyone we meet feels that we're interested in their lives.
Money can so easily be used to isolate people from other people,
rather than to bring them together. We want the way we live to
include others.
　　　　　—Phyllis and Merle Good, Kate and Rebecca,
　　　　　Lancaster, PA

12.

Cultivating Faith

Modeling _____

▼ When the children were small, we sometimes had family worship,
   although we seemed to have difficulty maintaining it on a regular
   basis. We tried to live out our faith in Christ on a daily basis.
   —*Leroy and Sarah Miller, Chesapeake, VA*

▼ We allow lots of questions about faith; we discuss issues such as
   abortion, killing, and ethics. We still struggle with not making
   things too black and white for them. We see lots of "gray" in life,
   and we don't use religion as a fix.
      Passing on the faith is a challenge. I try not to preach, but share
   my own faith struggles. Very few of our children's peers are
   Christians, so we assure them that our prayers follow them daily,
   and that the "Hound of Heaven" follows them everywhere and will
   never leave them. It's our understanding of giving them back,
   spiritually, to God.
   —*Marvin and Rachel Miller, Indianapolis, IN*

▼ Our family worship and prayer time consists of sharing together and
   taking turns at mealtime leading in prayer. Cultivating our
   children's faith happens in our walk and talk and listening to them
   daily, particularly at mealtime, or right after school, or right before
   bedtime.
   —*Millard and Pris Garrett, Kimmi and Krissie, Lancaster, PA*

▼ I believe in the "teachable" moment and I believe every single day is
   peppered with these moments. It is my belief and hope that if we
   can connect faith to life's ordinary moments, we will integrate
   natural faith-building with life so that it becomes the children's
   livable faith.
   —*Mark and Leone Wagner, Lititz, PA*

▼ We like to say "God bless you" to each other. It seems more
   meaningful than a simple good-bye.
   —*Phyllis and Merle Good, Kate and Rebecca,*
   Lancaster, PA

▼ More important than the form of family prayer is to strive for "worshipful" behavior. Most basic is respect and consideration for one another, with the example being set by the parents, of course. We do have a song or a grace or just a moment of silence before mealtime, and try to have one-on-one prayer before bed with each child. This varies a lot according to the individual child with no set form. Even though we are not a very "singing" family, we do sing together simple songs, in unison, sometimes with a recorder or guitar. Singing is good for families! We look for opportunities to support faith in a child without forcing religion.
— David and Louisa Mow, Farmington, PA

▼ We have tried to de-emphasize the academic rat race by suggesting that, while we should all do our best in life, grades aren't everything. Accordingly, our girls know that we as parents always go to conferences with their schoolteachers with one question at the top of the list—"Do you have suggestions on how our child can grow in her respect for others, even if her report card doesn't measure that?"
—Phyllis and Merle Good, Kate and Rebecca,
Lancaster, PA

▼ Cultivating our children's faith came largely from trying to teach Christian values and being the best examples we could in our limited ways. We encouraged them when they were discouraged and prayed audibly with them and for them at mealtime and bedtime (the latter when they were younger). Now, as young adults, they are open to dialogue we couldn't have earlier discussed.

▼ While living in Nigeria we spent time with missionary friends who allowed us to join them in family devotions. They had a notebook full of photos of people they wanted to pray for. Their children enjoyed choosing whom to pray for.
—Jim and Dee Nussbaum, Kidron, OH

▼ I guess the greatest way we cultivate our childrens' faith is by attempting to live exemplary lives. We do often have dialogue at the table with frequent guests, adding variety to our table discussions.
—Roy and Hope Brubaker, Mifflintown, PA

▼ We attempted various forms of family worship in a formal sense. None of these lasted a long time, but were valuable for a certain period. More effective seemed to be the spontaneous times of worship in a beautiful outdoor spot, a time of rejoicing as we came through a difficult time as a family, or with an individual in the family.

▼ We found praying with a child experiencing the hurts of relationships in school, fears about exams, times of being treated unjustly, or times of parental failure, were more crucial in the development of the children's faith than formal family worship, although that, too, is important.

▼ Example, perhaps, is the best way to cultivate your child's faith; therefore, some of your own struggles, fears, and victories need to be shared.
    — *Norman and Ruth Smith, Ailsa Craig, ON*

▼ We cultivate our children's faith by noting when our behavior does not seem to fit with what we are trying to teach our children. My hardest task is consistently celebrating life, staying open to whatever experiences are there for me to savor.
    —*Donna M. Froese and Don E. Schrag, Samuel and Joseph, Wichita, KS*

▼ It has always been the custom at our evening dinner table to have all members of the family share the experiences of their day. During the elementary and high school years our children asked many questions: "Why do we do it this way?" "What do we believe about this and why?" These questions often extended into hour-long discussions arising out of our daily happenings.

Family experiences varied from dealing with one son who was beaten because he would not salute the flag, watching an infant being baptized in the United Methodist church we were attending, seeing this same congregation take the lead in working positively and actively to cool tensions during the first years of school busing for integration, dealing with the disappointment of having a church person, who should have been a model, work with duplicity.

We made a major effort not to hand the children simple, pat answers which they would later feel they had to reject because they didn't make sense. We tried to be honest about our own questions and faith struggles. Our children came to see that a faith that has not been questioned is a faith not worth holding. In turn, they developed the courage to ask questions within a church community that itself was struggling to be faithful to the God in whom we place our trust.
    —*Wilma Beachy Gingerich, Harrisonburg, VA*

▼ We've tried to expose our children to powerful, spiritual role models. At suppertime we have a Bible story and prayer, with prayer again at bedtime until they reach age 11 or 12.

▼ We have many informal discussions about faith and try to answer questions as they arise.

▼ We've given each child a notebook of recorded stories, hopes, dreams, and advice from us parents. We each wrote Anthony a long letter about faith, sex, drugs, and alcohol on his 15th birthday.

▼ We have bought the children good Bibles. Kate wants to read her *Adventure Bible* on her own. We buy Anthony devotional books for teenage boys.
> —*Shirley and Stuart Showalter, Goshen, IN*

▼ We've found a four-year-old asks a variety of faith oriented questions, some very difficult to answer. We work hard to discuss those questions and not pass them off.
> —*Kelli Burkholder and John King, Jacob and Suzanne, Goshen, IN*

▼ Our children beg to hear stories about when we were young. This is a good chance, not only to tell funny stories, but stories of our faith development.
> — *Roger and Pamela Rutt, Lancaster, PA*

▼ We try to talk to our three-year-old about what he learned in Sunday school.
> —*Richard Harris and Caprice Becker, Manhattan, KS*

Praying

▼ For grace, we hold hands and try (about half the time) to pray about things an 18-month-old will understand—incorporating new words, his friends, etc. He enjoys grace. He usually gives a round of applause after the "amen," and we often join him.
> —*Ann Becker and Byron Weber, Kitchener, ON*

▼ We started holding hands around the table to pray when we had toddlers' hands that needed help to be calmed! The tradition has continued through all of us reciting "God is Great" together, to now, when Larry leads in prayer or asks one of our children (ages 16-23) to pray.
> —*Larry and Evie Hershey, Atglen, PA*

▼ We often go around the circle before our meal, giving one-sentence prayers to a lead-in such as, "I am grateful for. . ."
—*Janice Miller and David Polley, Ann Arbor, MI*

▼ We have family prayers before meals. We enjoy giving our four-year-old son the chance to lead the prayer.
—*Jim and Carol Spicher, Mountville, PA*

▼ Once our children were out of grade school, they took their turn in leading prayer.
—*Monroe L. Beachy, Sugarcreek, OH*

▼ Our son and daughter-in-law encourage their daughters, ages 10 and 11, to make up their own lists of persons and matters for which they want to pray.
—*H. Howard and Miriam Witmer, Manheim, PA*

▼ We try to use prayer requests that were mentioned in our church "sharing time."
—*Mr. and Mrs. Nelson Schwartzentruber, Lowville, NY*

▼ If there is a crisis in our family, we meet to pray together.
—*Lorna Sirtoli, Cortland, NY*

▼ We are expecting our third child. As a family we are praying daily for the baby. Everyone lays their hand "on the baby," and one, two, three, or all of us pray. This has helped our children express their fears about the baby and to share in the nurturing of the unborn child. It was the kids' idea to add a kiss after the prayer.
—*Ellen Herr Vogts, Newton, KS*

▼ Being present during a nightly prayer time for each child is very important for us. A parent always gently rubs the child's back during prayer and our ending song, "When Nighttime Comes." We always try to include a prayer for someone from our church or local community, and always pray that a Muslim family member will learn to love Jesus. We try to keep prayer time a mix of special concerns and routine requests and thanks.
— *Gretchen Hostetter Maust and Robert Maust, Keezletown, VA*

▼ Children learn to pray by hearing others pray. We also try to teach them the importance of church attendance *and involvement*—there's a difference! We also hope they observe the way we live and react in day-to-day situations.

> —*Jay and Linda Ebersole, Rosalyn, Randy, and Ryan, Lancaster, PA*

▼ After our memorized nighttime prayer, *everyone* is encouraged to add his/her own concern, praise item, or request. Those memorized prayers may be a comfort, even at 20 years of age, in the midst of a dark hour, as they have been for me.

> —*Katherine Hogue, Springstein, MB*

Devotions _____

▼ We wake our children each morning by playing Christian music and hymns. After eating breakfast together we have devotions, using a children's devotional periodical that addresses everyday situations our children may have to deal with.

> —*Galen and Jeanette Miller, Joas, Joel, Shonda, and Shanelle, Clymer, NY*

▼ I always find it challenging to organize a family worship time that is meaningful to the children with their varying ages and abilities. One summer when the children were nine, seven, and four, we had a worship time after breakfast. They each brought their Bible or Bible story book. We also used a prayer book and song book. Each morning the children took turns choosing a Bible story (reading it if they were able), song, and prayer. They really enjoyed helping to decide what we did.

> —*Sue Aeschliman Groff, Kinzer, PA*

▼ I grew up in a family that had devotions every morning. We were made to listen, bow for prayer, plus help along with the Scripture reading. When I became a parent, I wanted to have family devotions, but didn't want it to be as structured and demanding as my experience as a child. With our children at breakfast, I read a devotional book or a Bible story as they were eating. We also always prayed for them before they left for school.

> —*Sam and Joyce Hofer, Morton, IL*

▼ Mornings before breakfast we take 10 minutes to read from a devotional magazine for children. Then we take turns drawing a Bible verse out of a little box and read it, and that same person leads in prayer. Evenings when we're all together (our kids are teens now and not at home every evening anymore), I read aloud from a Christian novel and follow that by reading a chapter from the Bible that we discuss and ask questions about as we go. We close with prayer requests and prayer.

▼ When the kids were little, we sang around the piano. Sometimes we'd tape it and send it to Grandma.
    —*Judy Stoltzfus, Colorado Springs, CO*

▼ We like to have both devotional reading and prayer at breakfast. Now, though, with high-school-aged girls, we aren't always able to do that. On those days, we try to remember to read at supper. We find it better not to be legalistic about when we read, although we do like to start the day with it as much as possible.
    —*Janet E. Dixon, Berne, IN*

▼ We read a Bible passage at the breakfast table, and sometimes discuss it, or the children recite Bible verses they are learning. We often discuss matters of faith at mealtime. We often talk about the Sunday sermon at Sunday lunch or about our Sunday school class discussions. The children are also often very interested in my sermon preparation and try to influence the process. We often pray for our children's special needs and always tuck them in at night with prayers.

▼ Bonita plays worship songs on the piano almost daily. The children often join in or gather around to listen.
    —*Ervin and Bonita Stutzman, Mt. Joy, PA*

▼ We use the *Rejoice* devotional magazine at breakfast and a different devotional book at bedtime. We often sing before meals, especially when married children or guests join us, and in the evening.
    —*LaVerna and Lawrence Klippenstein, Winnipeg, MB*

▼ We had our worship in the evening after our meal. This kept the family together at the table.
    —*John and Marilyn Burkhart, Mt. Joy, PA*

▼ When I was growing up, we had family devotions following the evening meal. Dad and Mother introduced "Name That Tune" long before it was a popular television game show. Dad would begin singing in the middle of a song, and the first person to identify the title could lead in prayer or read the Bible story.
    —*Melvin Thomas, Lancaster, PA*

▼ We take turns praying at the dinner table. We also sometimes sing our prayers. We have read Bible stories and stories of people of faith, from C. S. Lewis series to biographies to Cornelia Lehn and C. J. Dyck books.
> — *Lois and Jim Kaufmann, New Paris, IN*

▼ For years we've had family devotions at suppertime when we could. Often sports events took one or more away, but we tried to retain it as much as possible. Often we sat at the table talking afterwards, especially when the kids were older.
> —*Jim and Dee Nussbaum, Kidron, OH*

▼ We have mealtime prayer and devotions and also talk about God and pray at "ordinary times." We do some singing together.
> —*Beth Schlegel and David Stoverschlegel, North Wales, PA*

▼ During the summer, our best intentions and attempts fall apart as the madness of the peaches, blueberries, tomatoes, and grapes is upon us. (We are fruit and vegetable farmers!) But our usual practices are, at the beginning of each month, to all help to choose songs, one for each day of the week, which we sing for prayer at our evening meal as we join hands around our table. Following this we have a moment of quiet, which is open for anyone to offer audible prayer. During our meal, one parent reads a short selection from a devotional book, which we follow with conversation on the reading, or on the day's activities, or on just about anything.

We have found this to be good family time as we gather for a moment of togetherness in our usually busy day.
> —*Samuel C. and Margaret Wenger Johnson, Bart and Hannah, Keezletown, VA*

▼ We have had a practice of having short Scripture or devotional reading at the beginning of our evening meals.
> —*Jim and Janalee Croegaert and family, Evanston, IL*

▼ After the evening meal and before doing dishes, our family gathered in the living room for Bible or devotional reading, Bible Quiz Cards, singing, taking turns playing instruments on different evenings, and prayer. As the children grew older, they took turns planning and leading worship. We made tapes of some of the children's singing and playing.
> —*Marvin and Violet Jantzi, Medina, NY*

▼ We sing together before a meal. We use *Rejoice*, a devotional magazine, at breakfast and another devotional at bedtime. As a family we have read through many books. They have been a springboard for helpful discussions.

▼ We have subscribed to Christian magazines at the children's levels.

▼ We have provided books of prayers and encouraged the use of prayer hymns when our teens were not comfortable praying spontaneous prayers during family worship. We discuss Sunday school lessons and occasionally the sermon. We have a variety of good music and message tapes which we play during mealtime or chore time, now that our most lively conversationalists have left home.
— *LaVerna and Lawrence Klippenstein, Winnipeg, MB*

▼ We did small dramas from the Bible, then everyone had to guess the story.
— *Orpah and Elam S. Kurtz, Jefferson, NC*

▼ Find books such as *The Many Faces of Jesus,* and look at all the ways Jesus has been depicted through art over the years and in various cultures. It may inspire some artists in your household to try paintings or sculptures of their own!
—*Nancy Nussbaum, Elkhart, IN*

▼ We sing prayers before meals. We sing lots of Sunday school type songs together. We read Bible stories at bedtime. Sometimes we pray at bedtime.
—*Rod and Martha Maust, Indianapolis, IN*

▼ In my home we had family worship, singing one hymn for a month to learn it, and then learning memory verses. In our home we have had Bible reading and prayer regularly. The Bible memory and singing happened at other times, often while driving in the car. With four children, and often extra ones, the singing and reviewing verses reduced the bickering and teasing.
—*Laverne and Eldon Dean Nafziger, Hopedale, IL*

▼ We have taught our daughters numerous prayer songs which we sing before we eat. They take turns choosing a song.

▼ In the evening, each child chooses a Christmas card out of our designated basket and we pray for those families/individuals.

▼ We read a Bible or faith story at breakfast.

▼ We discuss their Sunday school lessons on the way home from church.

▼ In addition, we try to use ordinary happenings as opportunities for sharing our faith.
—*Wayne and Mary Nitzsche, Wooster, OH*

▼ Part of our daily family worship was singing two songs each evening from the hymnal until we sang through the book.
—*Iona S. Weaver, Lansdale, PA*

▼ When our four sons were ages six to 13, the older two were absorbed in world history and geography in school. We decided to tap into this interest by using selected segments of the *Macmillan Bible Atlas* in our family devotions. We read an *Atlas* entry each evening, followed by Bible passages which provided the context for that particular entry. We then discussed the historical, social setting in which the story took place. Together we would imaginatively seek to reconstruct the event. The 13- and nine-year-olds were interested and excited by this activity. But the enthusiasm of the older ones did not always bring the six-year-old along. So we alternated with several months of stories on a level which held his interest. But in the process, the imaginative reconstruction of the faith story took root.
—*Wilma Beachy Gingerich, Harrisonburg, VA*

▼ Make a family banner as a family worship experience.

▼ Memorizing Scripture should be a family affair. Put a Scripture verse on the bathroom mirror each week, and see how many people can recite it at the end of the week!
—*Nancy Nussbaum, Elkhart, IN*

▼ Our children enjoy setting up a church service at home. They put all the bears on the living room chairs and some small benches. Each one is given money. At the proper time the "ushers" collect it in two small baskets. (The children enjoy having this money to add to a project such as Bibles for Romania.) A footstool becomes the pulpit, which holds an open Bible and an object related to the story for the day. (A favorite is a metal ship that makes Paul's journeys come to life.) The service is full of their own ideas, and they spend a lot of time setting it up just right. I am invited to join them for it.

For the closing, we usually all sit quietly, with eyes closed, while we listen to a record playing the Lord's Prayer.
—*Mattie Miller, Sugarcreek, OH*

▼ When our kids were old enough, we took turns planning and leading worship, encouraging lots of variety. Sometimes we'd sing hymns with Mom or Daughter playing the piano. Sometimes we'd sing Scripture songs with Dad playing the autoharp. Sometimes we'd all get involved in acting out a Bible story. One Sunday morning we acted out two Bible stories to see if the congregation could guess the stories.
—*Mim and Roger Eberly, Milford, IN*

▼ We needed to keep adjusting our times for family worship. If morning breakfast didn't work, we changed it to suppertime when the whole family was together. Sometimes it was a bedtime experience. We usually read a portion of Scripture. Sometimes we memorized Scripture together; we especially used Old Testament portions, such as Isaiah 55, Psalm 103, Psalm 23, etc.

▼ Since our children are grown and gone, my husband and I always read Scripture together at breakfast and pray together. Saturday evenings we offer special prayer for the ministers where our children go to church.
—*Stephen and Sadie Yoder, Quarryville, PA*

▼ We had a family worship time while the children were growing up. They did not always appreciate this "special" time. One precious memory of our singing together was when Dirck (our retarded son) learned to play the piano well enough that he enjoyed playing for family worship.
—*Luke and Miriam Stoltzfus, Philadelphia, PA*

▼ We read a story and pray together before bed. In a year, we usually read one Bible story book cover to cover and several other noble stories—*Charlotte's Web*, C.S. Lewis *Narnia* tales, *Little House on the Prairie*, etc. We often sing a mealtime prayer—our four-year-old campaigns mightily for "Johnny Appleseed"—who can resist? For some reason when we sing we usually also hold hands.
—*Laura and Steve Draper, Winfield, IA*

▼ Each of our kids have their own time of day or night when they have their private devotions, using a devotional book or devotional Bible. When each turns 12 years old, I give them a notebook with

193

Scriptures to pray. It helps to teach them what and how to pray, and guides them in praising God.
—*Judy Stoltzfus, Colorado Springs, CO*

▼ At the time our children sometimes complained, but when we had a normal Sunday at home, the first thing we did after Sunday dinner was to play recorders. We'd arrange chairs and music stands in a circle, and we each had our own recorder: John played a bass recorder; I played a poor alto (which, in recent years when we play is a source of entertainment for the rest at my expense!); Carole played a fine soprano; Mark, a tenor; and Brian, a second soprano. In retrospect, I'm sure the greatest benefits weren't only musical, but more likely that it drew us together in a common activity. However, it gave me great satisfaction to notice that the recorder was often slipped into the backpack on a hiking trip or an overnight, and Carole has shared her playing in worship settings in her church.
—*John and Alice Suderman, Kalona, IA*

▼ When we take family walks in nature or visit a lake, we often talk about God's goodness and about God as the Creator of this wonderful beauty.
—*Elizabeth Weaver, Thorndale, ON*

▼ Most of our times of worship and prayer come from a continuous attitude that acknowledges God's presence and power in our lives. If the news has stories that need prayer, we stop and pray. If we hear a siren, we stop and pray for God's protection or comfort for whatever is going on.
—*Chuck and Robyn Nordell, Fullerton, CA*

Faith Development

▼ We have worked at faith development in several ways: reading Bible and faith stories as bedtime stories, having each family member take a turn praying audible prayers at mealtime, special devotional times at Advent, talking regularly about issues of faith and practice at the dinner table.
—*R. Wayne and Donella Clemens, Souderton, PA*

▼ Ask children of needs they may know about. As a family, develop a plan for service or outreach. Make sure everyone can contribute in some way to the project. Avoid doing service only during

Thanksgiving and Christmas. Retirement centers are wonderful places for outreach. Serve or make food for a homeless shelter.

Service should stem from the children's gifts, interests, and ideas.
—*Nancy Nussbaum, Elkhart, IN*

▼ Our intention in raising our family in a mixed neighborhood in the center city has been to introduce our daughters to the variety of economic classes and races in the human family, as well as learning to live with limited space and resources.
—*Phyllis and Merle Good, Kate and Rebecca, Lancaster, PA*

▼ We emphasized *praise* in cultivating our children's faith. We have taught them that God is loving and kind, that God is the Creator of all of life. The prayer we taught them before they were even able to speak was, "Thank You God For This Day. Amen."
—*Virginia Froese, Springstein, MB*

▼ We pray together at special moments on our travels or pause to pray at the edge of our newly planted garden. We've tried to emphasize the spontaneous occasions for cultivating faith.
—*Ernest and Lois Hess, Lancaster, PA*

▼ Children need a special place at home where they know they can go to be alone. If you have a special spot where you regularly spend time with God, help your children find their own special spots. Something this simple can have a tremendous impact on a child's spiritual development.
—*Nancy Nussbaum, Elkhart, IN*

▼ Cultivating children's faith in God is a constant activity, beginning early. One of my favorite things is to show our children the white swelling of a bud among the green leaves of the peace (or spathe) lily. We make frequent checks to observe its development and often remark, "God has made everything beautiful." At the same time, I try to teach the older children Ecclesiastes 3:11. We record and graph each flower's growth over a period of time. We may draw each day's bloom, based on its actual measurement, or take dated photos. It's been a good way for me to teach our children to believe in God the creator as a caring Lord, providing necessities plus decorations!
—*Anna Yoder, Millersburg, OH*

▼ We had suppertime devotions when our children were little; breakfast-time devotions when they were older. Increasingly busy schedules made it difficult to find the time when all of us were there for devotions.

▼ Our daughters know we pray for them whether or not they are at home. Our children have attended peace camp, which explored ways to deal with conflict and provided hours of discussion and activities centered around peace.
—*Paul and Elaine Jantzen, Hillsboro, KS*

▼ We try to sing daily, often a "table grace," but other times, too. We try to talk about God, but the subject is rather abstract, so sometimes we wonder if we are expecting too much of a three- or six-year-old. For example, we explained that God is both male and female (a concept I can scarcely comprehend). Jesse understood it. He said, "I get it. God has a mustache . . . and wears a necklace." Praying with the children has been difficult. It often feels manipulative. We don't do it often.
— *Anita and Randy Landis-Eigsti, Lakewood, CO*

▼ Ellis, as a pastor, made many visits to funeral homes, and when our children were preschool age, he and I took them with us. They weren't expected to be quiet. They could ask any questions they wished, and if they knew the families they visited with them. We felt they would benefit from seeing families cry and laugh together in the funeral home setting. We felt that, later in life, as they experienced the death of persons close to them, they would have something familiar to help color and soften their normal and necessary responses to those deaths. (When they were old enough to stay alone for short periods of time, they had a choice about whether or not to accompany us.)
—*Charlotte H. Croyle, Archbold, OH*

▼ We cultivate our children's faith by faithfully attending church on Sundays and also Wednesday evenings. We have started to have a catered dinner in our congregation on Wednesday nights (you can come anytime from 5:30 to 6:30 to eat), then at 7:00 there are Clubs, MYF, or Bible Studies for *all* ages. It's been a wonderful experience for our children to see and interact with church friends more than just on Sunday mornings.
—*Mike and Kim Pellman, Matt and Brooke, Bird-in-Hand, PA*

▼ Since our house church groups are small, we have replaced children's Sunday school with intergenerational activities. We may have a drama or activities center to stimulate thinking. The dramas are very simple and basic. We often rehearse them only once or twice prior to the service.

▼ We have a Teen Entry Celebration when a young person joins the church. The event is planned by the individual youth, parents, and the youth leader, and usually reflects the special interests of the child. Our son, for example, who is interested in sports, had a focus on the biblical virtues which can be developed and strengthened through sports.
   —Glennis and Mark Yantzi, Kitchener, ON

▼ One way to share enthusiasm for the church beyond our own congregation and conference has been to attend our denominational Assemblies every two years. We haven't missed any since Rebecca was 12 days old.

   The children's activites have been superb. Our girls have always enjoyed Assemblies, including the large evening sessions for entire families. They have friends from across North America whom they only see every two years at these events.

   We parents have been involved in a good bit of work on committees and boards at these meetings. One way to protect our family time has been to insist as much as possible on keeping mealtime for the four of us alone—no meetings, no guests—so we can visit with each other, free of other demands.
   —Phyllis and Merle Good, Kate and Rebecca,
   Lancaster, PA

▼ Every person in your congregation from first grade through college (and older!) should have a specific job to do. This could be making a banner once or twice a year, passing the offering plate, helping with children's time, rearranging furniture during the service, holding roving microphones when you have special guests, helping in the nursery or toddler room, making something special for fellowship meals, making Advent candles each year, illustrating the cover of your newsletter, reviewing children's books for the newsletter, reading Scripture, managing the overhead projector during singing, signing for the deaf, helping count the offering, etc.
   —Nancy Nussbaum, Elkhart, IN

Singing

▼ We have a hymn-singing evening at our house for friends on Friday or Saturday nights.
—*Christine Certain, Fresno, CA*

▼ One or more of us occasionally participates in our congregation's music group which Jim leads, and also joins when possible in Jim's engagements as a singer/songwriter: Janalee and Anna on vocals, Jubal for support and critique, Jacob on sax and/or bass. We work at the cultivation of our own and our children's faith through church involvement, discussions, and prayer.
—*Jim and Janalee Croegaert, Evanston, IL*

▼ During our children's growing up years, we chose a hymn to sing for a month during our daily devotions. It became a way of learning and memorizing new hymns.
—*Henry and Edna Brunk, Upper Marlboro, MD*

▼ We often sing "Bible School Songs" in the car. The children often come up with selections we had forgotten. It's a favorite activity, because it not only passes the time, but it also brings a true sense of togetherness.
—*Merv and June Landis, Talmage, PA*

▼ Our family loves to sing. We sing together around the table before the meal and sing for fun throughout the day. Even with young children we've picked out some easy hymns, and they learn all the verses very quickly just by hearing the words. We have several copies of a hymnal in our home, and even take some along in the car for longer trips. Our children take more interest in singing at church, now that they're familiar with the songbook.

We also love to read together. I remember as a child growing up with a diet of literature that was almost entirely Bible stories. While our children have a much wider assortment of literature, we try hard to have our library well stocked with good Bible stories which prompt good discussions.
—*John and Ruth Miller Roth, Sarah, Leah, Hannah, and Mary, Goshen, IN*

▼ Some nights, when I couldn't go to sleep, my mother played hymns on the piano for up to half an hour. When I would run out of things to do, she would give me a Bible verse to memorize. One of my favorites was Acts 3:6.
—*Carol Gail Eigsti*

Stories

▼ We had bedtime Bible stories every night. Our daughter now gives a copy of the book we read from as a baby shower gift to her friends.
—*Jim and Shirley Hershey, Bloomingdale, NJ*

Sundays

▼ When the kids were young, we tried to make Sunday mornings non-stressful. Angry feelings are not good preparation for praise and worship! Eliminating tension was not always possible, so we initiated singing on the way to church. There were those occasions when we needed a time of quiet before singing together felt appropriate. We would always sing, "I'm So Glad for Sunday," as soon as someone in the car could see the church building, concluding the song with our own fun ending!
— *Lois and Jim Kaufmann, New Paris, IN*

▼ We traveled 15 miles to church every Sunday morning. On the way I would ask questions about the Sunday school lesson or start a memory verse and have the children finish it. During the week I would write a quote or Scripture verse on the blackboard and encourage the family to memorize it.
—*David M. and Rhonda L. King, Cochranville, PA*

▼ One of the best ways to memorize Scripture is to sing it. Our 21-month-old daughter learned to sing Scripture songs, and now, at two-and-a-half, picks those Scriptures out when she hears them in other books or stories.
—*Brenda Augsburger Yoder, Lancaster, PA*

13.

Family Vacations

Car Travel

▼ We take along a bag of small gifts—gum, baseball cards, small travel games, and snack items—that have been wrapped in newspaper. It is fun to try and guess the contents and select one to unwrap every two hours. We also read our way through the miles. We recall the time I was reading about a skunk spraying in *Trumpet Of the Swan* by E. B. White, just as a skunk odor drifted through our window. We also borrow books or tapes from our public library.
   —*Suzann Shafer Bauman, Lima, OH*

▼ We prepared a bag of wrapped "gifts" for each child on a long car trip. They could pick a package each day after lunch. Gifts were usually comic books, pencils, and paper, or paperback books.
   —*R. Wayne and Donella Clemens, Souderton, PA*

▼ On long trips we took along little packages (number determined by the length of the trip) to be opened at intervals, also based on the length of the trip. These packages included such things as gum, a new book to look at or read, a game to play, magic tablets that revealed a picture when scribbled over with a pencil, etc. Singing rounds, playing 20 Questions, or telling continued stories became more popular as the girls got older.
   —*Herb and Sarah Myers, Mt. Joy, PA*

▼ We took presents for them to open as we traveled. ("When we get to Liverpool you can open Number One," etc.)
   —*Mark and Leone Wagner, Lititz, PA*

▼ Daryl made a couple of briefcase-like boxes: one to sit on top of the carseat for Yovana; the other to lay on Dagan's lap. We fill the boxes with paper and pencils and markers before each trip. The children have passed hours drawing. The boxes also make great tables for eating while we are driving.

▼ During trips we sometimes have storytelling times. Each person takes a turn at making up a story to tell the others. It is fun to see what each person's imagination produces.
　　　　—Daryl and Marlisa Yoder-Bontrager, Lancaster, PA

▼ We try to move people around so they are not in the same seat the whole trip.
　　　　—Phil and Penny Blosser, Beavercreek, OH

▼ While traveling, we rotated where each person sat. And we took along cookie sheets and playdough. We also had a "surprise" box. Each day they received a small gift that could be used on the trip.
　　　　—Bob and Doris Ebersole, Archbold, OH

▼ Our one daytime travel pastime was finding A-Z letters on billboards, signs, trucks, etc. (It was while playing this game, we discovered our third grade daughter needed glasses. She couldn't see letters at a distance like the rest of us could.) Our other most used card game was Crow. Each card had a picture of an object like a bicycle, clock, girl walking, railroad track, policeman, school bus, cow, bird flying, etc. When the item on the card was actually spotted out the window, the person with that card would say "Caw, Caw." We continued playing until all the items were seen.
　　　　—Lois Dagen, Lancaster, PA

▼ We played many games while riding in the car—counting how many white horses on each child's side of the road or counting silos as we drove through farm country.
　　　　—Jim and Shirley Hershey, Bloomingdale, NJ

▼ Players count certain animals on the side of the road closest to them (dogs, cows, horses), only one category at a time. The first side to reach 25 wins. Passing a cemetery cancels the count on the side of the road on which it appeared.

　　Add interest by assigning different numerical values to cows, horses, tractors, or cemeteries.
　　　　—Orpah and Elam Kurtz, Jefferson, NC

▼ Our kids developed the Counting Game to see who could get to 100 first by finding numbers in sequence from license plates, house numbers, street numbers, etc. All of us played that game and sometimes it carried on long after a trip when one of the boys would call to say they just found the number "42" on a license plate!
—*Jim and Dee Nussbaum, Kidron, OH*

▼ When the children were small, we played the ABC game—finding the letters on billboards, license plates, etc. Also popular was naming a country—or fruits or vegetables—for each letter of the alphabet. Rapid mathematical calcuation was fun; for example, $5\times5-1+3\times2-1+5=3$. These I made up as I said them, so no two were alike.
—*Daniel and Erma Wenger, Lancaster, PA*

▼ Count cars, trucks, buses, etc. Assign a set number of points for each kind of vehicle. Deduct five or 10 points for an ambulance, police car, tow truck, etc.
—*Robert and Miriam Martin, East Earl, PA*

▼ Singing stories, a joke/riddle book, tapes, the alphabet game with teenagers and adults, the word game "Ghost" —all pass the time. To play Ghost, the first player begins spelling a word by giving its first letter (but not disclosing what the word is). Each succeeding player adds a letter to continue building a word, but also trying to make the next player end the word.
   The player who has to end a word takes the first letter of the word GHOST. Each time someone ends a word she/he takes on an additional letter of GHOST until she/he has fully spelled the word GHOST. At that point, the player who has completed GHOST drops out of active play and sits there silently, listening like a GHOST! Play continues until all but one player become GHOSTS.
   Laura and Steve Draper, Winfield, IA

▼ We played "Rubberneck." You find the alphabet in out-of-the-car signs. You have to take the letters in A-B-C order. First one done hollers, "Rubberneck!" Two players can work together.

▼ We also played "Beaver." Every station wagon (or any designated vehicle) is a "Beaver." Whoever gets to 10 first (one point per vehicle) is the winner.
—*Mim and Roger Eberly, Milford, IN*

▼ This past March, the four of us drove to Florida. To pass the time, we played the license plate game—keeping track of all the different states and provinces. It was a real family project.

—*Mike and Kim Pellman, Matt and Brooke, Bird-in-Hand, PA*

▼ One game for riding in the car involves looking for objects or places on a list prepared ahead of time by parents. The first one to find all the things on the list earns points.

—*Richard and Betty Pellman, Millersville, PA*

▼ A favorite pastime on our long trips was to play Jotto, a word game. To play while traveling, give each person a piece of paper and a pencil. Each player chooses a 5-letter word (using no repeating letters or proper nouns) and writes it in a covered spot for private reference. The object of the game is to guess the words which the other players have chosen, by guessing only one letter per turn.

Players concentrate on one player at a time. For example, all players take a turn at guessing a letter player A might have in his/her word, and then all players take turns at guessing player B's letters. All that Player A or B needs to say when letters are guessed is "Yes" or "No" (truthfully), and no hints are given about where the letter is located in the word. Players get hints, of course, as they listen to fellow players guess, as well as from their own guesses. The game resembles "Hangman," but in "Jotto" one does not learn the order of the letters. That has to be figured out. The game moves very slowly, so it is a good time-killer on days when you have a 500-mile goal. It is also the kind of game in which one can be interrupted to see interesting scenery. The winner of the game is the person whose word is guessed last.

—*John and Alice Suderman, Kalona, IA*

▼ On long trips each person gets an opportunity to choose one fast-food place to eat. We watch for letters of the alphabet in road signs and license plates to spell each member of the family's name. Other adaptations can be improvised, the town and state where you live, each person's birthdate, etc.

—*Anna Yoder, Millersburg, OH*

▼ For long trips we try to find a new table game or card game to help pass the time.

—*Elizabeth Weaver, Thorndale, ON*

▼ Books have proved to be invaluable on our frequent trips to Pennsylvania. We take a bag full of books and when Michael starts getting restless we read to him. We also exchange toys with friends so that the children have toys which are new to them for the trip.
—*Bob and Jeanne Horst, Harrisonburg, VA*

▼ We read out loud in the car. Long trips are especially good because you can read the whole book.
—*Miki and Tim Hill, Woodstock, MD*

▼ We like to have either Mom or Dad read stories aloud when we travel.
—*Richard and Jewel Showalter, Chad, Rhoda Jane, and Matthew, Irwin, OH*

▼ I read some of our children's favorite books aloud on tape and rang a copper bell each time they were to turn a page. We took the tape and books along so the child could "read" any book she or he desired, independently, while traveling.
—*John and Trula Zimmerly, Jackson, OH*

▼ We listen to story tapes in the car. Walkmans allow each person to listen to their own choice of tapes. We've never had any trouble occupying our children on vacation.
—*Mark and Maxine Hershberger, Aaron and Stefan, Dalton, OH*

▼ Someone reads from a devotional book each day while we're traveling, now that the kids are older.
—*Mim and Roger Eberly, Milford, IN*

▼ On long trips we've told stories and memorized Bible verses and poems.
—*LaVerna and Lawrence Klippenstein, Winnipeg, MB*

▼ Singing has been one of the best ways to pass time on long trips. I also tell lots of stories—from my childhood, from other family members, from our own family. Sometimes we play "Guess who I'm thinking of" (only questions requiring "Yes" or "No" answers may be asked).
—*Rod and Martha Maust, Indianapolis, IN*

▼ We camped for years in a VW bus—the only way we could afford to travel. After the children were in bed, I told a story, since it was too dark to read. They would give me a list of characters and I would

spin a story. Not all stories were great successes, but enough were that it was fun for all.
>   —*Phyllis Eller, La Verne, CA*

▼ Traveling was the one main time we passed on our stories.
>   —*Mark and Pauline Lehman, St. Anne, IL*

▼ We have sung a lot on trips. That gives me a chance to teach the children songs I learned in my childhood. Now, in more recent years, we listen to tapes the children choose. We parents have learned a lot of songs we wouldn't have sought out ourselves and actually enjoyed them.
>   —*Ken and Eloise Plank, Hagerstown, MD*

▼ We listened to music during long hours in the car—the parents supplied one tape of music, and then the kids supplied the next tape. Neither party could complain about the music. The kids learned to appreciate classical music; the parents learned a lot about and came to appreciate much of the kids' music. All of our musical horizons widened!
>   —*Irvin and Leona Peters, Winkler, MB*

▼ When our children were younger, we did lots and lots of singing in the car, leaving out words that they then filled in.
>   —*Mark and Leone Wagner, Lititz, PA*

▼ In the car we sing songs, making up our own words. We also rotate the places where we sit.

▼ We keep a Trip Log, noting our routes, where we ate our meals, where we slept, what rivers we crossed, what sights we saw. We illustrate it with postcards of places we visited.
>   —*Ilse H. and Larry R. Yoder, Goshen, IN*

▼ While driving, we would help the children follow our route with the atlas.
>   —*Laurence and Marian Horst, Goshen, IN*

▼ We do crafts such as cross-stitch and needlepoint in the car.
>   —*Tom and Lois Marshall, Spruce, MI*

▼ During long car trips we always stop for a "get physical" session at a roadside park.
—*Jenny and Dave Moser, Bluffton, OH*

▼ On long car trips, a Mom-designed bag hung from the back of the front seat with three pockets for each child in which to keep games and activities suitable for travel and souvenirs acquired on the trip. We kept a family diary on trips. Mom was the scribe, but all contributed ideas. We read books on trips. Some of them became family friends.

▼ We played car bingo. For that, cards were made up listing particular things to watch for that could be marked off as they were seen. Another game involved choosing a sign or object in the distance, having everyone close their eyes and then yelling "Now," when they thought the car was even with it. The driver, of course, was the judge!
—*Norman and Ruth Smith, Ailsa Craig, ON*

▼ As we traveled, each child kept a scrapbook, writing in their memories of the day and including postcards of places we had been. By encouraging their buying postcards with their travel monies, we tried to have them reinforce their memories.
—*Henry and Edna Brunk, Upper Marlboro, MD*

▼ When we drive, the children take walkmans for individual music listening, special travel kits with games and toys, pillows for sleeping, books on tape, and snack food.
—*Shirley and Stuart Showalter, Goshen, IN*

▼ We play the "family guessing game" while driving. One person chooses a family we all know. The rest of us may ask yes or no questions to try to guess which family has been selected. When we guess the right one, it becomes someone else's turn. On long trips, each child packs his own bucket of entertainment—things like pencils, pads, masking tape, matchbox toys, etc. The buckets stay on the back seat with the children.
—*Kenny and Rachel Pellman, Nathaniel and Jesse, Lancaster, PA*

▼ Sometimes we played imaginary games with our younger children, such as, "Where am I hiding?" We'd think of a place in the car to hide, such as in the keys, or light, etc., and the others would guess where we were hiding.
—*Stephen and Sadie Yoder, Quarryville, PA*

▼ Before one 20-hour trip we made an idea box that everyone was requested to contribute to. No one else was allowed to read the ideas until we were actually traveling. Then when people started getting scrappy we pulled out an idea. Everyone had made an agreement that everyone would participate, whether they felt like it or not. Ideas ranged wide—singing, reading aloud, arm wrestling, finger wrestling, Who Am I? (guess by yes or no answers), standing on your head while staying in your seatbelt, etc.
—*David and Martha Clymer, Shirleysburg, PA*

▼ As we traveled to reunions we would name the relatives, aunts, uncles, and cousins we expected to see.
—*Clayton and Ruth Steiner, Dalton, OH*

▼ We play "capping"—saying words beginning with the last letter of the previous word—or "idea capping," saying a word that is related, idea-wise, to the word that just preceded it, while still having it be a word that begins with the last letter of the word that went right before it.
—*Ellen Peachey, Harpers Ferry, WV*

▼ A favorite game that we frequently played is a word game called "On the Whole or Beheaded." "It" thinks of a word that becomes a different word when its first letter is removed ("Beheaded"). "It" then gives hints for both words and the other players try to guess. ("On the whole" I'm thinking of a word that is part of your house—wall; "Beheaded," it means everything—all. Or "On the whole" I'm thinking of a large animal—bear. "Beheaded," it's part of your body—ear.)
—*Mary and Nelson Steffy, East Petersburg, PA*

▼ When traveling, we look for interesting and humorous signs. We photograph them and add them to our family collections.
—*Cornelia and Arlie J. Regier,*
Overland Park, KS

▼ A few times I took a cassette recorder along. The children could record "everything" that went on.

▼ Traveling with binoculars is a lot of fun.
—*Edwin Miller, Wellman, IA*

▼ We assign jobs on a rotating basis on long-distance car trips. One child, with their choice of parent plans the meals for a day on our budget of $35.00 for six of us. We have two meals and a snack daily. They choose when to get food at a grocery store for picnic supplies, or McDonald's, or whatever.

One child is in charge of car cleanup and is the map watcher.

One child is responsible for devotions/activities.

We keep a visual map/record on the ceiling of our car on black construction circles—from the driver's position to the rear of the car. We tape pictures of significant sights, sayings, experiences, meals, and pictures of our campsites. As the kids get older their art improves, takes up more time, and is definitely worth keeping!

—*Bylers, Williamsport, PA*

▼ When we did travel, which was seldom, I made Bingo cards with cows, birds, and signs with Q. I also made charts to mark everytime they saw a church or school or bus.

▼ We let the children follow a map and tell us what the name of the next town would be.

▼ We took along school activity books, usually a grade level below the one the child just finished so she or he could easily figure out the answers. It was a subtle way to review information, also.

—*Hazel and Glenn Miller, Hudson, IL*

▼ A few years ago I bought each child a spiral bound sketchbook to use while traveling. They are now almost full. I encourage them to date the drawings and often they reflect some place we've been. Sometimes a cousin has drawn in them. Since I'm an artist I would occasionally draw a picture and then they would color it.

—*Harvey and Lavonne Dyck, Christina and Colleen, Viborg, SD*

▼ Kirsten made many attractive and entertaining books for her small brother, Zachary, to take along on trips.

—*Ken and Helen Nafziger, Jeremy, Kirsten, and Zachary, Harrisonburg, VA*

▼ We have had a regular "time out," a 10-minute silent time in the car that anyone can request, to deal with tension or other needs for space. We often have had a mid-afternoon ice cream break that we all look forward to on days when we drive most of the day.

—*Keith Schrag, Ames, IA*

▼ My family traveled to Kansas every summer to see our relatives. When we were young, the trip seemed unending. As we got a bit older, we began to enjoy the time in the car, reading a book out loud and listening to episodes of "A Prairie Home Companion." We established traditions of always staying at the same motel, eating at one of three favorite restaurants, and always stopping at a homemade ice cream stand. The trip itself began to be as much fun as our time in Kansas.
   —*L. Lamar Nisly, Newark, DE*

▼ We have found traveling with small children, especially on long trips, goes much better when we drive at night while they are asleep.
   —*David and Louisa Mow, Farmington, PA*

▼ We start long trips at 2-3:00 in the morning so that when they wake up we are halfway there!
   —*Mary Hochstedler and Ruth Andrews, Kokomo, IN*

▼ While we waited during a two-hour layover at an airport last summer, a bottle of bubbles entertained our one-and-a-half-year-old for quite a while! I also borrow toys from other friends, which keeps costs down.
   —*Brenda Augsburger Yoder, Lancaster, PA*

▼ To create a sense of progress down the road, we celebrate every 100 miles with some type of praise for another 100 safe miles.
   —*Ann Martin Kauffman, Goshen, IN*

▼ When the boys were little, and even now, it helped(s) to tell how long the day's travels are expected to take. "We should be there by supper time" helped to avoid a lot of impatient questions. Our younger son always traveled much better if he knew what type of sleeping arrangement he was headed for—a motel, someone's house, etc.
   —*Nancy and Clair Sauder, Lancaster, PA*

▼ On long trips (four-plus hours) we give each child a coin purse with 20 dimes. Each time there is griping, teasing, picking, or other behavior unacceptable to a parent, a dime fine is charged to one or both children and is put in the parking meter drawer (sometimes called an ashtray). When we reach our destination, the children get the remaining money—usually $1.90. It is amazing how the car atmosphere has changed. They actually discuss disagreements amicably and resist urges to pick and complain. If they argue with me when the fine is levied, I double it.

—*Gretchen Hostetter Maust and Robert Maust,
Keezletown, VA*

▼ While traveling we tried to stop at our campground early enough in the day so the children would have time to play before supper and bedtime.

—*Ken and June Weaver, Harrisonburg, VA*

Destinations _____

▼ My husband learned his leisurely style of vacationing from his family. They always left plenty of time to explore things that were not on their original itinerary. By practicing this together we have enjoyed lively county fairs, witnessed spectacular sunsets, discovered petting zoos, and new museums, and learned a great deal of history and folklore from roadside markers. Done this way, getting there really is half the fun.

—*Kristine Griswold, Falls Church, VA*

▼ We have taken our children back to the places they were born or where we have lived.

—*LaVerna and Lawrence Klippenstein, Winnipeg, MB*

▼ Because of our limited finances we rarely took vacations. We did go on picnics, took day trips to a special place, and visited out-of-state friends.

—*Jim and Dee Nussbaum, Kidron, OH*

▼ When the children were babies, we either hired the children of our friends or kept our friends' children in exchange for their keeping ours, for one week each year, giving us some freer time alone and our children time with other children. As the children got older (three to five years old), they went to their grandparents' farm. That was their idea of "heaven." When the children reached the age of five, we started camping trips and going on houseboats, always visiting friends along the way.

—*Marvin and Rachel Miller, Indianapolis, IN*

▼ One of our best mini-vacations was when our fifth grader asked if we could visit Monticello to help him prepare for a history project.

We figured we could drive there in one day and decided to make it a long weekend trip. We all enjoyed learning about Monticello and, as a bonus, found the McCormick Museum in Virginia as well, which tied into our eighth grader's term paper on American farm equipment. In the past we have gone to the library to get books about the state or region we plan to visit and have driven out of our way to stop at historical sites the books mentioned.
> —*Nancy and Clair Sauder, Lancaster, PA*

▼ We're glad we spent so much time in history museums and art museums when our girls were younger. They both now seem very interested in connections between people and places, and both enjoy art.
> —*Phyllis and Merle Good, Kate and Rebecca,*
> *Lancaster, PA*

▼ We began planning for our trip to Florida by requesting brochures from the different chambers of commerce along our proposed route. Next, we asked the children to help plan one thing that each was interested in doing.

▼ How could we possibly go by train and keep a three-year-old, a seven-year-old, and two teenagers happy? Each person was given a suitcase that she or he could carry. We carried extra clothing for the little ones with us. We chose our motels within easy walking distance of the train. On our first day at Disney World, the little ones wanted to stay on the merry-go-round while the rest were anxious to do more and bigger things. We solved that with one parent going with each group. The teenagers didn't finish in one day, so we agreed they could go back by themselves the next day while we took a tour to the Cape. We turned off the lights at 10:00 p.m. because we all slept in the same room. I remember coming home and saying "My, what a big house we have."
> —*Sam and Joyce Hofer, Morton, IL*

▼ While I like to camp, my son David and I have not yet ventured out together. We often stay with friends, and last year we traveled to Chicago by train. We did not have a sleeper car but chose to stay in the seats. There were other children aboard so that made it fun. We had packed a number of "surprises"—small toys or activities to pass the time. What was nice about the train was that David could walk around, and I could spend time with him instead of doing the driving.
> —*Beth Schlegel and David Stoverschlegel,*
> *North Wales, PA*

▼ We have found that many families come back from vacation as tired as when they left. Two of our favorite vacations (our children agree) were ones when we really rested and were "recreated." We went to a friend's cabin in the mountains where it was quiet and beautiful. We took along a lot of books, games, and food. There was no phone, no schedule, and no traffic. We spotted lots of deer, hiked, went swimming in a mountain river, played games, read to our hearts' content, and snacked. We also had special family devotions.

We each hunted for something in the wild to present to each family member, affirming them and telling them why that particular thing reminded us of them. We also took slides along. It was a good time to view family slides which sometimes we are too busy for at home.
—*Verna Clemmer, Leola, PA*

▼ With our busy lives we want consciously to teach our children to enjoy "down time," quiet time as a way to relax and refresh oneself. We generally spend a week at the ocean and then another five to seven days camping somewhere different each year. We *all* like biking and swimming. We schedule very few activities, but rather do what we "feel like" day to day.
—*Elizabeth Loux and Don Kraybill, Matthew, Micah, and Ashley, Harleysville, PA*

▼ Being dairy farmers with no regular hired help, we needed to "squeeze" vacations in when we could, so we went to a state park for a day between milkings. Also, we rented a cottage or tent at a local camp so that Daddy could go home to milk evenings and mornings. We even set up a tent in our meadow and slept there with some friends for a few days.
—*Arlene S. Longenecker, Oxford, PA*

▼ Our family has been going to a cabin in the mountains of Lycoming County, Pennsylvania, for the last number of years. We started this with the pleasant memories my husband had of his childhood, and much hesitation on my part! The cabin has electricity, but no running water. Our children (now four-and-a-half and almost seven) look forward to these weekends with much anticipation! Sometimes we take cousins or friends of theirs along, or other adults. Once a year in the fall we take both grandmas (bless their adventuresome hearts)!
—*Allen and Roseanne Shenk, Strasburg, PA*

▼ When children are smaller, it's much easier to go to one place and stay there, rather than traveling constantly. We find camping or renting a cottage is one of our favorite activities. The water is a natural and excellent entertainer of children, be it a lovely beach somewhere or the ocean. A shovel and bucket are the only toys you need.
—*Elizabeth Weaver, Thorndale, ON*

▼ Every summer we rent a cabin in the mountains for one week. Each year we invite a different family to join us for the first three days. Usually we invite friends who have children our kids' ages, and we all have a great time together. Then for the last four days we stay just as a family, playing games, hiking, etc. We've found this combination of friends/alone time is perfect!
—*Miles and Dawnell Yoder, Lancaster, PA*

▼ We go camping on vacation. We try to locate near a town with lots of things for the kids to do. When we stay at state parks they usually have a nature program. On long trips we take tapes, books, and car games.
—*Phil and Penny Blosser, Beavercreek, OH*

▼ We discovered that motel vacations didn't offer enough activity for our two active boys. When they were still toddlers, we bought a tent and started camping. Later we moved up to a tent camper. Campfires took a huge chunk of our sons' camping day as they gathered wood, got it burning, kept it burning, played musical chairs trying to escape the smoke, and actually cooked food over the fire.
—*Dick and Nancy Witmer, Manheim, PA*

▼ We enjoy camping because being together outside provides opportunity for the children to play creatively. We found that when we stay in a motel we are being pressured to go somewhere or do something. And the TV is always there.
—*Galen and Marie Burkholder, Jed, Kara, and Gina, Landisville, PA*

▼ As parents we never had the urge to take our young'uns camping. But our teens wanted to try camping, so we told them they would have to teach us how. They decided where to go and what to take. We had such a wonderful weekend we decided on a repeat for the next year. So long as it is their project, they arrange their schedules for the weekend they want and plan the place they want to go.
—*Mrs. Robert Sauder, York, PA*

▼ Once a year, we go to a mountain home with two other families. It's been a tradition for about seven years. We go fishing and hiking and have a great time. In the summer, we go to the shore with each extended family—often going to the same restaurants year after year, biking to the same spots, and enjoying our parents and grandparents.
　　　　—Mike and Kim Pellman, Matt and Brooke, Bird-in-Hand, PA

▼ We tented all over North America, splitting the places to stop between the children's interests and the parents' interests.
　　　　—Irvin and Leona Peters, Winkler, MB

▼ We have taken an annual camping trip to distant areas. Sometimes the trip has a specific theme: Native American Awareness—Colorado, Nebraska, South Dakota — or New England.
　　　　—Keith Schrag, Ames, IA

▼ We have a small vacation budget and my husband and I both enjoy the outdoors. So we have chosen to camp on our vacations. The children love it!
　　　　—Virginia Froese, Springstein, MB

▼ Most vacations were camping trips, many times three or four days only and several times a year. We did this to visit family in other states.
　　　　—Harold and Rachel Ruhl, Ronks, PA

▼ Some years our whole family went to a church camp for a week, with us parents volunteering to be on staff as nature director, Bible class teacher, or crafts teacher.
　　　　—Dick and Cathy Boshart, Lebanon, PA

▼ Since my husband passed away eight years ago, my son and his family and my daughter and her family spend Christian Family Week together with me at our church camp.
　　　　—Grace Brenneman, Elida, OH

▼ For many years our family vacations were planned in conjunction with church functions—retreats, summer camps and conferences—or, in a few cases, family reunions. To add variety to the thousand-mile trek from Alabama to Pennsylvania, we took different routes, stopping at attractions of interest along the way, when time allowed that diversion.
　　　　—Lois Dagen, Lancaster, PA

214

▼ We planned vacations around traveling to annual church conferences. Our sightseeing took place to and from the convention.
—*Dick and Cathy Boshart, Lebanon, PA*

▼ Our main family vacation each year is spent going to our local church conference where children's activities have delighted all but our youngest.
—*Rod and Martha Maust, Indianapolis, IN*

▼ We spend a week in July at our church camp. Family camp is very informal—we do as much or as little as we wish. The highlight of the trip is a day-long visit to the sand dunes and beach of a Michigan state park. At camp there is swimming, volleyball, golf, frisbee, boating, crafts, campfires. Because our kids are young, we do most things as a family unit. As they get older they can easily make their own choices about how they'll spend their time at camp.
—*Jenny and Dave Moser, Bluffton, OH*

▼ Family camp at a church camp is becoming an annual tradition. There are activities for all age groups, as well as fun for the whole family to do together. No cooking or washing dishes all week is a real treat for all of us. It's a wonderful opportunity for us to make new friends, as well as renew friendship from past years. There is good "spiritual challenge" and discussion from the daily morning sessions. Our children's grandparents come for the week and enjoy time with the grandchildren.
—*Roger and Pamela Rutt, Lancaster, PA*

▼ Every other year our whole family—three married children and seven grandchildren—all meet at a church camp in western Pennsylvania. We share one big cabin for a weekend. We eat our main meals in the camp cafeteria.
—*Elmer S. and Esther J. Yoder, Hartville, OH*

▼ Because we had a dairy, we seldom had more than a day's vacation at a time. After we had no dairy, we enjoyed spending time at our church camps, and we also went on camping trips.
   Especially memorable for us were two canoe camping trips we took in the wilderness areas of Minnesota and Ontario. The last time there were 19 of our family involved, including seven of our married children and four grandchildren. This is a great way to relate in-depth and at leisure with adult children no longer living at home.
—*Iona S. Weaver, Lansdale, PA*

▼ We want to have a week of extended-family vacation—now and in the future. We generally rent a cabin for the week that the person with the tightest schedule has free. Not everyone can come everytime, but they try.
—*Charles and Ruth Lehman, Chambersburg, PA*

▼ My extended family, now totalling 12 adults and nine grandchildren, vacations at the beach for a week. We choose to live in one house. Having seven children under the age of five makes the week lively and interesting.
—*Jim and Carol Spicher, Mountville, PA*

▼ Our favorite family vacation that we do for one week each summer is going to the beach in North Carolina with another family. We rent a house together next to the beach. It is a very leisurely, fun time for all of us—for one week everyone is allowed to do what they want, when they want to. We make very few definite plans.
—*Heidi and Shirley Hochstetler, Kidron, OH*

▼ The beach is our favorite. We usually take one-week vacations, staying at one location and taking day-long trips from there. We rent a place with a kitchen so we can cook our own meals.
—*Mark and Maxine Hershberger, Aaron and Stefan, Dalton, OH*

▼ We don't drive on long trips. We like to vacation with our extended family. We usually go and stay with them and visit, play, and tell stories, rather than going to Disneyland or other attractions.
—*Tom and Karen Lehman, Corbett, OR*

▼ Our vacations usually consist of visiting relatives. We're so thankful the children can build meaningful relationships with their cousins, aunts, uncles, and grandparents.
—*Galen and Jeanette Miller, Joas, Joel, Shonda, and Shanelle, Clymer, NY*

▼ Traveling to see family has been our main vacation.
—*Anita and Randy Landis-Eigsti, Lakewood, CO*

▼ We enjoyed house-sitting for grandparents who lived in another area so they could "get lost" together, and our children could explore and become acquainted with an area where one parent grew up.
—*Richard and Betty Pellman, Millersville, PA*

▼ We took the children's grandparents along on a five-week family trip to the West. It was a good way for all of us, especially grandchildren and grandparents, to get better acquainted. We stopped in motels, "Mennonited Our Way" and stayed with friends and relatives. Motel swimming pools were a wonderful way to relax at the end of the day.
—*Mr. and Mrs. Nelson Schwartzentruber, Lowville, NY*

▼ Vacations can be lots of fun, yet economical by taking day trips from home. Kids of most ages weary of much travel. Why not try nearby restaurants at the beginning and/or the end of the day? Patronize local Bed and Breakfasts? (On the other hand, returning home to sleep each night is a big cost cutter.) The anticipation and mystery about where we will go each day is exciting for the children, but requires good planning and organizing on the part of parents.

We live in an area with easy access, north, south, east or west, to museums, art galleries, industries, gardens, zoos, sports arenas, and on and on.
—*Richard and Betty Pellman, Millersville, PA*

▼ At the beginning of the summer we make a summer jar of "day trips." Sundays are especially good days to pull a slip out of the jar and enjoy a quick "surprise" trip. Favorite repeats each year were collecting a variety of leaves at a local state park and following a nearby creek.
—*Janice Miller and David Polley, Ann Arbor, MI*

▼ Because of Ken's work we have been fortunate to have spent extended time in Europe about every five years. These visits included ballet, language study, museums, art, culture, and history which have filled our childrens' memories and influenced their lives and choice of work.
—*Ken and Helen Nafziger, Jeremy, Kirsten, and Zachary, Harrisonburg, VA*

▼ Vacations can include ministry. When our kids are older, we plan to go to an area where help is needed in a Vacation Bible School.
—*Chuck and Robyn Nordell, Fullerton, CA*

▼ Fifteen adults from our church flew to Nicaragua as a work brigade to build houses with Habitat for Humanity. We paid for all materials needed to build one house, helped pour concrete, built walls, hauled materials, went sightseeing, and returned after eight

days. In the group was a father with his two sons and one daughter-in-law. The experience of "walking in someone else's shoes" and working side by side with them made a profound difference in our understanding of being a global citizen.
—*Cornelia and Arlie J. Regier, Overland Park, KS*

▼ We have made our vacations opportunities for education or visiting church work. The children helped plan the itineraries and did research on the places we visited. This always added to the anticipation and excitement of going, as well as to the learning. When the children were little, each child took a turn in helping us decide where we would eat, what places we would visit, and what motel we would choose that day.
—*R. Wayne and Donella Clemens, Souderton, PA*

▼ We read through the "Little House" series two complete times. One year we went west by way of DeSmet, South Dakota, to see the surveyor's shanty. We ate our lunch where the four cottonwoods stood and looked up some of the grave sites of Ingalls family members. Coming home on the southern route we stopped at the family museum in Springfield, Missouri. We found Nellie Olson's name card along with many other memorabilia. It was one of our best trips.

▼ One summer we and our four children (ages four to 11) took care of a hostling camp on the hiking trail from Colorado Springs to Pikes Peak. For eight weeks we lived there, receiving weary hikers as they came through. Sometimes we provided food and often overnight shelter. Much of the time we cleaned up around the area. There was also time for hiking many nearby trails. Nineteen years later we backpacked our way there again to relive some of the pleasant memories. That time there were 12 of us! We were happy to find the camp still serving its original purpose and being well taken care of.
—*Bill and Phyllis Miller, White Pigeon, MI*

▼ We tried to allow time to find something for each child's interest on long trips. Of our five children, some were interested in drama and musicals, so we tried to find that in historical areas. Others enjoyed nature, fishing, game playing, singing, and reading. Each child learned to "give and receive" of their time and interests to the others.
—*Henry and Edna Brunk, Upper Marlboro, MD*

▼ Some vacations are reserved for "mystery" trips of two or three days. Each member gets one choice of a place to go, but does not tell the

rest of the family. Children who do not drive share the secret with one parent, so that parent knows where to drive and make reservations as necessary. This exposes children older than seven to some of the responsibilities of planning. As preparations are made, all persons are informed concerning special items to pack. Children and adults attempt to solve the mystery of where they are going. This promotes awareness of geography and of local places of interests.
        —*Anna Yoder, Millersburg, OH*

▼ Going as a family to professional meetings is interesting.
        —*Ilse H. and Larry R. Yoder, Goshen, IN*

▼ We do some separate vacationing. Last year I took Kate to some local historical sites, and Stuart took Anthony to ball games. This year Stuart will take both children by Amtrak to Montreal because I have to be in Chicago at the same time. We like to go to Chicago together, once a year.
        —*Shirley and Stuart Showalter, Goshen, IN*

▼ Now as older adults, we take separate vacations some summers. My husband likes to travel and see the country and hike. I like the beach and reading, conferences and retreats. We appreciate our differences, and celebrate that we can each explore areas important to us and have something to share with each other when we're together.
        —*Shirley Kirkwood, Mt. Solon, VA*

▼ We vacation with friends from our single days. We adults have fun and get reacquainted, while our children learn to know each other. Our family also enjoys vacationing with my parents.
        —*Lorna Chr. Stoltzfus, New Holland, PA*

Souvenirs

▼ On long trips we gave each child a predetermined amount of money to use for souvenirs. What they bought was left up to them, unless they asked for advice.
        —*Norman and Ruth Smith, Ailsa Craig, ON*

▼ The children each made a scrapbook and kept a diary to help pass the time. Our daughter collected placemats—they were no-cost mementoes of places we had seen. Our son collected matchbooks

from places we visited, again at no cost. Each child received an allowance and funds to spend and budget throughout the vacation.
—*Dick and Cathy Boshart, Lebanon, PA*

▼ We make a theme photo album after our trips to display our pictures. I hand-cover these albums with fabric to show the theme of the vacation. For example, red, white, and blue print fabric will represent our Virginia trip to Williamsburg.
—*Marie Palasciano, Hazlet, NJ*

▼ We make a scrapbook for every trip we take. It is both a memorabilia scrapbook, and a journal photo album as well. Each person is responsible to write/draw in the book every day. And as we meet people, we invite them to write in our book as well.

▼ A favorite activity of our children (who love to write stories) is to start a progressive story at the beginning of our trip. One person starts, then stops, leaving the story hanging. The next person continues the story. As we travel around, different people we visit/meet, add to the story, moving it through many bizarre twists and turns. The stories often trigger specific memories of special people we've met through the years.

Throughout the winter, our family goes back to these scrapbooks and remembers the good times. We are now on our twelfth scrapbook.
—*Jane-Ellen and Gerry Grunau, Winnipeg, MB*

Meals

▼ We ate one meal a day in a restaurant. The other meals we ate from food we packed in our cooler, replacing the ice daily.
—*Dick and Cathy Boshart, Lebanon, PA*

▼ We usually have picnic supplies (paper plates, cups, tablecloth, etc.) and foods along for one meal a day. Around noon, everyone is busy looking for the best picnic spot. We take turns choosing where to eat. Sometimes it has to be on the grass.
—*Mim and Roger Eberly, Milford, IN*

▼ On long trips with preschoolers, we ate lunch in the car while driving. Then we stopped at a park to play. After being in the car, they were *not* interested in sitting in a restaurant.
—*The Baker-Smiths, Stanfield, OR*

▼ We lived in Europe during the time that our four sons ranged in age from two to nine. During this time we often traveled together by car. By noon we would find we needed to take in food and allow for some output of pent-up energy. The milieu of European restaurants fit neither into our budget nor time schedule. So before leaving home, I packed a lunch. At noon we stopped at a scenic spot off the main road. The boys scavenged for small sticks and dead wood while Ray started the fire and I spread a cloth and the food. Then we all gathered around to fry hamburgers or eggs in a cast-iron skillet set on the fire, or to roast wieners (Würstchen). With fresh vegetables and fruits and home-baked cookies, we had a nutritious meal within an hour, the boys had run off their excess energy, the fire was safely extinguished, and we were packed up and ready to move on again.
—*Wilma Beachy Gingerich, Harrisonburg, VA*

▼ Our food tradition on vacation is to eat breakfast and lunch from our cooler, and have dinner in a restaurant in the evening.
—*Millard and Pris Garrett, Kimmi and Krissie, Lancaster, PA*

Responsibilities _____

▼ When our children were young, they had a subscription to *Golden Magazine*. Each month it had an article on a different state. We took along the issues about the states where we were traveling, and as we entered a new state, we read and learned about that particular place. It made the article and the state more real.
—*Roy and Carol Sprunger, Monroe, IN*

▼ Our family camped. Each of us (including our four children) had a certain job in setting up camp—pounding stakes, blowing up an air mattress, getting water, etc.
—*Bob and Doris Ebersole, Archbold, OH*

▼ When we arrived at our campsite, Dad and Son set up the tent; Mom and Daughter made supper. In the morning, Dad and Son took down the tent; Mom and Daughter made breakfast. We had a great system.
—*Jim and Shirley Hershey, Bloomingdale, NJ*

▼ We have regular chores (setting up tent, meal preparation, etc.) that each of us looks forward to and performs with lots of positive feedback.
—*Keith Schrag, Ames, IA*

▼ We like to vacation by going camping with another family or several families. We involve the children in the packing process of getting ready to go, and when we arrive at the campground, the children help to set up the camper. We always roast marshmallows and make "mountain pies" for some lunches; the children enjoy making their *own* food the way they like it.
—*Joan and Jim Ranck, Christiana, PA*

Preparation

▼ To keep costs down, and because our time has been limited, we have always had ultra-planned vacations! We have prepared well, also to get the most out of them. Homeschooling has allowed us to do great preparation. (My teenaged daughter recently told a teacher that hers is the only family she knows of that has required reading beforehand.) We tend to choose places of historic significance or natural wonders.
—*Lois and Jim Kaufmann, New Paris, IN*

▼ In my cousin's family, each person was assigned a state or states to research and report on as they passed through or visited that state.
—*Mim and Roger Eberly, Milford, IN*

▼ During the weeks prior to a long trip, our children selected an assortment of items for their travel bags—books, markers, puzzles, games, and tapes.
—*Marlene and Stanley Kropf, Elkhart, IN*

▼ Before going on a trip, each child who was going along made their own travel game. They cut out pictures of things we would likely pass, to see who could find their objects first.
—*John and Marilyn Burkhart, Mt. Joy, PA*

▼ Each person helped when camping. Everyone packed their own suitcases with a basic list taped inside the lids. As they got older, the children took along their guitars and flutes so we could have music.
—*Harold and Rachel Ruhl, Ronks, PA*

14.

From Generation to Generation

Food Traditions _____

▼ A "rule" in one of our homes was that each person at the table had
to try a little of all the foods served at a meal. That practice has
carried through to our present family; as a result we have children
who are a delight to cook for—not snoopy eaters like many we meet
today.

As each of our children entered different cultures, they didn't
hesitate to try strange foods.
—Jim and Dee Nussbaum, Kidron, OH

▼ I am single and past 70, but I have really appreciated the attitude of
my parents toward food. Likes and dislikes are often instilled by
parents. At our house all food was good for you and tasted good. If
something did not taste good, there was something wrong with the
child! One was expected to eat of everything on the menu, at least a
small portion. Very little was said, no nagging, no fussing. If the
plate was not cleaned, that person had no dessert. Only late in my
life did I learn that both my father and my mother had certain
dislikes, but they never divulged them.
—Elma Esau, North Newton, KS

▼ We grew up having waffles (with sauce) and pancakes for dinner
rather than breakfast. We still do!
—Christine Certain, Fresno, CA

▼ We carry on traditional foods. Chinese noodles is a favorite from my
extended family. It's what we nearly always eat for Saturday
evening if we're all together. When our son set up housekeeping in
graduate school, he took the recipe with him.
—Marlene and Stanley Kropf, Elkhart, IN

▼ In the first years of our marriage, with our children at home, we
attended a mission church about 12 miles away and drove extra
miles to pick up and take home folks from the community. We were
"starved" by the time we got home. Our meal was ready in the oven.
I would put a roast of beef in a pan, add potatoes, several onions,

and/or carrots or string beans; a slow oven did the rest. With dessert prepared the day before, we dined royally.

The Sunday noon meal has always been special in my life. My mother would say, "I cook 20 meals a week; Sunday evening is my time off. Get what you want." We always had a hot main meal after church. So for supper, we would put out cake, fruit or whatever, without apology, before leaving for church in the evening. We thought everybody else did it that way, too.

—*Edna Mast, Cochranville, PA*

▼ Egg sandwiches on Sunday night—Bonita grew up on a poultry farm. Popcorn on Sunday—that was Ervin's family menu.

—*Ervin and Bonita Stutzman, Mt. Joy, PA*

▼ At mealtime we always join hands in a full circle when we pray. We include guests when we have them in. This is something my family always did, and something we still do when we go home. Our children automatically reach out to whomever is beside them when we sit down at the table.

—*Ellen Vogts, Newton, KS*

▼ We sing a Spanish praise song before evening meals. Keith's family served as missionaries in Mexico.

—*Keith and Brenda Blank, Rebekah, Laura, and Matthew, Philadelphia, PA*

▼ I usually try to make springerle Christmas cookies for the holidays, a practice we had in my family home.

—*Grace Brenneman, Elida, OH*

▼ We continued baking Russian paska at Easter.

—*Harvey and Lavonne Dyck, Christina and Colleen, Viborg, SD*

▼ Each year Grandma filled an Easter plate for each grandchild. We returned the plate to Grandma before the next Easter for a refill. Years later, we fill these same plates for our grandchildren, who return them to us for the annual refill.

—*Edwin and Rosanna Ranck, Christiana, PA*

Birthdays _____

▼ The holiday and birthday celebrations and family vacations in the home in which I grew up were very special. We passed some of those ideas and practices on to our children, and they in turn are passing some of them on to their children, in spite of the societal changes with each generation.
       —Richard and Betty Pellman, Millersville, PA

▼ We always make a big deal of birthdays. Even though we have several birthdays close together, we celebrate each one separately. Birthdays were eventful for me as a child, and we have continued the traditions of a cake, candles, and singing.
       —Larry and Evie Hershey, Atglen, PA

▼ Birthdays were always special in my family, and I continue to make it a special day for our children. This does not mean they get a mountain of gifts, but we just remind them throughout the day in little ways that it is their day.
       —Merv and June Landis, Talmage, PA

Reunions _____

▼ Because our families were close growing up, we want to continue to get together with our siblings who now all have families of their own. Cousins are blood, and our kids love getting together.
       —Miki and Tim Hill, Woodstock, MD

▼ When I was a young girl, my mother's family spent several days together each summer in a big, old house in Ship Bottom, New Jersey. We've done it every year for 28 years. One year, when the owner rented the house to another family for the same week, we didn't give up the time together. Instead, we went to a motel. Last year my grandmother died the week before we were to go, but we went anyway. It was difficult, but we were all together, remembering our wonderful years together. Over the years we got to know our cousins, aunts, uncles, and grandparents in a way we never could have otherwise. Now our children learn to know their second cousins, great-aunts, -uncles and great-grandpa in a way they talk of fondly (already!). I can't imagine having a summer without our Ship Bottom experience. Also, the local pizza man looks for our gang to move in. If business was slow, it isn't after we show up!

—*Mike and Kim Pellman, Matt and Brooke, Bird-in-Hand, PA*

Christmas Traditions_____

▼ Christmas traditions tend to continue more than any others in our family. Growing up, we each always had a Christmas stocking. Inside we would place small gifts that related to each person. We could always count on an orange and a piece of coal besides the gift. This tradition began when my mother was a little girl. Her parents were extremely poor, so for them an orange was a treat and the coal was a joke. If you were not good, coal would be left instead of a gift. The coal was always there!

Somehow the simplicity of an orange and a small gift can be more appreciated than tons of gifts at Christmas. The idea is that Christmas should be more giving than receiving. One year, instead of giving a gift that we purchased, we wrote love notes to each other and stuck them in the stockings. We wrote about how much we appreciated each other. I'll never forget that Christmas.

—*Brenda Augsburger Yoder, Lancaster, PA*

▼ We are now taking our grandchildren along to choose a Christmas tree at a tree farm early in November and to cut it early in December. It's not quite the same as going to one's own pasture or woods, but it is a meaningful time, nonetheless.

—*Paul and Elaine Jantzen, Hillsboro, KS*

▼ We borrowed the Christmas story reading from the Bible and singing of Christmas carols by candlelight from my husband's family, although we read only the account in Luke 2.

—*Lois and Jim Kaufmann, New Paris, IN*

▼ We continue the tradition of opening a Christmas gift Christmas Eve, accompanied by traditional refreshments like eggnog and cookies.

—*Robert and Miriam Martin, East Earl, PA*

▼ We've continued many holiday family traditions—Advent calendar, cookie-baking, and family cookouts on special days.

—*Wendy Patterson, Shelby, NC*

▼ We have a traditional Christmas Eve dinner that we make, although I am much more relaxed about it than my parents were. We have fewer different dishes, and, in some ways, I'm ready to begin our own Christmas Eve dinner tradition that would require less work that night!
—*Patrick and Gina Glennon, Carolyn and Steven, Turnersville, NJ*

▼ When I grew up, our Christmas gifts were not wrapped, but displayed on a table by the Christmas tree on Christmas Eve. They were covered with a blanket, and on Christmas morning they were uncovered. My sister saw in a moment her beautiful doll and doll house, while I saw my train, already on the track and ready to go. It seemed that our parents had much fun assembling them and setting them up. We still have the fun; we just wrap everything now in paper.
—*Jake and Dorothy Pauls, Winnipeg, MB*

▼ We did not have a Christmas tree in my family, but my husband did in his family. We continued the Myers tradition for our children and added stockings to be filled Christmas Eve after everyone was in bed. We have since added stockings for all the in-laws and grandchildren.
—*Ben and Lorraine Myers, Dillsburg, PA*

▼ From my father's family we have continued a Christmas Eve tradition which was practiced in some Alsatian homes: the Psalm Bag. We assemble the numbers one through 150 in a small cloth bag which is tied with a black shoestring. Before gift-opening, each family member chooses a number (beginning with the oldest in the circle) and then reads the corresponding Psalm. The length of the Psalm is a preview of whether one's year ahead will be short or long.
—*Alice and Willard Roth, Elkhart, IN*

Entertainment

▼ Both our parental homes included reading "chapter books." Despite the pull of TV, we have worked at finding great books to keep interest high.
—*Lois and Jim Kaufmann, New Paris, IN*

▼ From Mark's family—singing. From my family—playing board games and Rook. We also do well at having work days at the homes of our aging parents.
—*Glennis and Mark Yantzi, Kitchener, ON*

▼ On a snow day, we still try to read a book aloud.
   —*Charles and Ruth Lehman, Chambersburg, PA*

▼ My mother was widowed when I was young. She regularly read to
   us from church papers and books. This was pre-radio and TV,
   and we had no automobile. We developed a strong reading program
   with our own children. Each evening we went to the living room
   immediately after the evening meal and read aloud to the children.
   This tradition continued until the children were in high school.
   Sometimes we visited the places we read about. We have continued
   reading to our grandchildren when they are with us.
   —*Russel and Martha Krabill, Elkhart, IN*

▼ When I was growing up in the '30s and '40s on a farm north of
   Toronto, ON, our holiday of the year was a trip to the beach of Lake
   Ontario. When the harvest was finished, Dad would proclaim a
   holiday, and we would gather up the beach gear—tire tubes to ride
   the waves; long, one-piece black bathing suits for the men; very
   modest attire for the girls, with Mother deciding she would only
   wade in her longish dress. We took a picnic lunch with plenty of
   marshmallows and set off in our 1936 shiny Dodge for the beach.
   Our cousins and best friends had done the same in their home and
   joined us for this long anticipated day.

   We changed in the bushes or a makeshift tent by the car and spent
   the afternoon riding the tubes, jumping the waves, playing
   beachball, getting a "doozer" of a sunburn. It was worth the
   sunburn just to feel my dear aunt smooth Noxzema over my
   shoulders at home that evening.

   Before our children left home, we spread our vacation time over a week
   or more and took trips to the east and west of Canada. Those times
   were much enjoyed, but no more fun than that one day at the lake.
   —*Harvey and Erma Sider, Fort Erie, ON*

▼ The day is July 4, 1939, and I awaken early, excited that we are
   going on a family outing. I know my father will be all geared up to
   get the milking done, finish up the chickens quickly, and pack his
   wood for our picnic fire. My mother will probably remark that she
   doesn't see why we should go away when there is farm work to do,
   and other farmers wouldn't think of taking off. That fact made it all
   the more special to me, because I knew there was work to do, but
   we were having a holiday.

   This I have not forgotten during all my years and have continued
   the tradition of making holidays special. To this day, we plan a

picnic or go away and make the day different than the usual routine. I am thankful to my parents for setting such a good example.

—*Sam and Joyce Hofer, Morton, IL*

▼ Long walks on the farm, playing certain table games, and reading aloud to each other are things we did growing up. We now do those activities with the extended family, and we find them happening sometimes now with our own children. Table games, in fact, are almost a ritual—they entertain, pass time together pleasantly, include adults and kids together, and provide a relaxed forum for either "meaningful" or "insignificant" conversation.

—*Laura and Steve Draper, Winfield, IA*

Work

▼ We've taught our children to share household chores as we did growing up.

—*Robert and Miriam Martin, East Earl, PA*

▼ We garden and can like Rod's family did; we also bake bread, as his grandmother did.

—*Rod and Martha Maust, Indianapolis, IN*

Special Activities

▼ We continue something I did as a child—we have secret pals for the week before Valentine's Day. A week before February 14, we pull names, much as one does for Christmas. For the next week, we each do little deeds of kindness for our pals, as secretively as possible. On Valentine's Day we have a special meal. Red and white foods, and foods shaped as hearts or decorated with hearts, dominate the menu. During the meal, we reveal our secret pals, if they have not already been guessed.

—*Herb and Sarah Myers, Mt. Joy, PA*

▼ We continue prayers and stories at bedtime, and "God bless you" as our final words after hugs and kisses.

▼ Scrapbooks. Our children love to look not only at the ones we keep, but at the one my mother kept for me.

▼ We try to carry on hospitality. My mother always invited single women to our Thanksgiving and Christmas dinners, and we have done some of that. We supported a Chinese student and have given shelter to some needy students.
—*Shirley and Stuart Showalter, Goshen, IN*

▼ Many things we did as children ourselves, we did and sometimes still do with our own children: baking date-nut pinwheels and decorated sandtarts every Christmas. Painting Easter eggs and hiding them Easter weekend. A summer beach trip. Participating in summer Bible School. Gardening, canning, and freezing food—smaller amounts than our parents, but always the same things.
—*Stan and Susan Godshall, Mt. Joy, PA*

▼ We continue many patterns from our childhood homes: going on vacation each year, eating together, celebrating birthdays with immediate family only, going to church and Sunday school regularly, and working together to get jobs done.
—*Mark and Maxine Hershberger, Aaron and Stefan, Dalton, OH*

▼ Both of our families are musical, so we sang and played a lot in our own family. (All the children took piano). And we played for the children and the neighbor's children. One tradition our parents had was having a simple meal of buns, butter, and tea on Sunday morning. We kept that in our own family.
—*Helen and Jack Wiebe, Selkirk, MB*

▼ We loved to travel and go camping. Our children do the same with their families. Storytelling is also being passed on.
—*H. Howard and Miriam Witmer, Manheim, PA*

▼ The week at the ocean was Mom's family tradition, and it truly isn't summer without it!
—*Elizabeth Loux and Don Kraybill, Matthew, Micah, and Ashley, Harleysville, PA*

▼ In my parents' family, all of us children went to bed after lunch for one hour of rest. I did that with each of our sons till they started school. Each one had to spend one hour alone in a room, either sleeping or reading a book. That was my time for rest and relaxation. What a happier family we all were when we awakened.

▼ Every Sunday everyone was expected to attend church and Sunday school on *time*! The only exception permitted was sickness, and that seldom happened—the house was too quiet and lonely!
—*David M. and Rhonda L. King, Cochranville, PA*

▼ While growing up, we had a favorite wintertime project: making a crystal garden using coal from the coal bin. My parents still have a coal furnace, and fortunately we live close enough to get coal from the bin each winter to make a crystal garden with our children.
—*Lois and Randy Zook, Lancaster, PA*

▼ My mother always made chocolate candy Easter eggs with our names on them. Now I have the joy of making them for our children, in-laws, grandchildren, and some friends.

▼ Mother also put the usual dyed eggs in a special footed glass bowl. I have that cherished bowl to continue that tradition.
—*Bill and Phyllis Miller, White Pigeon, MI*

Connections

▼ I (Erma) lived on a farm until I was six. Each spring after we moved away, we returned to the farm to hike and pick wildflowers. Several times we've taken our children to the farm to hike, cross the creek on a log, and climb around on the covered bridge nearby. Our children have also had the privilege of seeing Dan's childhood home in Tanzania, hiking up to the "Giant Shoe," eating ugali, experiencing that culture as he did.
—*Daniel and Erma Wenger, Lancaster, PA*

▼ We've found letter-writing a good way to communicate for several generations, now. My family lived in India, so that was the only way we had to know the relatives. We still write every week to our children. They wrote home faithfully in college, and now our away children write regularly. My husband's family all live close and still get together to celebrate birthdays, holidays, graduations, and sometimes just because they like to be together. Singing together has been important.
—*LaVerne and Eldon Nafziger, Hopedale, IL*

▼ My sister-in-law has six children and they have all kinds of fun. One year on her wedding anniversary, Barb dressed in her wedding gown, her oldest daughter wore a bridesmaid's gown, one son

played "Here Comes the Bride" on the piano, another son acted as an escort, and the little girls dressed up as flower girls. A bunch of silk flowers served as the bridal bouquet. Dad, the "groom," had been ushered to the living room to watch the whole procession, which was a complete surprise for him. At the end of the event they had cake and ice cream.
—*Nancy and Clair Sauder, Lancaster, PA*

▼ Some of our birthday and Christmas ideas (like a gift on the bed) are from our families. We're trying to create our own to pass down. We have enjoyed learning more about our heritage, which (contrary to our last name) is largely Scottish on both sides of our families, by going to Scottish games and reading about that history and tradition.
—*Phil and Sandy Chabot, Becky and PV, Cromwell, CT*

▼ We took in foster children, trainees, Fresh Air children. Our four children are now grown and married. We have six grandchildren. Now the enjoyment seems to be just sitting and talking about growing up and how spouses' families were the same or different.
—*Harold and Rachel Ruhl, Ronks, PA*

▼ On Sunday evening (between four and six), I remember that my mother called my grandmother on the phone, and they would chat for up to half an hour. I now do the same with my mother when I'm home. If I don't call, she does. Through the week our schedules are both hectic, and that is a time when we can talk as long as we want.
—*Jay and Linda Ebersole, Rosalyn, Randy, and Ryan, Lancaster, PA*

▼ Our own children had a very interesting rock collection—fossils, special rocks that looked like the sole of a shoe complete with a heel, one the shape of a bare foot, a hollowed out canoe, a cookie, an ice cream bar with a stick, a rock for Jacob's pillow, coral, to name a few. That same collection is very much in use today. Each rock is there, either because of its shape or the location where it was found. The grandchildren know the stories and have added some rocks of their own.
—*Mattie Miller, Sugarcreek, OH*

Values _____

▼ Both my husband and I grew up in families where church leaders, school teachers, civic authorities, and elderly people were held in respect, where honesty and integrity were practiced, hard work was honorable, being a good neighbor and sharing with those in need was a way of life, and, most important, the Bible was believed and obeyed as they understood it. We have tried to live and pass on these values to our children.
  —*Iona S. Weaver, Lansdale, PA*

Spiritual Activities _____

▼ Family devotions were always a part of our growing up. We read Bible stories or other stories before bedtime, and I understood the value of that, even though I did go through a stage as a teenager when I thought it was a little too much. Later I saw how it bonded my family, and I knew I wanted that for our family. We have adopted that idea and changed it, but it was the foundation for our present times together. As a child, I understood most clearly from my parent's prayers at morning devotions their values and beliefs. It was in that setting that I learned to pray as I took my turn. Our children have also learned to pray during our morning family devotions.
  —*Loretta and Roy Kaufman, Sterling, IL*

▼ The practice and tradition of going to church and being involved in church were a critical part of our growing up. We have embraced that with high priority. Family time around mealtime is another priority we learned in childhood.
  —*Millard and Pris Garrett, Kimmi and Krissie, Lancaster, PA*

15.

Creating
a Sense of Family

Meals_____

▼ We try our best to have everyone together for our evening meal.
That's when we catch up on the happenings of family members.
>   —*Marian Bauman, Harrisonburg, VA*

▼ We tried hard to preserve breakfast and the evening mealtime
together as much as possible. The Sunday noon meal was a
particularly high priority.
>   —*Ernest and Lois Hess, Lancaster, PA*

▼ We tried to eat at least one meal together each day, usually in the
evening. Sometimes we would play the game, "Trading Characters,"
at these meals. To trade characters, two persons simply exchange
their regular places at the table (Son sits where Dad usually sits and
Dad sits where Son usually sits). Then each person tries to act like
the character who usually sits in that place. We found this to be
quite revealing about how parents are perceived by children, and
vice versa. We always did this in fun and with some exaggeration.
We learned a lot!
>   —*Glen and Thelma Horner, Morton, IL*

▼ We have a high priority on evening family dinner, although keeping
that is a terrific challenge. We never watch TV while eating, not
even when the Colts are playing football!
>   —*Marvin and Rachel Miller, Indianapolis, IN*

▼ We always eat supper together as a family, even if it's rushed to
accommodate schedules.
>   —*Roger and Pamela Rutt, Lancaster, PA*

▼ We have tried to minimize commitments by kids or parents that take
us away from home at the evening mealtime. We also let our
answering machine do its work between six and seven p.m. (with
some exceptions) to minimize interruptions. Attending Sunday

morning worship and related events has been quite significant for us, although it's easy to take that for granted.
—*Jim and Janalee Croegaert, Evanston, IL*

▼ We ate evening meals together. Sometimes a child who was working or involved in school activities missed this time. I can't remember any subject about which we forbade discussion. We had very lively table talk.

As parents we helped in special church youth projects, frequently providing transportation.
—*Harold and Rachel Ruhl, Ronks, PA*

▼ When my farmer husband is working in the fields, we pack a supper and all go out to eat with him. I make it a priority to rearrange schedules so we can all eat together.
—*Joan and Jim Ranck, Christiana, PA*

▼ We've enjoyed having a picnic in the wheat field during harvest. The children (now grown) still like to come out during harvest.
—*Wilma Schmidt, Walton, KS*

▼ Our two married daughters live within five miles of us. They and their mother work full-time. More than two years ago, they decided to take turns cooking supper. On Monday, my wife cooks enough for everyone. The girls or their spouses stop by for their share. Tuesday and Wednesday they take their turns cooking. Friday and Saturday we eat leftovers or go out to eat. We believe it's more economical this way, and the cooks have learned it's easier.
—*Leroy and Sarah Miller, Chesapeake, VA*

▼ In an effort to create a sense of global family, we prepare a meal from another country once a month. After we eat together, we read about the country and find it on a map of the world.
—*Wayne and Mary Nitzsche, Wooster, OH*

▼ Until the children were in high school, we always ate our breakfasts and evening meals together. Even though Mom and Dad both had to go to work, we ate together and said good-bye to each other as we left for our different places of responsibility.
—*Allen and Doris Schrock, Goshen, IN*

▼ A priority for us was eating breakfast and dinner together. Until our children were out of high school, they participated with us in a weekly small group with other families from the church. This was an important way for us to be together, as well as stay close to a few other families.

—*Marlene and Stanley Kropf, Elkhart, IN*

▼ Time around the supper table after everyone is finished eating is often a relaxed opportunity for stories about other times and places, sharing memories of our vacations, or talking about current issues. Many times I have supper alone with the boys, because Clair is working, and those are the times we often talk about values, setting standards for oneself, and how to handle peer pressure. If I ever start to "preach," though, the mood is broken and the time is over!

—*Nancy and Clair Sauder, Lancaster, PA*

▼ We like to go out for meals (often breakfast) before someone leaves for camp, college, Voluntary Service, etc. That way it's only our family, we're free of interruptions at home, and there's a sense of who we are before someone leaves. We plan these times *well* ahead and get them on everyone's calendar.

—*Richard and Jewel Showalter, Irwin, OH*

▼ We try to remember all ages. This past Saturday night our son and family, who live two hours away from here, called and said they would be here at 12:00 o'clock Sunday. Immediately, without telling them, we invited the rest of the family to come. We were 20 here for dinner, with the help of freezers, chicken, pork chops, potatoes, corn, homemade rolls, etc.

—*Milton and Ella Rohrer, Orrville, OH*

▼ I serve many homemade soups, often cooking chicken for chicken corn soup or chicken noodle soup. No matter how hard I tried, invariably I would miss picking out all the bones, and the children would complain and I would feel guilty. Then I devised this system: the first person who discovered a bone in the soup or casserole received a quarter. Additional discoveries were worth a nickel. No one ever complained again. In fact, they wanted to find a bone. When they eat at our home now (as adults), they are still offered quarters and nickels. While they rarely accept the offer now, a bone wakens many fond memories/stories!

—*H. Kenneth and Audrey J. Brubaker, York, PA*

Fairness

▼ Younger children want to have, and often do have, privileges equal to their older siblings. This problem is difficult. We attempted to give younger ones *different* privileges. We treated both genders the same: the boys cooked; the girls drove trucks.

▼ We insisted on knowing where each child was every hour of the day and expected them to call us if their plans changed.
—*Grace Kaiser, Phoenix, AZ*

Homeschooling

▼ Homeschooling has definitely helped us develop a strong sense of family.
—*Lois and Jim Kaufmann, New Paris, IN*

Work

▼ Having a garden and preparing food to freeze and share has been a special family activity.
—*Shirley Kirkwood, Mt. Solon, VA*

▼ Dave includes our preschool girls in farming activities when it's safe and when the big push to plant or harvest is behind him.
—*Jenny and Dave Moser, Bluffton, OH*

▼ One family of seven children and working parents posted a menu on the refrigerator. Whoever got home first started the meal.
—*John and Trula Zimmerly, Jackson, OH*

Limiting Schedules

▼ Except for music lessons and church clubs, we chose not to involve our children in many after-school activities. They were on a few sports teams for a few seasons and in school dramas, but we did not chauffeur them to practices six days a week.

▼ When they were small we arranged our schedules so as not to need outside child care and seldom had sitters. We encouraged our children to have friends over, and hosting them was a major joint

Sundays

▼ Going to church together Sunday morning is part of who we are as a family and has not been challenged by the children. Also important to Sunday is a home-cooked dinner and a long time sitting and talking at the dinner table. The older the children get, the longer the talk.
    —*R. Wayne and Donella Clemens, Souderton, PA*

▼ Eating supper together with plenty of humor is a valued time, even by our teenagers. Sunday afternoons have been our times for table games (after parents' naps!). Other activities also take place, but we parents have tried to make this family time.
    —*Lois and Jim Kaufmann, New Paris, IN*

▼ The most difficult time for us has been the children's high school years because of sports and music. Sunday evening happens to be a time when nothing is regularly scheduled, and so that has become a somewhat sacred time of the week. We do not always do something together, but we're all home, and usually have something special to eat. We may watch a couple favorite shows together. There's a certain comfort in knowing we'll all be around Sunday evening, getting ready for another week. I think families need to look for opportunities to be together.
    —*Linda and Ron Gunden, Elkhart, IN*

Reading

▼ We like to find and read library books together, related to special interests, specific seasons, events (books about zoos in connection with a trip to the zoo or a picture book about parades after attending Old Settler's Day Parade), or even world news events.

▼ Trips provide many memories for children and a whole family.
    —*Paul and Elaine Jantzen, Hillsboro, KS*

▼ My mom read lots to us in the evenings when I was a young child, and I have practiced that with my children. I have said no to mar evening obligations in an effort to be home most of the time.
    —*Judy Stoltzfus, Colorado Springs, CO*

activity. We also hosted Fresh Air children and handicapped adults during the summer.

▼ We have said no to organized sports on Sunday, after one of our boy's games hurried us all home from church, and the ongoing schedule would have meant leaving church early many Sundays.
　　　　—*LaVerna and Lawrence Klippenstein, Winnipeg, MB*

▼ We limit each child to one sports activity and one or two music activities at a time. Since the older two drive, our youngest child has picked up more after-school activities—children's choir, music lessons, sewing, etc.
　　　　—*Marvin and Rachel Miller, Indianapolis, IN*

▼ We have tried to limit the number of extra activities the children are in, so they can have time at home. They can choose two sports a year; so far they've only chosen one. We let them know it is okay not to be in everything. We have, at different times, coached the boys' soccer team.
　　　　—*Jim and Nancy Roynon, Brad, Taryn, Drew, and Colin, Archbold, OH*

▼ I hate meetings. Every night should be family night with perhaps one exception. Most of us rip and tear around all week, then frantically try to have a "family night" or day together (Sunday), rushing off to "worship." We have two sons. They are allowed one extracurricular activity per year. They have each picked soccer. They play fall season, not spring. Music, baseball, swimming, are all done spontaneously or "sandlot"-style with the neighbors.
　　　　—*Tom and Karen Lehman, Corbett, OR*

▼ I weigh in my mind, how much is too much? Year-round sports? Gymnastics and piano and sports? I see so many children, with adult-like schedules, I just want to be able to guide our children, so that they can discriminate between activities and decide that even if they don't do something this year, they can do it next year, or never for that matter.
　　　　—*Merv and June Landis, Talmage, PA*

▼ I say no to a lot of evening meetings. I feel the kids need us at home to help with homework.
　　　　—*Tom and Lois Marshall, Spruce, MI*

▼ We both work part-time to allow more time at home. We have done this since our first child was born. This gives us much more flexibility, and we have more energy available for stressful times. We have each also said no to invitations to be on committees in the larger church.
—*Rod and Martha Maust, Indianapolis, IN*

▼ Our children were born while we were living in South America. Upon returning to the U.S., we decided that only one of us would take a job. This has allowed us to use very few babysitters. One of us is usually at home with the children, but we still feel like we have a full schedule. We try to make sure we have time for our family to be alone together. Meals are one of those times. It is difficult, however, since we live in the city where there are lots of other children knocking on the door and asking our kids to come out and play. We often need to say that our children need to be with us for awhile.

▼ We also go on regular picnics. Those times have been some of the best ones for our family time together. In a park we are all away from the things that busy us in our house, whether it is the jobs that we do, or the children that ours play with.
—*Daryl and Marlisa Yoder-Bontrager, Lancaster, PA*

▼ We say no to a 40-hour week (it's not easy but it is possible), as well as church committee meetings and TV.
—*Anita and Randy Landis-Eigsti, Lakewood, CO*

▼ Stuart and I have both said no to jobs with more prestige and pay, in order to give priority to our family. We still struggle with the many demands in our lives, but one of us (and both as often as possible) has weekend and evening time enough for the children. I have been a "working mother" for nearly 16 years. I estimate that I have spent about five hours a day with each child (preschool), and about two hours a day in direct child-centered contact since each of them has been in school. Stuart has spent about half to two-thirds of that time, also, depending on the arrangements of a particular year. This is our version of quality time.
—*Shirley and Stuart Showalter, Goshen, IN*

▼ Say no to too many long-term obligations. We are not very involved in community or school organizational programs because we both work. Our time is limited to church and our children's individual interests.
—*Mark and Maxine Hershberger, Aaron and Stefan, Dalton, OH*

▼ In our current jobs, Stan and I travel for the church. We say no to trips that take us out of town over our childrens' birthdays.
—*Marlene and Stanley Kropf, Elkhart, IN*

▼ We say no to Sunday evening activities. We keep that as a family time, so we can regroup before beginning a new week.
—*Mark and Leone Wagner, Lititz, PA*

Be Deliberate!

▼ Each family has to find what works best to gather their family. The main thing is to be deliberate and willing to sacrifice our own personal time for it.
—*David and Louisa Mow, Farmington, PA*

▼ We worked at enjoying our children.
—*LaVerne and Eldon Nafziger, Hopedale, IL*

▼ By living out in the country on a farm, having a big garden, and building our own home, we have made a major decision to make family, along with our farm community of six families, a priority. This has been a major commitment for all of us and is not taken lightly. Just the existence of Hidden Meadow Farm has said much to our families and the many people with whom we have contact. I think it is possible for people in other living situations to also make a choice for family and community in their own unique ways.
—*Gretchen Hostetter Maust and Robert Maust,*
Keezletown, VA

▼ I try to make time for the girls each evening (during the school year), even if I have papers to grade or other homework. Bedtime can be good "talk time." Having devotions together, and bedtime prayers, help us belong together. We say no to things which seem to espouse values we don't agree with, or to things that encroach upon our time or an already planned event.
—*Janet E. Dixon, Berne, IN*

▼ My husband has his office in our home, and usually he is available to our family. We homeschool our kids. I also have a craft business and work out of our home.
—*Melody Hall, Goessel, KS*

▼ On days when I am home, we "hit" the sofa in the living room after school and sit together to talk about the day—theirs and mine. I think it's important to tell them about the good and bad things which happened in my day, so they will learn the "two-way-ness" of communication in a family.
—*Jane-Ellen and Gerry Grunau, Winnipeg, MB*

▼ We try to accept that all of us do not have to be together to feel like a family. And we mean to accept and celebrate that society is different than it was when we grew up. So, we try to reach out to one another whenever we bump into each other in our busy lives. We read together out loud. We eat together. We sing together. We take walks together. We bike together. We swing together. We attend church together. We clean house together. We do laundry together. We visit friends together. We visit family together. We travel together. We vacation together. We laugh together. We talk together. We cry together.
—*Donna M. Froese and Don E. Schrag, Samuel and Joseph, Wichita, KS*

▼ We enlist technology to protect us from technology—in the form of an answering machine. When the phone rings during supper, bedtime stories, or other special times, we let the machine pick up the call. (Since Ann is a pastor there are lots of calls.)
—*Ann Becker and Byron Weber, Kitchener, ON*

▼ It is encouraging to see young parents, in spite of their busy schedules with both working outside the home, take time to talk to children. A real education can take place while driving in the car—to be telling, showing, explaining, listening. Being very careful and selective about choosing good child care persons when it is necessary for parents to be absent—whether at work, involved in church or community activities—is so vital. Planning vacations that include the whole family is important, but they should be planned with the interests of each child considered. There may be times when it is suitable for them to help in the planning.
—*Richard and Betty Pellman, Millersville, PA*

Special Family Activities

▼ We talk openly about everything. We share our feelings, concerns, and solutions. The kids know they are deeply loved, even though we have our share of battles of the wills. We do silly things, act

silly—and generally enjoy life. I volunteer once a week at a nursing home, and I am reminded weekly about how short life is.
—*Patrick and Gina Glennon, Carolyn and Steven,*
Turnersville, NJ

▼ Be sure to get everyone away from civilization together—it's especially important with teens—or from anyone who might know us, for at least a few days. That creates special memories and "in-family" jokes.
　　Backpacking together is great. Camping out. Long trips in the car! Eating supper in Daddy's office lounge when he can't come home! Having subs or pizza (special deals in our town) the day Mom works and gets home late! We hold family conferences where we plan at least a once-a-month special experience. The treasurer keeps track of budget—one month may be free tubing in the creek and one month cross-country skiing for just our family.
—*Bylers, Williamsport, PA*

▼ Developing a sense of family is a struggle, especially as our 10-year-old daughter finds her eight-year-old brother "weird" and "embarrassing!"
—*The Baker-Smiths, Stanfield, OR*

▼ An after-school/after-work shared snacktime (usually a bowl of ice cream) provides a catch-up talk time that allows everyone to tell about his/her day.
—*Janice Miller and David Polley, Ann Arbor, MI*

▼ We bought a pass to the zoo. We can now go for just an hour or two to get away and not feel guilty about spending so little time for the money.
—*Christine Certain, Fresno, CA*

▼ We visit with grandparents, aunts, and uncles. That teaches children family traditions and history. Because their grandparents lived with us, our children got to know more distant relatives who came to visit the grandparents.
—*Monroe L. Beachy, Sugarcreek, OH*

▼ Both Bonita and I have a high tolerance for interruptions. I do as much of my work at home as possible, and Bonita is a homemaker. Our children have worked alongside us as much as a farmer's children usually do. Our boys are often in the office when I'm working. When they were small, they played in the sewing room with Bonita, since she did a good deal of sewing/tailoring. We often talk about being family, our individual traits, strengths, and weaknesses.

One of our favorite activities is family drama, enacting situations. We enjoy listening to American Broadcasting Company ("Prairie Home Companions") on Saturday nights. In the past, we have listened together to a variety of other radio programs. We enjoy singing together spontaneously. We have said no to some activities which take children in different directions, such as evening sports activities.
—*Ervin and Bonita Stutzman, Mt. Joy, PA*

▼ We have attempted to incorporate many kinds of activities into our family time, rather than assuming that all of these need to be provided by outside clubs, lessons, etc. (These have their place, but can reduce parents to chauffeurs.) We try to do art, music, and gardening at home with the children, and go with them to museums (brief visits), nature centers, etc. These have been good learning times for us as well, and fun to do together. Some things can be enjoyed at various levels and despite age differences—aquariums are a good example. Flexibility in accommodating different attention spans are needed though!
—*Susan and Scott Sernau, South Bend, IN*

▼ We have a master calendar where we put everyone's activities. Each person has a different colored felt pen. Because of our business, evenings at home and days with nothing scheduled are precious to us as parents, and this has rubbed off on our children.
—*Jim and Nancy Roynon, Brad, Taryn, Drew, and Colin, Archbold, OH*

▼ When one child is invited away, the one staying home gets special attention. Staying home alone with parents can be as much fun as going away. We have food chosen by the child, and we may watch a video together or go somewhere special.
—*Kenny and Rachel Pellman, Nathaniel and Jesse, Lancaster, PA*

▼ When I would go away for a few days to a writers conference as the children were growing up, Alvin would plan a day trip with them; for example, visiting the General Motors plant in Wilmington or going to an airport to "see jets fly." Eating out at a fast-food place was a highlight of that day. (We also always stopped for soft ice cream on the closing night of summer Bible school!)
—*Edna Mast, Cochranville, PA*

▼ We have enjoyed taking day trips to see local spots of natural or historical interest, many picnics, and have attended concerts as a family since the children were babies.
—*Ken and Helen Nafziger, Jeremy, Kirsten, and Zachary, Harrisonburg, VA*

▼ A couple of years ago—before any of our children were married—we took them all to Florida. This was the first time our one son discovered his youngest brother was a person worth getting to know. The best part of the trip was watching this relationship grow. We traveled in a station wagon and were very tight for space, but it was a wonderful week!
—*John and Marilyn Burkhart, Mt. Joy, PA*

▼ To give our children a sense of family, we sometimes shared private matters which we called "family secrets." They proved to be trustworthy at those times and were rewarded with some sort of celebration, such as going out for dinner to a special place, for example, when we cleared the mortgage!
—*Richard and Betty Pellman, Millersville, PA*

▼ When I was a child, my dad, who was a minister and bishop, had frequent speaking engagements—especially on weekends. The rare Sunday evenings that he had free were special times for the entire family. A special event on such a Sunday night was when Dad took his reel-to-reel tape recorder into the parlor, that special room entered only on special occasions, and, beginning with the youngest family member, interviewed us—individually. We would all sit with Mother in Dad's study as she monitored the traffic flow and told the next family member when it was his/her time to enter the parlor for a private minute with Dad. The suspense and anticipation were almost unbearable! The questions from Dad were different for each member of the family, and were always directed to something pertinent or relevant in our experience.

Then after all the children were hosted, Mother and Dad had a few minutes to talk by themselves. They then called all of us back into the parlor, and we listened as Dad played back the interviews. The baby (and there was always one or two, it seemed) would utter little more than a "da-da" or coo, and we were delighted. Some would sing a song. When all the children were through, Mother and Dad would come on, telling us what wonderful children we were and how grateful they were to be our parents. Then Dad would say, "It's been a long day and since you were good boys and girls, Mother has a

popsicle for each of you," and would assign a family member to go to the cellar and get them from the locker. It was always a wonderful surprise because we had no idea there were any popsicles on the premises. It all ended too quickly.
—*Melvin Thomas, Lancaster, PA*

▼ I believe one of the most important strengths in our family is a sense of humor and fun. Our girls even comment now, as they visit friends' homes, that we have fun together. It's not that we do anything special; it's just an attitude of being able to laugh at ourselves and situations. Often it helps the girls do chores and things that they don't care to do—through finding the humor.
—*Harvey and Lavonne Dyck, Christina and Colleen, Viborg, SD*

▼ A crazy tradition we have that probably no one else quite understands involves the Russian egg cup. When my son was 12, he used plastitak to stick a wooden egg cup (brought from Russia by my parents) to the wall of the house. This egg cup traveled from room to room, and finally one day ended up on the ceiling by the stairs. It delighted me to find it in a new place each day, and I think he did it to hear me laugh.

After a period of troubled transition in our lives, during which we left the house where the egg cup appeared on the walls and ceilings, we lived in many houses and the children grew up and away. Finally I moved into a house, much like the one that held our favorite memories. When Mike came to visit, the egg cup was stuck to the ceiling in the living room by the stairs, just as it was in that happy house.
—*Ann James Van Hooser, Princeton, KY*

▼ Periodically we have family meetings to discuss specific issues.

▼ Since our children are older, we have incorporated students who attend Rockway High School into our family—two years ago we had one from mainland China; this year one from Korea. Our children are quite involved with this decision and have been enriched by other cultures.
—*Glennis and Mark Yantzi, Kitchener, ON*

▼ At this stage in our lives, we try to create a sense of family by having special times when all the children and their families come together. Our once-a-year Thanksgiving and Christmas combination usually has interesting treasure hunts for the

several age groups of grandchildren. They have become a tradition with prizes for everyone. The children would feel unfulfilled without the hunt.
—*Stephen and Sadie Yoder, Quarryville, PA*

▼ Singing together has always been a part of our biannual Martin family reunion. At the initiative of one of the cousins, we formed a choir last Christmas and gave two concerts of selections from the "Messiah." The choir was comprised of cousins and/or spouses and some of their young adult children for a total of 50 singers. We recruited non-relatives as three of the soloists, the organist, and a seven-piece string ensemble. We repeated the concerts at Easter and forwarded donations we received to Mennonite Central Committee. Practicing and singing together were wonderful worshipful and community-building events. Relatives who participated came from a radius of 120 kilometers.
—*Arlene Kehl, Kitchener, ON*

Networking via Phone, Mail, Visits

▼ Our five children tried their wings and "flew" to Boston, Los Angeles, Phoenix, and Chicago. Our family stays closely knit in spite of distances. The network is connected by telephone, visits, letters, shared pictures, and briefing each other on immediate concerns—joys, sorrows, and disappointments.
—*Roger and Rachel Wyse, Wayland, IA*

▼ We say no to most outside obligations, with the exception of extended family activities. If we have extended family activities, we encourage our daughters to attend with us. We always try to keep them abreast of family news, so they know what is going on in the lives of their grandparents, aunts, uncles, and cousins. The majority of our outside activities are family related.
—*Clive and Margaret LeMasurier, Plainville, CT*

▼ One year, all the Nafziger brothers, their families, and Mom and Dad came from Ohio to Minnesota, where we were living, to celebrate Christmas. We hung a handmade stocking for each family member in our apartment. We rented a local college gymnasium for a day and had activities for all ages.
—*Ken and Helen Nafziger, Jeremy, Kirsten, and Zachary, Harrisonburg, VA*

▼ We've started a Christmas gift tradition where, instead of giving things, we give time gifts to parents. We just finished one such weekend at a cabin—we plan the time, prepare the food, and provide the space. It allows an extended time together to play, visit, and have fun. We've created some great memories.
—*Kenny and Rachel Pellman, Nathaniel and Jesse, Lancaster, PA*

Family Meeting

▼ We keep Friday night for "family night" and try not to let any other events interfere. We take turns choosing what to do—usually playing a game, but also going for a walk, out for ice cream, etc.
—*Phil and Sandy Chabot, Becky and PV, Cromwell, CT*

▼ We usually keep Friday night open for a family activity. It may involve games at home, going out for pizza, shopping for clothes, or an occasional game of miniature golf or bowling. Sometimes our family activity is with another family, but usually we spend the time as an immediate family unit.
—*Nancy and Clair Sauder, Lancaster, PA*

▼ Taking walks around the neighborhood, talking, and picking flowers are favorite activities for us during the summer. We try to have a family night each week, usually Fridays. We play games together, go shopping, and have fun snacks. Because our children are all preschool, we just enjoy a lot of little things, and the important thing is that we are all home together.
—*Keith and Brenda Blank, Rebekah, Laura, and Matthew, Philadelphia, PA*

▼ We are starting weekly family meetings as a forum for discussing issues of concern to each person.

▼ Since our daughter was very little, we have done a "family squeeze hug" where we stand, arms around each other in a circle, and squeeze three times, then kiss each other.
—*Phil and Sandy Chabot, Becky and PV, Cromwell, CT*

▼ We schedule what we call "Family Meetings" as needed. We reserve at least a half hour, and we all sit down together in our family room. These meetings often focus on a problem we're experiencing as a family, but which doesn't have a ready solution. By making an

248

event of the meeting, the problem gets special attention, and, more often than not, the girls are the ones who have come up with the solution! Examples: making mealtime less fragmented, setting bedtime, settling arguments, deciding on clothing allowance, making chores more fair. We have several rules for these meetings: no phone calls, no one leaves until a decision is made, and everyone must try to listen to the others.
>—*Phyllis and Merle Good, Kate and Rebecca,*
>*Lancaster, PA*

▼ We had family meetings. During these times we shared grievances and worked at ways to solve them, as well as just enjoyed being together.
>—*Loretta and Roy Kaufman, Sterling, IL*

▼ Differences, when they arise, are debated for a short time in our family meetings by each person (uninterrupted), and a vote is taken. The simple majority wins.
>—*Ron S. Jansson, Barnstable, MA*

▼ We always schedule a family retreat for the weekend of Good Friday and Saturday. We started this when the children were in their teens, and their dad traveled a lot. This became the highlight of the year for "only family" time. When our son was in his late teens and at university, we decided to make this time together intentionally "spiritual." At first our son was unhappy with that, but the first year, his "topic" was the highlight of the occasion. One family member/couple chooses the theme and we take turns describing our thoughts and feelings. We keep the theme devotional in nature, non-threatening—although it usually becomes an opportunity to share very personally. As our children married, their spouses joined in enthusiastically.

At first we went to a hotel, so no one would have to prepare meals. Now, with grandchildren, it seems simpler to have it in our home. For a special treat for the grands and all of us, we try to spend several hours at the local pool. We eat our main meals in a restaurant.
>—*Harvey and Erma Sider, Fort Erie, ON*

Support

▼ At this point, only our eight-year-old has an "outside" schedule, so we've made his soccer and baseball games family events, thus encouraging support for each other. We also try to do what we can

to support Dad's church involvements. Talking about what he does and where he goes helps us be supportive of him and doesn't isolate his activities from us.
> —*Galen and Marie Burkholder, Jed, Kara, and Gina, Landisville, PA*

▼ When one younger child is learning to ride bike or master other skills, we encourage an older sibling to "teach" as much as we parents. Our youngest has loved it, and now is beginning to turn the tables. She often wants to teach us a song she learned or will make up a game to play and instruct us. In this way we all benefit from each other's different interests and abilities.
> —*Elizabeth Loux and Don Kraybill, Matthew, Micah, and Ashley, Harleysville, PA*

▼ We try to treat each child as an individual who has talents and personality to bring to our family team. As each is encouraged to do her/his best, the team works better and better.
> —*Chuck and Robyn Nordell, Fullerton, CA*

▼ We've said no to more than one organized sport per child. The sport chosen becomes a family affair. We attend practices together (we're fortunate that both boys chose soccer) and enjoy attending games together.
> —*Kenny and Rachel Pellman, Nathaniel and Jesse, Lancaster, PA*

▼ We believe it is important to attend functions in which our children are involved: school activities, choral groups, dramatic presentations, and competitions, in an effort for them to feel our interest, support, and approval.
> —*Richard and Betty Pellman, Millersville, PA*

▼ We attended as many of our sons' activities as possible—they were in music and sports, and we wanted to share their activities with them.
> —*J. Herbert and Cleo Friesen, Mt. Lake, MN*

▼ We parents try to attend our grown sons' baseball games to let them know we care.
> —*John and Marilyn Burkhart, Mt. Joy, PA*

▼ We lived in a home that was "clean enough to be healthy; dirty enough to be happy." But one time we could count on the house being spic-and-span was when a member of the family returned from a trip. The clean house was always a special welcome treat for the traveler, and, with the work already done, we were all ready to hear stories of the trip.

—*Janice Miller and David Polley, Ann Arbor, MI*

Quality Time

▼ Even though we do not have children, we have had to work at finding time for one another in the midst of busy careers. When our schedules become so hectic that we continually miss one another during the week, we implement the Friday night date. We set this night aside exclusively for each other. The specific activity we choose to do is much less important than the fact that this time allows us to catch up with one another and rekindle romance.

—*Cheryl and Jerry Wyble, Salunga, PA*

▼ When our children were young and we were both working, there seemed to be no spare moments. But that's when we as parents needed most to cultivate our relationship. And so we tried to have "Mommy and Daddy dates" at least twice a month. Often we went out to eat, which involves a bit of expense. But we decided early on that if we both worked, part of that extra income needed to be set aside to cultivate our own togetherness. We've never regretted it.

—*Phyllis and Merle Good, Kate and Rebecca,*
Lancaster, PA

▼ Jim cares for Jonathan while I work two evenings a week. This decreases our total family time, but it gives them some valuable time together.

—*Jim and Carol Spicher, Mountville, PA*

▼ Bob, a physician, had Tuesday afternoons off, and we all kept that free—no meetings, etc. In the summer we would go to the lake. The guys golfed, and the rest of us were on the beach. We always had a picnic meal as part of the day.

—*Bob and Doris Ebersole, Archbold, OH*

▼ We told each child every day that we loved them, and we still do in every phone conversation.

—*Mary and Nelson Steffy, East Petersburg, PA*

About the Authors

Phyllis Pellman Good and Merle Good have teamed together on a variety of projects, beginning in the early '70s with an experimental theater.

Today, they jointly oversee the operation of The People's Place, a heritage interpretation center about the Amish and Mennonites, in Intercourse, Pennsylvania, a village in eastern Lancaster County. They also operate The Old Country Store, Old Road Furniture Company, The People's Place Gallery, and a variety of other shops located nearby.

Merle Good is the publisher of Good Books and Phyllis Pellman Good is Book Editor. They are also the publisher and editor of *Festival Quarterly* magazine. Together and individually they have written numerous books and articles, many of them interpretive, about the Mennonites and Amish.

The Goods live in the city of Lancaster with their two daughters and are members of the East Chestnut Street Mennonite Church.